IN THE PRESENCE OF DINOSAURS

IN THE PRESENCE OF DINOSAURS

JOHN COLAGRANDE AND LARRY FELDER

Illustrations by Larry Felder *Foreword by Jack Horner*

TIME-LIFE BOOKS, ALEXANDRIA, VIRGINIA

To Sandra, who encouraged, tolerated, and understood.

J. C.

To Edwina, a kind and wonderful person,
and a beautiful soul.

L. F.

Time-Life Books is a division of Time Life Inc.

TIME LIFE INC.

Chairman and CEO Jim Nelson
President and COO Steven L. Janas

TIME-LIFE TRADE PUBLISHING

Vice President and Publisher Neil Levin
Senior Director of Acquisitions and Editorial Resources Jennifer Pearce
Director of New Product Development Carolyn Clark
Director of Marketing Inger Forland
Director of Trade Sales Dana Hobson
Director of Custom Publishing John Lalor
Director of Special Markets Robert Lombardi
Director of Design Kate L. McConnell

IN THE PRESENCE OF DINOSAURS

Editor for Special Markets Anna Marlis Burgard
Technical Specialist Monika Lynde
Production Manager Carolyn Bounds
Copyeditor Lise Lingo
Design by Phillip Unetic, 3r1 Group
Quality Assurance Director Jim King

Printed in China
10 9 8 7 6 5 4 3 2 1

LIBRARY OF CONGRESS CATALOGING-IN-PUBLICATION DATA

Colagrande, John, 1945
In the presence of dinosaurs / John Colagrande and Larry Felder; illustrations by Larry Felder; foreword by Jack Horner.
p. cm.
Includes bibliographical references.
ISBN 0-7370-008909
1. Dinosaurs. I. Felder, Larry, 1958- II. Title.

QE861.4.C65 2000
567.9—dc21

CONTENTS

JACK HORNER, MUSEUM OF THE ROCKIES

FOREWORD

The Paleontological Paradigm Shift

Many years ago, when I was a boy of eight or so, I would take "expeditions" to the hills surrounding my hometown of Shelby, Montana. I had been told, by my father or by one of his friends, that the hills were made of shale, and that the shale had been mud at the bottom of a great ocean that existed in the middle of North America during the days of the dinosaurs. I didn't know much about geology or biology at the time, but I did have a passion for collecting fossils. On my outings I learned to look for large, gray limestone nodules in the shale. With a hammer or another rock I would crack open the nodules and dig out the fossil clams and ammonites and occasional bone fragments of marine reptiles. For several years I dragged the fossils home, did my best to identify them using books from the local library, and then cataloged them into my "basement museum of antiquity."

As I got older, I talked my mother into driving me to other areas a hundred or so miles from home, where I would collect dinosaur fossils. By the time I was in high school I had accumulated a fairly representative collection of Mesozoic fossils from northern Montana and southern Alberta. Throughout this period I also had collected all the dinosaur models and toy figures I could find in stores and catalogs, and I would play with them in the treelike fireweed thickets around my house. Together with the fossils I collected, the toy dinosaurs were imagination fuel, and the more fossils I discovered, the more vivid the imagined scenes became. I would dig a big hole in the backyard and fill it with water to make the inland sea. I would imagine the giant clams, ammonites, and plesiosaurs, and other creatures both wonderful and scary, lurking in the puddle's depths. In the "forests" around the "ocean," sluggish, tail-dragging reptiles battled one another in their struggle for survival.

I had read *All About Dinosaurs* by Roy Chapman Andrews, and it was clear in my mind that dinosaurs had been living, breathing, cold-blooded monsters, living up to their name, the "terrible lizards." Outdated behemoths that waded recklessly through the Mesozoic awaiting their destined extinction. That was the opinion of the time. Most paleontologists didn't think dinosaurs were of much scientific interest, but agreed that dinosaurs were great exercises for kids' imaginations. And, of course, if an interest in dinosaurs persisted past childhood it was clear to most everyone else that the dinosaur lover was simply a "big kid." In 1964, when I was in high school and clearly too old to be still thinking about dinosaurs, I created a science fair project with many of my fossil discoveries, comparing the dinosaurs of northern Montana with those of southern Alberta. With my fossils and many quotes from Edwin Colbert, a renowned paleontologist from the American Museum of Natural History in New York, I attempted to give the observer, and the science fair judges, the fuel for their imagination so that they too could "see" the dinosaurs of Montana and Alberta, roaming the forests along the east coast of the inland sea. The project was a winner, and I got to go to the state science fair at Montana State University (now the University of Montana) in Missoula. There I received an invitation from one of the professors to come to Missoula and major in geology, where they taught paleontology courses. From that point on, my life focus was on becoming a dinosaur paleontologist and attempting to re-create scenes of extinct dinosaurian ecosystems, based on real scientific studies.

By coincidence, 1964 began what Bob Bakker would eventually call the dinosaur renaissance, the rebirth of scientific interest in dinosaurs. John Ostrom and his field crew, which included Bakker, would discover and name *Deinonychus* and recognize its affinities with birds. Ostrom would also reveal evidence that dinosaurs didn't drag their tails, and that they might have been herding animals. A couple of years later Bakker would begin promoting the idea of hot-blooded dinosaurs. The hot-blooded, cold-blooded debate was on. Those scientists reluctant to budge from their views of dinosaurs as sluggish and "reptilian" argued adamantly against the Ostromonian and Bakkarian notions of active, agile, and birdlike dinosaurs. And until 1978, I was one of them, because I had learned about dinosaurs from Andrews and Colbert, and I had imagined these beasts in my backyard, and knew them to have been brainless and slow, but really cool nevertheless. But in 1978, it was all to change with a discovery in a rock shop. Bob Makela and I met Marion Brandvold of Bynum, Montana, who showed us some small bones. We determined that they were the bones of baby dinosaurs, and that began a new chapter in paleontological history.

Many years later, I found myself sitting on a hill, less than seventy miles from my hometown, imagining a scene similar to those I had "seen" as a boy. Only this time I and my colleagues had gathered and studied the rocks and fossils making the imagined interpretation possible. The year was 1984, six years after discovering baby dinosaur bones in the rock shop, five years after my crew of students and volunteers had discovered the first clutches of dinosaur eggs found in the Western Hemisphere, and one year after discovering the first dinosaur embryos found anywhere. From the hillside, I could look out at the Willow Creek Anticline and strip away the rocks in my imagination, revealing sequences of prehistoric times and entire ecological systems. Not scenes of constant ferocious battles by stupid, giant, lumbering monsters, as I had imagined as a boy, but the lives of amazing and splendorous creatures.

The sediments reveal a sequence of events and activities unlike anyone had ever imagined: gigantic nesting grounds filled with twenty-five-foot-long, honking, duck-billed Maiasaura parents guarding six-foot-wide nests filled with eggs or babies. Adults bringing food to their twenty-odd hatchlings, each a foot and a half long, each squeaking and bellowing. Just above the nesting ground, in sediments laid down hundreds or thousands of years after the *maiasaurs* had left, another scene unveils itself. A layer of dark mudstone reveals thousands of maiasaur carcasses strewn across a devastated plain. A catastrophic event, related to volcanism or a violent storm, or some other catastrophe, annihilated what appears to have been a herd of migrating dinosaurs. Above the devastation, in sediments deposited later, a third layer reveals a scene of large alkaline lakes with island nesting colonies of the meat-eating dinosaur *Troodon*. Constructed mud nests, neatly arranged eggs, and carcasses of small plant-eating dinosaurs all attest to the attention of the parent troodons toward their eggs and offspring.

Only in retrospect is it possible to see how a sequence of events can lead to a paradigm shift, but in a sense that's what happened. Throughout the seventies and eighties, our discoveries of eggs and babies and nesting grounds, together with John Ostrom's studies of bird-dinosaur relationships and Bob Bakker's "hot-blooded" theories, fueled a rebirth in dinosaur interest. The image of dinosaurs changed in people's imaginations, from slow, stupid monsters searching for a place in time to go extinct to agile, parental, attentive ancestors of birds.

In the Presence of Dinosaurs is the culmination of this paleontological paradigm shift. The incredible artwork of Larry Felder is jet fuel for our imaginations and, with the words of Felder and John Colagrande, will lead you on a time-travel journey through 155 million years, representing some of the most significant discoveries in our most recent understanding of the age of dinosaurs. You will begin your travels in the Triassic, visiting the forests of what is now present day Arizona, and the rift valleys of Connecticut. From there you will move up into the Jurassic, visiting the Morrison Plain of Utah and Colorado. Moving further in time, you will visit the Cretaceous ocean I had tried to envision in a puddle when I was a boy. Then you'll travel sideways into the Cretaceous, viewing the east coast of West America, where you'll see the dinosaur nesting grounds and the herds, and all the magnificence of my favorite geological time. You continue forward in time and latitude to the north slope of Alaska during the end of the Cretaceous, and finally witness the reign of the *Tyrannosaurus*. It's an imagination journey that is as close to reality as our geological and paleontological information allows. And it's a journey that will set a new stage for children of all ages sitting on hillsides, digging holes in their yards for oceans, or just walking around thinking about those spectacular and magnificent ancestors of birds, the dinosaurs.

INTRODUCTION

A Celebration of Prehistoric Wildlife

Nature stages few more spectacular events than the annual migration of wildebeest and zebra across the Serengeti plains of east Africa. More than a million animals journey across the grasslands of Tanzania and Kenya, following the rains and the wave of new green growth they usher in.

The African migrations are the largest movements of large animals on the face of the earth, and naturally attract a like amount of attention. In addition to the vast herds traversing their time-honored routes, recent years have witnessed a newer kind of migrant, as herds of naturalists, photographers, filmmakers, writers, and artists chronicle the lives of these animals on their arduous treks. Through the observations of professionals that study this area, the lives of zebras, lions, and wildebeest are often better known to the average person than the lives of the animals in their own backyards. This comes as no surprise. The journeys of thousands upon thousands of large animals, the lives they lead, the challenges they face, and the habitat they are a part of add a sense of wonder about the world we live in.

Now imagine treks of animals *ten times* the size of a wildebeest, moving not across expansive grasslands, but over an entire continent. Think for a moment about the impact of hundreds of thousands of three-ton, thirty-foot-long animals on the environment. Consider the intricacies of their lives: their behavior, interaction, appearance, sound, smell, and feel. Envision the look of the land before and after they passed, the rising dust, the muddied tracks, the stripped trees. And finally, imagine your own reaction if you could have experienced all of this. This is what *In the Presence of Dinosaurs* is all about: not an account of extinct animals so much as a celebration of life. It is a wildlife book whose subjects include dinosaurs, and the creatures that coexisted with them.

Dinosaurs have been described as all sorts of things, from dead-end mistakes to Nature's special effects. But above all, they were animals. And, if the bones they left behind hint at anything at all, they were very special animals indeed. Compared to mammals, the ruling land animals today, dinosaurs were for the most part larger, more elegant, and, in the end, more awe-inspiring.

Compare a medium-to-large sized plant-eater today, a horse, for example, to a medium-to-large sized plant-eater eighty million years ago, a *Maiasaura*. There is nothing particularly outstanding about the skeleton of a horse. It has a rather wide body, four thin legs, and a short tail. Yet the horse, when we see it in the flesh running across a field, all of its muscles moving under a glistening coat, is one of the most elegant animals alive today.

Contrast this with the skeleton of *Maiasaura*, which was a twenty-five-foot long denizen of the late Cretaceous Period. It had a long, proportionally tapering tail, which nicely offset the animal's body. Its forelimbs were much smaller than its hind ones, creating a nice contrast, indicative of an animal that could effortlessly rear up on its legs. It was also proportionally thin, making the horse look almost squat by comparison. By any measure, prehistoric life would have equalled, or even surpassed, life today, in its ability to both inspire and fascinate us.

Perhaps you've seen a flock of pelicans flying in slow formation over the waters of Florida. Now picture a flock of *Pteranodon*, with their twenty-five-foot wingspan, flying wing to wing, doing the same thing. Many of us have watched wildlife shows with a sense of fascinated horror as a pride of lions runs down a zebra, pulls it to the ground, and begins to feast on the bloodied, barely dead animal. Now, imagine a pack of tyrannosaurs running down a herd of horned dinosaurs until they are able to cull one unfortunate animal away, and tear off chunks of flesh from it.

Many animals alive today are breathtaking, as is much of the landscape that serves as the backdrop to their lives. The same thing must have been true during the time of the dinosaurs—magnificent animals against majestic scenery. That is what we have endeavored to create here. We begin with the part of watching animals that is the most enjoyable to us: observing the way they live and interact in their environments.

The chapters of *In the Presence of Dinosaurs* are based on ecosystems. Instead of sections based on time periods, each chapter of the book focuses on a different type of ecological system that existed during the Mesozoic Era. Each system, because of its unique environmental conditions, played host to a unique group of animals, which adapted to life there. In our world today, animals that live in deserts, rain forests, and grasslands, for example, sport adaptations that enable them to survive in varied conditions. The same was true of animals that lived in the past. We have created a plausible view into ecosystems as diverse as barrier islands, woodlands, rift valleys, and plains, and the scores of animals and insects that populated them.

The behaviors we ascribe to the animals are by nature speculative, but are no more "radical" than some of the forms of behavior exhibited by modern animals. The feeding techniques and courtship rituals associated with some of the animals living today are so bizarre or inefficient that if they were not yet known, and were theorized by some zoologist, that person would be ridiculed. Yet, in the animal world, truth is often stranger than fiction.

Animals that lived millions of years ago may remind us of animals that are familiar today. But in reality, many animals living today are just contemporary expressions of forms that appeared a long time ago. Rhinos are a mammalian version of a body plan that was invented by horned dinosaurs almost one hundred million years ago. Ostriches are just modern versions of a successful body plan that was invented and perfected even earlier. And birds as a whole are really just a living fraction of the incredible diversity that once were dinosaurs. Some dinosaurs may seem birdlike, but actually, birds are dinosaurlike: Watching an emu or a hornbill walking around the grounds of a zoo is a hint at what once was the state of affairs on our planet.

Many of the illustrations in this book are images of animals involved in the course of their daily routines. Some of these behaviors are generalized, such as herbivores eating plants and carnivorous animals eating meat. But many are more specialized, or subtle, such as grooming, courtship displays, and hierarchical interactions. All are important aspects of behavior in today's animal kingdoms, and no doubt played an equally critical role with prehistoric wildlife.

You may wonder about the "hair" or "fur" on some of the animals. We are firmly in the camp of those who believe that dinosaurs were alert, active animals that were probably warm-blooded. The warm-blooded/cold-blooded debate has been raging for many years now, and this is not the volume to debate its merits. (Although the announcement in early 2000 of the discovery in South Dakota of the fossilized remains of a dinosaur with a preserved four-chamber heart—complete with aorta—strongly supports the belief that dinosaurs had a warm-blooded metabolism.) We readily acknowledge the vast difference in metabolism between a warm-blooded mouse and a warm-blooded elephant (or a warm-blooded *Coelophysis* and a warm-blooded *Brachiosaurus*, for that matter).

Speculation, though, in illustrations as highly detailed as these leaves little room for equivocation. Flipping through these pages, you'll see dinosaurs with hairy feathers, and pterosaurs with fur. They are the adaptations of small-to-medium sized animals with high metabolisms in an environment that is subject to change. There is no need to insulate large animals that live in warm environments, and the fossil evidence so far clearly shows that large dinosaurs were covered in scales. But with the discovery of a number of fully-feathered small dinosaurs in China since 1996, it can now be stated unequivocally that some small dinosaurs were walking around looking a lot more like ground birds than the lizard-like creatures they were thought to be by so many. It is persuasive evidence for those who argued for so long that dinosaurs are still with us in the form of birds. Many of the illustrations of small, feathered dinosaurs in this book were done before the Chinese discoveries, and it is gratifying to see the subject of one's speculations brought to life. Pterosaur fossils have been unearthed with fur, so they are illustrated with it here.

With a few rare and specialized exceptions, all small-to-medium-sized active animals today—birds and mammals—are insulated. It doesn't matter what the ecosystem is, or whether the animal lives in the bitter cold of the polar regions, or the broiling sun near the equator. There seems to be a weight barrier of about a ton-and-a-half that acts as a natural cut-off. Almost all animals below that weight are insulated, with fur on mammals, and feathers on birds. If dinosaurs were also warm-blooded, then a coat of hairy feathers would make the same sense for them millions of years ago that it makes for newly hatched birds today. It helps them regulate their body temperature, and prevents too much heat loss through their naked skin in the cold, or overheating when the outside temperature gets too hot.

But enough about theories and fossils. We hope that after reading through this book, you won't think of dinosaurs merely as skeletons, but as wild animals. You may come to share our vision of the richness of the life of the Mesozoic, but that is not our ultimate goal. Above all else, what we really wish for in the end is that you will have as much fun reading this book as we had creating it. This was a labor of love, the product of two grown-up kids who wanted to see their lifelong interests and ideas realized in book form. Enjoy it as we have.

1 NEW WORLD ORDER

245 Million Years Ago

CHAPTER ONE

NEW WORLD ORDER

The Dawn of the Triassic Heralds a Rebirth of Life

PRECEDING PAGES
Above a misty wetland, a new morning dawns on the supercontinent of Pangaea. At this time, early in the Triassic Period, Earth was still emerging from the throes of its greatest mass extinction. Ninety-five percent of all animal species had disappeared. As a result, the plant life of the day, a mixed flora that included conifers, ginkgoes, cycads, horsetails, and ferns, had the world much to themselves.

OPPOSITE
Life in the Triassic was marked by innovation. One such experiment was webbing. This animal, having just caught a cockroach, is *Sharovipteryx*, from the Late Triassic of Kirghizia. The webbing—skin that stretched between the animal's limbs and tail—enabled it to glide between treetops.

There has never been a time in Earth's past that compares with the Mesozoic Era. The history of our planet is a rich and varied collection of stories, and each period of time through which it has traveled has its own special tale to tell. But between 245 and 65 million years ago, it was as if all the rules that had been running life were suddenly cast aside, and a whole new set put in their place. It was a time when superlatives became commonplace. Never before nor since have so many unique natural scenarios come together. The result was some of the most fantastic and fascinating wildlife that could possibly be experienced or imagined.

Even today, sixty-five million years after it ended, the Mesozoic continues to make its influence known. Effects first set in motion back then carry down to the present day in both plants and animals. The dominant animals in today's world—birds and mammals—both trace their origins to the Mesozoic. The dominant plants in today's world—angiosperms, which comprise more than ninety percent of plant species—arose over a hundred million years ago. Even conifers and ferns, which have a much longer history, underwent changes throughout the Mesozoic that are apparent in their descendants that we see today.

In a sense, we owe our very existence to events back then. If not for the progression of life throughout the Mesozoic—and particularly, the way in which the era came to an end—it is fairly safe to say that human beings would not now be on Earth. Our ancestors spent 150 million years of the Mesozoic hiding in the shadows of other life forms, waiting for their chance to break out. In the aftermath of the catastrophe that closed out the Period were sown the seeds of our birth as a species. Its story, then, is our story as well.

Among the wildlife groups that had made use of webbing, one form added yet another innovation to the experiment, the elongation of digits of the forelimb. In these animals, as the last digit of the forelimb was lengthened, the skin attached to it grew as well. The combination of an elongated finger and an attached membrane of skin created the first wing and allowed the first powered flight in the vertebrates. Thus were invented the first pterosaurs, of which *Preondactylus*, an eighteen-inch-wide flyer from the Late Triassic of Italy, was one of the earliest.

The history of the Mesozoic is a story of life's efforts to reinvent itself in the throes of a global cataclysm, and the heights it reached once it got itself up and running again. The era began in the midst of a once-in-a-half-billion-year occurrence, the reign of a supercontinent. The preceding Permian Period had ended with the largest mass extinction in the history of the planet. Upward of ninety-five percent of all the animal species on Earth disappeared. As the first period of the Mesozoic, the Triassic, began, the five percent remaining had free run of the land. This scenario, a single, worldwide landmass set for colonization by animals that could spread to its farthest limits, was new to the planet. It brought on a riot of evolutionary tinkering that produced entire series of never-before-seen wildlife. It was a situation ripe for rampant evolution, and evolve life did, as brand-new groups of crawling, burrowing, and—for the first time—flying animals appeared.

During the Triassic Period, innovation and experimentation were in vogue. If thought of in technological terms, as the Mesozoic progressed into the Jurassic, research and development moved into product testing. Having come up with newly invented wild animals, the physical limits of what had been produced were stretched to their limits. Load-bearing tests became popular, and the results were the largest animals Earth has ever seen. Time and again, wildlife appeared that pushed the envelope of how big a land animal could really get, and the kind of impact it could have on its environment. In the Cretaceous, the final period of the Mesozoic, size was co-opted by finesse. Giants still walked the planet but, more and more, sophistication and high drama won the day. Yet again, a new series of wild animals appeared and populated Earth's ecosystems. Displaying an elegance and beauty never before seen, terrestrial wildlife grew in variety and refinement to heights that were scarcely hinted at when the era began. And then, it was over.

Throughout the Mesozoic, North America occupied a particularly important position in the drama that unfolded and played host to some of the planet's most spectacular wildlife as the era progressed. It also bore the ignoble distinction of hosting the event that is generally credited with bringing the curtain down on the 180-million-year run of the Mesozoic, the Yucatan Meteorite Impact. As a result of this

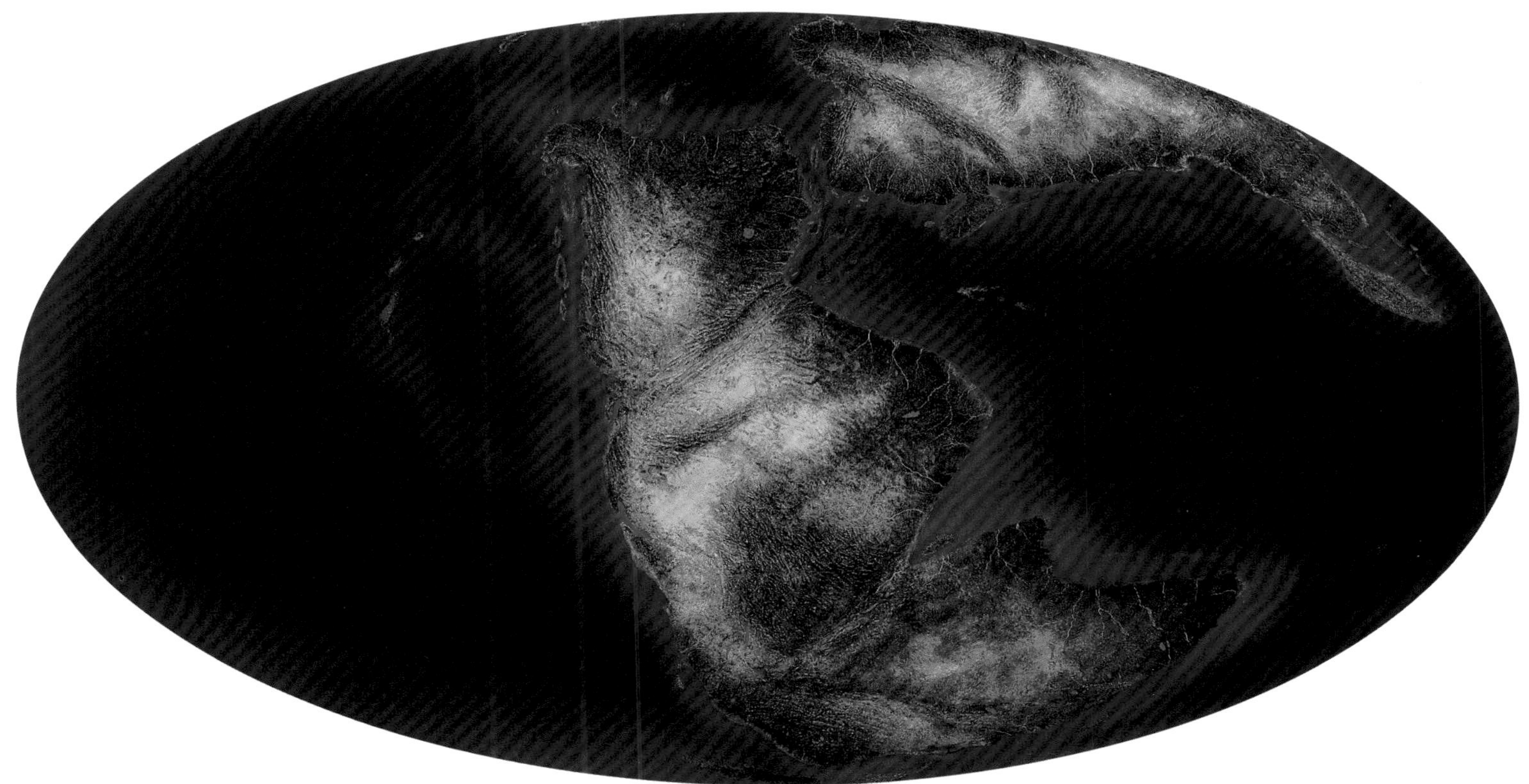

event, the moment when the Mesozoic Era ended and the Cenozoic Era began was particularly hard on this continent. Extinctions across North America were greater than those anywhere else in the world.

Having hosted some of the great dramas of the era, North America, in the end, played host to the greatest of them all. At the height of their glory, when the wildlife of the continent had achieved wondrous new levels of diversity and creation, it all ended in a geologic instant. It was an abrupt end to a period that had seen so many renewals over the eons. But perhaps it is fitting. The story of the era contains no memories of obsolete failures, quietly fading into oblivion. When the history of North America is finally written, the period between 245 and 65 million years ago will stand as a time when life pulled out all the stops. The dinosaurs went out at the top of their game.

As the dawn of the Mesozoic slowly broke across the face of the planet, it revealed a quiet and lonely Earth. The end of the Permian Period had seen nineteen out of every twenty animal species wiped out. Those that were left were, for the most part, small animals. Some had managed to stay in the background while their larger neighbors died out; others were simply lucky to have been generalized animals. This means that they were able to squeak through the extinctions because their lack of specialization made them less vulnerable to sudden environmental changes.

The end of the Permian Period had coincided with a number of factors that combined to create a world in distress—so many, in fact, that these events *define* the end of the period. A general lowering of sea levels eliminated many shallow marine environments. A vast outpouring of lava from volcanic eruptions on the plains of northern Asia pumped millions of tons of noxious gases into the atmosphere. Finally, a sharp rise in global carbon dioxide levels caused by an increase in deep ocean circulation wreaked havoc on marine and terrestrial habitats alike. These events created an environmental catastrophe. Life all across the planet was decimated, both on the land and in the seas. Many forms that had thrived in marine ecosystems for hundreds of millions of years, such as the trilobites, disappeared completely. On land, long-established groups, such as the therapsids, the mammal-like reptiles, saw their ranks either severely depleted or, in the case of the pelycosaurs, the fin-backed reptiles, completely annihilated.

The supercontinent Pangaea as it appeared during the Triassic, the first of three periods that comprise the Mesozoic Era. When the Mesozoic broke 245 million years ago, Pangaea was an immense but quiet land, with little in the way of wildlife throughout its expanse. As the Triassic progressed though, entirely new groups of animals would appear on the supercontinent: pterosaurs, mammals, and dinosaurs. The pterosaurs would take to the air and become the largest animals ever to fly. The mammals would find refuge in the shadows, surviving mostly as small, nocturnal, insect-eating wildlife. The dinosaurs would go on to rule the land as the largest terrestrial animals in the history of the planet.

Garjainia, a five- to six-foot-long archosaur from the Early Triassic of Russia. The archosaurs were another group of wildlife that had managed to survive the Permian extinctions. Although overshadowed by the therapsids early in the Triassic, they hung on. As the Triassic wore on and some groups of the rapsids died out, the archosaurs diversified and were able to radiate into the newly available niches. By the time the Triassic drew to a close, they were the dominant group of wildlife on land.

The period that follows an environmental upheaval is typically a time of quiet and rebirth. This was the case at the beginning of the Triassic. The wildlife that survived the Permian extinctions found itself on a planet with one huge landmass and one massive ocean. The world of the past was gone, and with it went the established and mature ecosystems of which its inhabitants had been a part. Those that emerged from the transition—a few kinds of therapsids, early members of the reptilian archosaurs, various other groups of reptiles, and some amphibians—were thrust onto a stage that had been cleared of all its traditional players. The roles of predator and prey had to be recast. The hierarchies that had developed in previous dynasties of animals had disappeared, and what was left was a world of varied habitats, extending from pole to pole, with very little in the way of animal life to fill them.When Pangaea formed at the beginning of the Permian Period, 290 million years ago, the separate landmasses that created the supercontinent brought along their own collections of plants and animals, which were then free to intermix and interact. In the process, some habitats were destroyed or eliminated, while others were created or changed. For a time, life went through a sorting-out period, as some species adapted to the new conditions, while others disappeared. Although there had been other supercontinents in the past, the Early Triassic was the first time in Earth's history when a supercontinent stood poised to be conquered by populations of new vertebrates, animals that could disperse rapidly throughout the virgin territory and, literally, take over the world.

Giving a group of small, generalized wildlife free reign over an immense landscape guarantees that there will be innovation and diversification—in a word, evolution. The intermixing of animals, especially those that hunt similar prey or eat similar vegetation, often leads from interaction to competition, as they vie for the same resources and territory. Where the lifestyles of small animals are not suppressed by their larger neighbors, opportunism becomes a favorable trait. Animals quickly push the boundaries as they exploit their environments. They radiate into new surroundings and habitats and diversify, evolving into new wildlife in the process.

After a modest beginning at the start of the Triassic, the reptiles that survived the Permian extinctions were beginning to diversify, and conditions appeared that would give them a leg up

on their amphibian neighbors. As the centuries of the Early Triassic wore on, Pangaea began to creep slowly northward until it lay right across the equator. Although wetlands were still widespread, the vast lowland bayous and swamps of giant scale trees, ferns, and tree-sized horsetails that had dominated the supercontinent for so long were slowly disappearing. As the period progressed, large, arid areas began to appear, especially in the interiors of the immense landmass. Cut off from moisture-ladened marine air, parts of the supercontinent began to dry out. Hardier ferns and gymnosperms—plants with thick needlelike leaves and scales, and woody bark to conserve water—became more common. In addition, their embryos were contained in seeds that could remain dormant until conditions were right for growth.

As Pangaea's climate became more arid, reptile groups quickly showed themselves to be up to the challenges of the newer habitats. More and more, they began to replace amphibians in many ecological roles. Amphibians found refuge in some marginal environments, usually the wetter coastal plains and the ever-diminishing wetlands, and tried to regroup and reorganize by evolving to meet the demands of the habitats in which they remained. But even though some were changing into predominately terrestrial forms, complete with armor, their reproductive strategies were still tied to wetlands. The reptiles adapted better to the increasingly widespread drier areas. One of the most important reasons for their success was the shelled egg. Those animals that used this innovative egg had a big advantage in taking control of the new drier environs, since shelled eggs can be laid anywhere on land. Such eggs meant that reptiles were no longer tied to the water to reproduce, so they could move into areas that amphibians had found off limits. As the supercontinent drifted toward the tropics, these animals found themselves well situated to take advantage of the changed environments.

By the time the Triassic was ten million years under way, reptile groups had radiated throughout much of Pangaea. The therapsids had evolved into many carnivorous and herbivorous forms and filled the niches they occupied quite comfortably. Large browsers and medium-sized root-foragers were being hunted by efficient therapsid predators. Ranging in size from inches and ounces to yards and tons, the mammal-like reptiles dominated the plains, the deserts, and the forests of early Triassic times. Another thriving group was the archosaurs. First appearing in the Permian Period, they had managed to survive the extinction event as denizens of wetlands. They all had the same basic reptilian body plan and habits, but with a more efficient bite, and a propensity for bipedalism, they were predisposed for success.

Both the therapsids and archosaurs, with their more advanced and efficient feeding and limb arrangements, thrived in the early years of the Triassic. The habitats and environmental roles opened up by the Permian extinctions had created an opportunity, and the two groups took advantage of it. While busy exploiting the new habitats available to them, they began experimenting in other areas as well.

Over the eons, animals had gotten by with an ectothermic metabolism, one that made each individual rely on its environment and sunlight to regulate its internal body temperature. Much of the animal's behavior, such as basking in the sun, was geared to maintaining its temperature

PRECEDING PAGES
As the archosaurs diversified throughout the ecosystems of Pangaea, among the new groups that evolved were the dinosaurs, of which *Eoraptor* was one of the earliest. First appearing in Gondwana, the southern section of Pangaea, they were a relatively minor wildlife group of the Middle Triassic. But despite its modest three-foot length, it was an alert, active animal, and the basic body plan of the group would prove to be a great success in the years to come.

RIGHT
Among the most successful group of animals in the Early to Middle Triassic were the therapsids, the mammal-like reptiles. *Cynognathus*, a three-foot-long predator from the Early Triassic of South Africa, illustrates the mix of reptilian and mammalian traits that characterize the group. Though closely resembling a mammal and sporting a furry coat, it still retained its reptilian semi-sprawling stance.

at optimum levels. As time wore on, though, several groups began tinkering with new approaches. By the middle of the Triassic, both the therapsids and archosaurs had independently evolved a basic form of endothermy, the ability to maintain body temperature at a constant level. The basic activity levels of the animals rose accordingly, because now they could remain active for longer periods of time in more varied conditions. There was a price to be paid, however: Greater amounts of fuel were required to stoke these internal fires.

Animals also began experimenting with insulation. Therapsids and archosaurs were originally clothed in the standard reptilian mosaic of scales. Scales are a versatile body covering. The basic material of which they are made, keratin, can be molded and shaped in a variety of ways. Random genetic changes over time brought the debut of elongated scales, fancy scales, overlapping scales, fringed scales, and countless other innovations. Many of these experiments turned out to be dead ends, offering no particular advantage or disadvantage. In an animal with a revved-up metabolism, however, any overlapping, frayed scales that trap dead air next to the animal's body make a great insulator. The same holds true for small sensory filaments that sprouted between the scales on some animals. Thus were created feathers and hair. By the Middle Triassic, both types of animals had independently come up with different forms of insulation, hair in therapsids and hairlike feathers in archosaurs.

Yet another group of archosaurs had developed stretches of skin between their limbs. Capitalizing on the increased levels of activity available through their new metabolism, and covered with their own particular style of fur, they began to exploit a habitat that, until then, had been the exclusive domain of insects. And so, less than fifteen million years after the Triassic began, a new type of animal, pterosaurs, became the first vertebrates to take to the air with powered flight.

For the first part of the Triassic, the therapsids seemed to have the upper hand; however, following a new series of extinctions, spaced over a few million years, the balance of power effectively shifted to the archosaurs. Again taking advantage of the opportunities presented by newly vacant niches, by the middle of the Triassic, therapsid groups shared habitats with a number of equally advanced groups of archosaurs. One offshoot of the therapsids had by now come on the scene: the true mammals, which were for the most part small, nocturnal, egg-laying, and insectivorous animals. At about the same time, in the southern part of Pangaea, a group of archosaurs broke off and began its own evolutionary path, likewise as small animals. These were the dinosaurs.

As the Mesozoic progressed and the Triassic began to wind down, Earth was a much different place than it had been when the era first began. Whole new populations of wildlife had evolved to fill the empty spaces left by the Permian extinctions. Typically, they were faster, more alert, more adaptive, physiologically more advanced, and better equipped to tackle the habitats around them than any animals before them. Therapsids, mammals, pterosaurs, dinosaurs: In the space of twenty-five million years, totally new kinds of animals had evolved and wasted no time in spreading throughout the world that had been opened to them. They would spend the next 155 million years ruling the Mesozoic Era. As Pangaea broke apart and North America drifted off on its own, with it went populations of animals the likes of which had never been seen before. The story of the Mesozoic, then, is the story of the wildlife, and how it survived and thrived in this new world.

By the Middle to Late Triassic, one group of therapsids had branched off and became true mammals. When the therapsids finally became extinct in the Middle Jurassic, their mammalian descendants managed to live on and are today the dominant land animals on Earth. This is *Megazostrodon*, a shrew-sized Late Triassic mammal, also from South Africa.

2

VEILED WOODLANDS

225 Million Years Ago

CHAPTER TWO

VEILED WOODLANDS

Wildlife Thrives in a Triassic Rain Forest

PRECEDING PAGES
Early morning sunlight reveals a Late Triassic stream and rain forest in equatorial Arizona. No longer hidden by the darkness of night, the land is still shrouded in a dense mist, due to the high humidity of the rain forest. In what amounts to a daily ritual in this area near Pangaea's western coastline, the fog will burn off as the sun moves higher in the morning sky.

OPPOSITE
The most common large predators of the extended Arizona wetland ecosystem are the phytosaurs. Superficially resembling the crocodilians, they are actually no more than distant archosaurian cousins. Several species inhabit the freshwater rivers and lakes of the region. Though each has its own preferred hunting habits and prey, all include fish as part of their diet, as this Rutiodon has done with the coelocanth Chinlia.

A few degrees above the equator, along the middle of the west coast of Pangaea, lies a wide, round, shallow depression. It is bordered by uplands and mountains on the north, east, and south and by the single worldwide ocean Panthalassa on the west. Here, in what is Late Triassic Arizona, isolated from the harsher, arid conditions that dominate the interior of the supercontinent, a sheltered woodlands harbors teeming communities of plants and animals in its wetlands and forests.

Viewed from above, the woodlands are an impenetrable green mass, with wisps of white and gray mist filling the low-lying areas. The air is warm, thick, and humid, moving little, if at all. Within the greenery, patterns emerge. An extensive system of rivers and streams cuts long, sinuous paths through the otherwise unbroken forest. Originating in highlands a few hundred miles to the south and east, these rivers and streams empty into a large lake far to the north and into the great ocean to the west. The waters meander northward, following the gently sloping floor of the woodlands.

High humidity and a relatively-high water table make the normally dappled forest canopy quite dense. The forest consists predominantly of conifers, some well over one hundred feet tall, most topped with clusters of branches whose ends are covered with overlapping scaly leaves. Scattered throughout are shorter cycads and cycadeoids, sheathed in a tough, deeply sculpted armor of old leaf bases and crowned with tufts of sharp-tipped, palmlike leaves. Ferns and fernlike plants—some as tall as thirty feet—form a solid green carpet wherever sunlight breaks through to the ground.

Many trees are covered with low-light-loving plant growth that anchors itself to a host tree by wrapping its roots around the tree's branches or penetrating its bark. Much of the green coloration of the canopy is due to these squatters. So dense is this epiphytic growth that in some places it reaches a mass of hundreds of pounds per acre.

On the forest floor, sparse and stunted ground-hugging plants try to survive in the shade. Randomly scattered in this perpetual gloom are bright oases of light. Hundreds of club mosses, rushlike horsetails, and ferns, along with the occasional cycad, blanket the ground wherever a hole in the canopy lets sunlight break through.

Sounds and breezes are quickly absorbed; the air is often dead silent, but the stillness is an illusion. The plants of the woodlands grow at a frantic rate, for a forest. Holes in the canopy fill quickly. Spindly saplings scattered through the understory reach up through the deep shade with their sparse needles and scale leaves waiting for a lightning strike, a windstorm, disease, or insect infestation to create an opening. Seeds and spores wait with mindless patience for a shaft of strong sunlight to spur them into growth. When an opening appears, the saplings race toward it, often reaching it in only a few

years. The winners spread their branches as wide as possible in the life-giving light. The losers are left to eke out an existence just under the recently patched gap by poking the odd branch through tiny openings, or to slowly die back into the perpetual twilight.

From a distance, the endless green of the forest may look monotonous, but a closer look reveals a palette of infinite diversity: Blue-green ferns and young yellow-green leaves are interspersed with the subtle, rich siennas and umbers of branches, tree bark, and leaf litter. And when the ebb and flow of sunlight through the mist and cloud cover strikes the occasional patch of dew-covered vegetation, the light sparks new color in the understory.

The forest—hot, humid, dim, and musty—stands in sharp contrast to the well-lit, breezy, open spaces of the riverside flood plains. There, brightly lit thickets of young conifers, cycads, cycadeoids, and scrub growth, with an abundance of ferns and water-loving, segmented, reedlike plants—some as tall as a tree—offer a change from the towering old-growth forests that close in on either side. On the flood plains trees rarely reach higher than twenty feet because of the ever-changing paths of the rivers and their destructive effects. But close to the rivers, large stands of horsetail reeds grow more than thirty feet high, their tops set gently waving

Phytosaurs congregate in a wetland surrounded by tree ferns, conifers, ginkgoes, and a multitude of flying insects backlit by the morning sun. Much of their activity in the day to come will consist of alternating between basking in the hot sun, mouths agape, and submerging in the water to cool off. A lot of the behavior of the big reptiles is geared toward regulating their body temperature, which is dependent largely on the environment.

back and forth by the slightest of breezes. These elegant plants can be seen from quite a distance, making the exact location of every river easy to determine for flying creatures looking for a meal.

Farther from the water grows a tangled mix of plants of all kinds: slender cycads, both branched and unbranched; squat cycadeoids with their massive trunks; short ginkgolike trees; sapling conifers sprung from seeds from the nearby forest; and the ever-present ferns, some simply set with lobed leaflike fronds and others intricately divided into a delicate lace of hundreds of leaflets.

Numerous trails crisscross the brush in an intricate maze. Established through long years of constant use, most of these head to and from the rivers, but many others lead to places where food or cover can be found, and still others range up into the forest. The trails are liberally dotted with droppings, left behind as animals amble from one feeding place to another.

As green and lush as the forest may appear, it cannot support a large, permanent population of herbivorous vertebrates, because the bulk of the edible plant parts grow high out of reach. So the majority of the vertebrates in the woodlands live near, along, or in its many rivers and lakes. In these flood plains, much of the vegetation is easily accessible to herbivores of every size—and many of the herbivores are easily accessible to the animals that prey on them.

Billions of plant-eating beetles and other insects sustain a fairly large population of small reptiles, mammals, long-legged crocodiles, young dinosaurs, and even fish. Larger predators include six- to ten-foot-long bipedal dinosaurs as well as the fearsome archosaurian rauisuchians, which, at nearly twenty feet in length, are quite capable of taking down any local herbivore. Then there are those like the fabrosaurids, omnivores that will eat almost anything found in and around the woodlands.

In the many lakes, bogs, swamps, and streams live myriad small, algae-eating arthropods and mollusks. They support a large population of small bony fish which, in terms of sheer mass, constitute a large but unseen part of the food chain that keeps the woodlands' aquatic ecosystems running. They provide food for larger freshwater sharks, lungfish, carnivorous dinosaurs, pterosaurs, the giant amphibian metoposaurs, and—easily the most common large vertebrate in the woodlands—phytosaurs.

As a river meanders, two distinct banks develop. On the outside of the curve, where the water travels faster, erosion forms a steep embankment, continually undercutting and carrying away the soil and vegetation. On the inside, where the water moves much more slowly, a wide crescent of gently sloping beach forms. It is here that phytosaurs are likely to be found.

Members of the large and diversified archosaurs, phytosaurs occupy the top freshwater predator spot in almost every river and pool in the flood plains. They are very territorial; a large phytosaur in a well-stocked wetland is extremely difficult to dislodge. Its size and hunting technique are more than enough to explain the odd behavior of most woodlands residents when they venture to the water's edge. Just the sight of an expanse of water may trigger reflexive changes: walking speed slows, with frequent pauses every few steps, accompanied by furtive glances and a quick side-to-side swivel of the head. Even larger pools and rivers are approached with caution because of what may lurk within.

The elongated bodies of these crocodilelike reptiles are supported by four short legs, with the hind limbs somewhat longer than those in front. Clawed toes interconnected with short webs of skin provide traction while walking across the muddy riverbanks, or along the silty bottom. Almost half of a phytosaur's heavily armored, twenty-foot-long body is tail. On land, phytosaurs occasionally assume an unhurried, almost stately, "high walk," with their legs held almost directly underneath them, but usually they just slide along the slick mud on the polished scales of their bellies. In water, they hold their limbs back against their bodies, sculling through the water at considerable speeds with their powerful tail muscles. Their narrow, much-elongated snouts slice through the water with ease, and their jaws sprout a battery of sharp teeth. Their nostril openings lie almost between their eyes, rising above the top of the snout, allowing them to

both breathe and see while remaining almost completely submerged.

Although well adapted to stalking, capturing, and eating a variety of prey, most species of phytosaurs primarily eat fish. These they round up by patrolling the shallows along riverbanks and lakeshores. Swimming parallel to the shore, they force fish toward the land, then quickly twist their bodies to one side and snap them up with a rapid, sideways movement. Some species of phytosaurs are more opportunistic, taking anything they can get hold of, subdue, and swallow. Just about any animal that enters or even approaches the water will attract their attention. With hardly a ripple, these phytosaurs slowly draw near their intended victim, size it up, and decide if and when to strike. As it gets closer, the stealthy predator submerges completely, jaws agape. Then, a few powerful strokes of its muscular tail propel it forward in a great spray of water. The tooth-lined jaws snap shut so forcefully that the victim is sometimes killed instantly. If not, it is dragged back into the water and held under until it drowns.

Once the struggling has stopped, the phytosaur swallows its prey whole or, if it is too large, dismembers it. Since phytosaur teeth are conical and sharply pointed, they are ideal for holding onto slippery prey but totally inadequate for cutting or chewing. Fish are usually swallowed whole; raising its jaws high above the surface, the phytosaur throws the meal down its throat with several jerks of its head. Larger prey must be torn apart. This rather inelegant feat entails holding the prey firmly while rotating rapidly in the water until the current mouthful separates

In a fish-eye view, a *Eudimorphodon* snares a *Semionotus. Eudimorphodon* are the most common pterosaur here and feed almost exclusively on the abundant freshwater fish in the lakes and ponds of the region. The pterosaurs fly close to the surface of the water, using their tail rudders to stabilize their flight, and dart their heads into the water, where their tooth-lined jaws hold fast to the many fish that often gather at the surface. At the moment of capture, the pterosaurs' eyes close, protected at that instant by a "third eyelid" called a nictitating membrane.

A large armored *Desmatosuchus* gnaws at a tree root it has just unearthed. Strictly herbivorous, these large twelve- to fourteen-foot-long animals are from a group known as aetosaurs. Built low to the ground, they browse on ferns and other vegetation and seem particularly fond of buried treats such as roots, rhizomes, and tubers, which they get at with their upturned snouts and claws. They have a considerable ecological impact, mostly negative, in that in their pursuit of their favorite foodstuffs they make a general mess of things, often damaging more than they consume.

from the rest of the carcass. Turtles, pterosaurs, dinosaurs, and any of the woodlands' wildlife—if they are the right size—will pique the interest of at least one of the larger phytosaurs. Smaller phytosaurs are fair game, too, so when phytosaurs bask on the bank, they congregate only with others their size.

Just as the wet season is winding down, and the rivers are at their highest, female phytosaurs take over the portions of the riverbanks closest to the scrub cover of the flood plains as nesting areas. Nesting must coincide with the greatest volume of a river; too early and the river will drown the nests, too late and the falling water level will leave the hatchlings dangerously vulnerable to predators on their dash to the relative safety of the river.

To avoid problems with potentially cannibalistic males, prowling juveniles, and other predators, the females nest only at the farthest landward reaches of certain beaches. Given a chance, vegetation will grow right up to the river's edge. However, phytosaurs on their way to and from the river to bask disturb the soil on their favorite beaches, so the plant cover there is sparse for quite some distance from the river's edge—if, indeed, there is any at all.

Over a period of a few days, the female phytosaurs all leave the rivers in the heat of the day and select a place for their nests. They use their powerful hind legs and strong claws to dig a hole a foot deep in the loose sand and clay. Within minutes, they fill it with several dozen white, shiny eggs and quickly cover it with a thick layer of soil. Each nest is effectively guarded by up to one hundred vigilant, easily provoked phytosaurs, who remain nearby to keep watchful eyes on their nests. They dig the nests as close together as they can be without risking serious confrontation with one another. That way, if one phytosaur has to leave to cool off, potential predators might be chased by neighboring phytosaurs defending their own nests.

Other animals that roam the flood plains are the dicynodonts, herbivores that reach lengths of up to twelve feet, weigh in at close to two tons, and bear daggerlike canine teeth. These formidable-looking therapsids are the few remaining evolutionary stragglers of once more widely scattered and more successful mammal-like reptiles. During the Permian Period, dicynodonts made up over eighty percent of the animal life in certain environments. Now they are all but gone.

Not very common in the woodlands, the dicynodont *Placerias* spends considerable time in and near the water, wallowing and using its great tusks and horny beak to feed on the luxuriant plant growth and dig into the soil for roots and tubers. Both the inaccessibility of adequate forage in the extensively wooded forests and the exceedingly thick and tangled plant growth on the flood plains tend to discourage large herds of large animals. Small groups of placerians can sometimes be found along the rivers because the banks are not everywhere accessible or easily negotiated by their short, stocky legs. Here they eat, all day long, almost every part of whatever plants they choose.

This often puts the largely innocuous dicynodonts right in with the basking phytosaurs, but animals the size of adult *Placerias* usually prove too daunting even for the larger phytosaurs. A colony of nesting phytosaurs, however, might deny a group of dicynodonts access to the river, if the lumbering herbivores chose that place and time to wallow or drink. Although confrontations in and out of the water do occur, active conflicts are rare.

Inland from all the activity of feeding dicynodonts and phytosaurs jockeying for the best spots on the beach, several yards into the heavy brush, things quiet down quickly. Here, not only are the rivers lost to sight, but even the sounds of the water are hushed. Occasionally, the gentle whisper of the breeze is interrupted by the rustle of an animal moving about in one of the thick stands of scrub. As often as not, the rustling indicates the presence of *Calyptosuchus*. Belonging to a group of archosaurs known as aetosaurs, they are heavily armored above and below with bony plates embedded in their skin. Equipped with a tail powerful enough to break bones, these otherwise harmless and dull-witted herbivores have few enemies.

Calyptosuchians use their unusual upturned snout, as do all other aetosaurs, to root through the loose, loamy soil in search of underground stems called rhizomes, as well as roots and tubers. While feeding, they seem totally engrossed, plowing along, noses down, heads all but buried. Surfacing occasionally to chew some morsel with their peglike teeth, they look around and listen for signs of danger. Places they have already rooted through are easily recognized by their signature: shallow, meandering trenches plowed into the dark soil, punctuated every so often with small craters. As the first of the plant-eating archosaurs, these widespread and prolific aetosaurs have the rooting/low-browsing niche pretty much all to themselves throughout the woodlands.

Another aetosaur spends much of its time in the more wooded areas. The narrow-bodied, long-legged *Desmatosuchus* is encased in armored plates like *Calyptosuchus*, but it also sports a pair of spikes jutting back from its shoulders as much as two feet. Also a loner, this twelve- to fourteen-foot-long reptile moves from clearing to clearing in search of ferns and other low-lying vegetation.

Often, these aetosaurs will come across the remains of some other inhabitant of the woodlands, rapidly being recycled into the local ecology by scavengers, insects, and the weather. Sometimes a long, tapered, serrated tooth, broken off at the root, lying near the scattered and broken bits of bone, held together by dried skin and sinew, bears mute testimony to the sudden and violent death of whatever wore the skin. The owner of the tooth, and the only terrestrial predator large enough to tackle and take down an animal as large as a fully grown aetosaur like *Desmatosuchus*, or a dicynodont like *Placerias*, is another archosaur, the rauisuchian *Postosuchus*. Reaching heights of five feet and lengths up to seventeen feet, these quadrupedal, carnivorous dreadnoughts, with their short muscular necks supporting high-sided heads equipped with daggerlike, serrated teeth, leave no doubt as to who is at the top of the food chain in this forest.

Rauisuchians occasionally wander in and about the woodlands and flood plains of the woodlands, raising havoc with the aetosaurs, phytosaurs, dicynodonts, and other inhabitants. Like their distant cousins, the phytosaurs and aetosaurs, the rauisuchians descend from

PRECEDING PAGES

A *Postosuchus* prepares to defend its bounty from thieving neighbors. The archosaur *Postosuchus* is the largest predator of the Arizona forest, often reaching seventeen feet in length. Although powerful enough to have taken down this catch, the large herbivorous therapsid *Placerias*, *Postosuchus*, like most predators, is not above turning its back on a considerable meal of carrion. As in most ecosystems, the majority of prey animals here die natural deaths, and a good percentage of the food that the predators here consume comes from carrion. However, just because no effort was expended in bringing down this meal, that does not alter the timeless etiquette around the meal. This *Postosuchus* will be no less vigilant in defending its prize, which means that the four terrestrial crocodilians *Hesperosuchus* and the lone dinosaur *Coelophysis* will have to be patient and wait their turn.

RIGHT

Most of the forest understory of Triassic Pangaea consists of various types of ferns. These large *Clathropteris* leaves, growing above smaller *Hausmania*, are among the many ferns that grow throughout the region.

bipedal ancestors, with their front legs shorter than the rear ones. However, unlike the phytosaurs' more sprawling posture, rauisuchians hold their limbs straight under their bodies like aetosaurs and are exceptional travelers. Covering a dozen or so miles in one day is not uncommon.

As juveniles, rauisuchians raid nests for the eggs and hatchlings of other woodlands inhabitants, dig up the burrows of still others, forage for big, juicy insects, or scavenge. As they grow, the size of their prey increases, but they do not disdain any of the smaller animals that previously sustained them. As adults, they are solitary hunters and patrol rather large territories. They eat whatever they can catch, kill, tear apart, and swallow: all sizes of aetosaurs, dinosaurs, phytosaurs, dicynodonts, and even, on occasion, fish.

Although they are not above scavenging and driving other predators from their kills, most rauisuchians hunt by ambush. Although ambushing requires less energy, it only works well where the movements and habits of the prey are predictable. The well-lit clearings with their thick undergrowth, to which desmatosuchians and other herbivores are instinctively attracted, are ideal places to lie in wait. It might seem impossible for an animal as large as an adult postosuchian to conceal itself well enough to completely surprise another animal, but the thickness of the plant growth in these clearings, the protective coloration of the rauisuchian, and its ability to lie absolutely motionless usually add up to a very surprised aetosaur.

When it comes, the attack itself is just a noisy blur. Although not built for prolonged pursuits, these animals can move at astonishing speeds over short distances. Once the prey is dead, the rauisuchian sets its forepaws on the carcass and starts tearing at it with its powerful jaws and forelimbs, dismembering the meal, and swallowing much of it as quickly as possible. The scent of blood travels far and wide through the forest, attracting others to the clearing. Once it has had its fill, or the prey is gone, the rauisuchian quits the area and often, sometime later, coughs up several wads of teeth, bone fragments, claws, scutes, and scales.

The remains, if any, and the material regurgitated by the rauisuchians are both quickly set upon by myriad insects ever on the alert

for such windfalls. From all over, they fly, crawl, hop, or skitter through the air or along and even under the ground. They come to feed or to lay eggs so that their larvae will be able to feed as they develop and grow.

The presence of carrion, and the activity it attracts, are often noted by still another archosaur: *Hesperosuchus*, a sometime predator, sometime forager, sometime scavenger. One or more of these sleek opportunists might slowly materialize from the gloom and cautiously approach the buzzing, humming feast. Almost half of the four- to five-foot length of these slender, long-legged, crocodilian archosaurs is tail. They walk upright, with their legs straight beneath them, delicately and soundlessly stepping closer, pausing in mid-stride at the slightest change in sound or movement. When startled, they can move very quickly, easily outrunning anything that tries to catch them. If all is well, they eventually approach the remains and use their short, sharp, conical teeth to tear off small bits of flesh.

A small gliding reptile, *Icarasaurus*, prepares to land on a tree branch. Although not capable of true powered flight, these common, small lizards are often seen gliding from treetop to treetop, in search of insects. Their "wings" are actually elongated ribs, between which is stretched a membrane of skin. With a "wingspan" of about a foot, they are a colorful addition to the forest canopy. The wings are also used in territorial displays and in courtship.

Also quick to partake of the feast is a foot-long lizard called *Icarasaurus*—sometimes scampering in from the darkness of the forest floor, sometimes gliding in from above on wings. These are actually greatly elongated, needle-thin ribs that extend several inches from the sides of its body. Once the animal has landed, these rib-wings fold nicely rearward and up to form a crest over its back. With tiny pointed teeth, the little lizard comes not for the carrion but for the insects it attracts. An icarasaur can open its mouth wide and easily ingest even the largest grubs and maggots—provided, of course, that it is not itself snatched up by a *Hesperosuchus*.

Icarasaurus has the honor of being one of the first vertebrates to take to the air, but, being a passive glider, it by no means dominates the skies over the woodlands. That distinction belongs to the pterosaur *Eudimorphodon*. With a wingspan of three feet or more, an adult eudimorphodon is quite adept at snatching fish from the shallows while on the wing. Deftly using its long, stiffened tail with the curious expanded tip as both counterbalance and rudder, the pterosaur maneuvers close to the water's surface and strikes out at its slippery prey with the very sharp teeth protruding from its upper and lower jaws. It then alights and transfers the fish farther back into its mouth where cusped teeth cut through the armored scales in a chewinglike motion before it swallows.

When cruising over a lake or stream, these extremely agile flyers constantly monitor the activity of the phytosaurs patrolling just below the surface. They watch for the telltale sign that the aquatic reptile is stalking fish: rapid swimming along the lakeshore or riverbank, as it herds the fish into shallower water. While the distracted fish are busy watching the phytosaur, the pterosaurs will swoop down and easily pluck them from the water.

Each wing of a pterosaur is formed by an extremely long digit on a short arm, both of which support a thin but tough membrane. Being warm-blooded, eudimorphodonts sport a furry coat unlike many of the scale-covered residents in the area. The sights and sounds of flocks of these noisy pterosaurs roosting along the shores of the larger lakes in the woodlands, carefully preening their fur and filling the air with their incessant chatter, add a pleasant flurry of activity to the normally placid and sedate rivers and flood plains.

The lakes of the woodlands abound in fishes, from the small, brightly colored, thick-scaled ray-finned fishes to moderately sized freshwater sharks, all the way up to larger streamlined lungfish and the deep-bodied coelacanths, with their distinctively lobed fins and three-pronged tails. The larger fish feed on the smaller and the smaller feed on the innumerable snails, clams, and small, swimming crustaceans. These small invertebrates, in turn, graze on the algae that thrive here and give many of the lakes a deep greenish hue. Sitting at the top of the lake food chain are the burly metoposaurs. Up to eight feet long, with four short, splayed legs, these large, flat amphibians lie along the muddy bottoms of rivers and lakes throughout the woodlands. Their large, bulging eyes sit well forward on their flat skulls and double rows of sharp, pointed teeth line the edges of their two-foot-wide jaws.

The more active side-snapping style favored by phytosaurs lies in sharp contrast to the metoposaurs' hunting style. Essentially, they slurp. Lying motionless in the fine mud at the bottom of a lake, even a fully grown adult's broad head and body are practically invisible. Any unwary fish that has the misfortune to venture within a yard of a concealed metoposaur simply disappears in a cloud of silt. By rapidly lunging forward and opening its long, wide jaws, the attacking amphibian creates a suction strong enough to draw in much of the water around its head, and everything in it—including the fish. Before the startled prey can react, toothy jaws close down, pinning it while the water is expelled. As an amphibian, a metoposaur's low metabolic rate only allows it very brief periods of rapid or strenuous activity and this technique suits it fine.

Occasionally metoposaurs can be found living alongside phytosaurs in one of the lakes, or in any of the slower-moving streams or rivers. Although there are more than enough fish to go around, relations between the two animals get a little strained during a prolonged dry season when shrinking habitats bring them closer together. But, except for occasionally eating a few of each other's offspring, neither of these formidable predators bothers much with the other, because they use different methods of hunting, and basically just stay out of each other's way.

Like the metoposaurs and phytosaurs, most of the wildlife in the woodlands is pretty much set in its habits and habitats. Each is a specialist of sorts, highly adapted for one lifestyle—and one lifestyle only. But there are some animals that are not restricted to a specific lifestyle

Upward of eight feet in length, another denizen of the Arizona wetlands environment is the large amphibian *Metoposaurus*. Burly, lethargic in appearance, they make their living by lying motionless near the bottom of a lake and literally "slurp" their meals in. Any fish or smaller animal that is unlucky to venture too close simply disappears in a cloud of silt, sucked in by the two-foot-wide jaws. A peculiar characteristic of these animals, and their relatives, is how incredibly flattened the animal's body is, particularly its head.

or habitat and, as it turns out, are just as successful. These unspecialized generalists make up still another group of archosaurs: the dinosaurs.

Dinosaurs descended from partially aquatic ancestors that had powerful tails and large hind limbs for chasing prey through water. When some of these animals moved back onto land in the southern half of Pangaea, ten million years earlier, they retained these tails and limbs and ultimately developed into small, lightly built, running bipeds. Since then, the early dinosaur descendants have spread north.

Fabrosaurids, although not at all common here, are still the most numerous full-time dinosaur residents. Equally at home in the forest, on a flood plain, or along a lakeshore, the three- to four-foot-long, predominantly herbivorous dinosaurs are quick and agile. They have to be: speed and agility are their best and only defenses against rauisuchians and other predators.

In sharp contrast to the basking phytosaurs or lumbering aetosaurs, fabrosaurids are always on the move. The long-necked, long-tailed animals forage actively, constantly dropping to all fours and using their slender flexible necks to poke their narrow snouts everywhere. Not very picky eaters, fabrosaurids will take young shoots, buds, leaves, some seeds, an occasional insect,

even carrion. Their small grasping forepaws scatter leaf litter and pull apart dead stems in their almost ceaseless search for food.

The *Coelophysis*, an equally active small dinosaur, is only an occasional visitor to the woodlands. Its normal range is the somewhat higher and drier area to the north and east. These six- to eight-foot-long animals wander into the woodlands only when pressured by a prolonged dry season or some other environmental calamity at home. About twice the size of the fabrosaurids, the nimble and carnivorous coelophysians use their speed and agility both to capture prey and to avoid becoming prey themselves. In the lowlands, they find a variety of food: fabrosaurid eggs and juveniles, crocodiles and aetosaurs—even an occasional small pterosaur, when they can catch them. In forays into the shallow waters of a lake, they often capture a few fish or even a metoposaur tadpole or young phytosaur. When a coelophysian captures its prey, or at least holds it down with its flexible fingers, it uses serrated teeth to tear off manageable pieces or, if the prey is small enough, like a tiny mammal, swallows it whole.

Since arising from therapsids during the Middle Triassic, mammals—warm-blooded, furred, milk-producing egg-laying animals—have spread rapidly across Pangaea and are now firmly established in the woodlands and elsewhere. A few inches long at most, quick and furtive, living invisible lives in a dark world, mammals are truly creatures of the night.

Darting through the underbrush, scrambling over twigs and through the leaf litter, noses twitching, in search of insects, millipedes, and other small arthropods, these nocturnal hunters are equipped with a full complement of night combat gear: keen olfactory senses, a touch-sensitive snout, and equally touch-sensitive whiskers, all of which make them look like little more than moving muzzles. Their acute hearing is aided by ears that can pinpoint the exact source of any sound, no matter how faint. This gear provides all the sensations that these relatively nearsighted and practically color-blind little hunters need to live their lives enveloped in the darkness of night or in their lightless tunnels and burrows.

Mammals' jaws are set with separate teeth for piercing, cutting, and grinding, arranged in that order, from front to back; ideal for catching, holding, cutting, dicing, crushing, and pulping the tough exoskeletons of the insects and other arthropods that make up their diet. Such highly nutritious food, combined with their insulating furry pelts, allows these warm-blooded animals to remain active during the cool of evening and the cold of night, when their distant reptilian relatives must reduce their activity to nothing more than shallow breathing.

Small size brings the safety of being unobtrusive in a predator-rich environment. To stay small, mammals stop growing at sexual maturity, unlike reptiles and archosaurs, whose growth may slow down considerably but does not stop completely. But small size requires adjustments elsewhere. Fewer, smaller eggs, with less nutrition for the embryos within these eggs, mean that the mammalian young, when they hatch, are extremely immature. They need a good deal of parental care, as well as a special diet, the milk produced by the mothers.

Now it has all fallen together for the mammals of the Late Triassic and, like the dinosaurs, they have established themselves as permanent, albeit small, members of Pangaea's wildlife.

During the Carboniferous and Permian Periods there had always been inhabitants of the swamps and lowlands of the planet. In the Triassic, these niches were, at first, filled by some holdovers, such as the large amphibian metoposaurs, dicynodonts and rauisuchids. But newer animals are now beginning to assert themselves. Originally trying to make a go of it in wetlands and swamps, they have slowly begun to alter the dynamic. As the dynasty of large, lumbering louts splash about in and near the lakes and streams of Pangaea, the offshoots of some of the newer lines are nipping at their heels. Left to lurk in the brush, these small animals wait patiently for their cue, ready to take the stage.

A pair of *Eudimorphodon* wing their way through a clearing among the great conifers. Shrouded by mist, veiled in a canopy of green, this ecosystem nonetheless supports a rich variety of wildlife throughout its expanse.

CHAPTER THREE

RIFT VALLEY

Dinosaurs Begin to Dominate the Jurassic Landscape

After eighty million years of stable existence, Pangaea is showing signs of breaking up. Deep under the supercontinent, thousands of cubic miles of hot, semi-molten, plastic rock are moving upward and outward, dragging the supercontinent apart. As the heat has been building, the rock underlying Pangaea has expanded. The continental crust has actually begun to rise at its center, bulging up by almost a quarter of a mile. Roughly parallel cracks are forming for thousands of miles up and down the middle of the continent, some running hundreds of miles long and tens of miles wide. The ground quakes almost daily somewhere along the fracture zone as paths are tested, in the process creating many rift valleys. When a path is finally chosen, the supercontinent will divide, spawning smaller landmasses and a new ocean. The rifting progresses unevenly. In some places, movement takes place along a single fault, leaving picturesque, nearly vertical escarpments. In others, hundreds of smaller faults result in barely perceptible slopes. No matter how tranquil they appear, these valleys are all products of violent, cataclysmic earth movements. As Pangaea splits farther, these valleys will continue to widen and deepen.

A few degrees from the equator, twenty-five hundred miles east of the mist-filled forests of the woodlands, and about as far from any ocean as it can get, lies a valley typical of the rift system. Running roughly northeast to southwest, it is watered enough during the rainy season to maintain several large lakes, numerous smaller ones, and enough forest, scrub, and fern prairie to support a sizable population of animals through the dry season. As the wildlife of the woodlands congregated in the relatively narrow flood plains, the wildlife here dwells in the relatively narrow confines of this valley.

PRECEDING PAGES
A clear, calm morning and a distant escarpment barely hint at the drama unfolding beneath this Late Triassic valley. This is the northeastern region of North America. Numerous scenes like this stretch on for thousands of miles to the northeast and southwest. They form a great system of rifts and leave no doubt that the great supercontinent of Pangaea is beginning to break apart.

OPPOSITE
A freshly made *Coelophysis* footprint lies almost hidden by a cycad frond. One of the most widespread and adaptable animals of this region, *Coelophysis* often leave their prints in the sandy soils and mud surrounding the many lakes and wetlands in the area. Notice the impressions of the animal's foot pads and claws.

An escarpment, formed by the steady dropping of the valley floor as the supercontinent is torn apart, looms dramatically and reaches beyond the horizons. The raw red-brown hue of this sheer scarp stands in sharp contrast to the uniformly green forest at its feet and the blue sky, studded with clouds overhead. A few green plants valiantly maintain a hold on the high, steeply sloping sandstone face. The eastern side of the valley rises gently, only gradually reaching an equal height, and it is swathed in vegetation, as is the valley floor.

Every afternoon during the rainy season the eastern skies cloud up quickly. With an occasional bolt of lightning tearing across the darkened sky and a rumble of thunder, the threatening gray clouds dump the moisture they have carried from the distant Tethys Sea bordering Pangaea's seemingly limitless eastern plains. Sheets of large falling drops, and a swirling haze of finer ones, at first form delicate tiny craters in the mud and then soak everything, cutting visibility down to almost zero. Within moments, countless cascades pour noisily over the escarpment, while countless rivulets trickle more sedately down the gentle slope opposite. Most of this water collects in the major and minor lakes that dot the length of the valley, growing deeper under the daily deluge.

The larger rift lakes run deep and still, and they may spread over several hundred square miles during the rainy season. Hundreds of feet deep in places, their poorly circulating waters bring no oxygen to their depths, so all life is confined to the sunlit surfaces, their extensive shallow shorelines, and the reed-choked marshes and swamps that abut them. All around a rich

smell rises—a mixture of damp soil, dripping vegetation, thick dark mud, and warm green water. Among the ferns, tangled scrub, and wooded groves of the valley floor, the torrid heat and high humidity close in and swarms of insects fill the air.

The plants and wildlife here are not quite the same as those of the woodlands of long ago. The valley lies far from the sea, and Pangaea's climate has become seasonally drier. Scale-leafed conifers, thick-cuticled seed ferns, and the cycadophytes, plants with large fronds and pithy stems, are thriving but plant diversity as a whole has dropped. As a result, large herbivores like the aetosaurs are dwindling in numbers. Others, like the dicynodonts, are gone—not just absent from the valley, but extinct. Their demise, and that of other large herbivores, has cut into the food supply of the larger carnivorous reptiles like the rauisuchians, and they too are in decline.

Most of the valleys of the rift system lie on the rainy side of the majestic, snow-capped mountains just to the west. They are relatively well watered, so they are full of fish, phytosaurs, and metoposaurs. However, increasingly arid conditions across the planet have placed the plants and animals in these valleys under a tremendous strain. Everywhere rainfall has become more cyclical. Superimposed on the annual wet and dry seasons, a much longer cycle now dominates the supercontinent's climate. During these longer cycles, alternating wet and dry phases take more than twenty thousand years to run their course. Terrible droughts decimate large areas for extended periods.

The therapsids and early mammals are having an especially hard time of it. They

Coelophysis are successful due in part to their ability to get by on a wide range of prey; basically, anything they can catch and eat will sustain them. Opportunistic, many are often seen at the first light of day, patrolling the shores of lakes and wetlands, in search of something to eat. That is when they leave their footprints, which harden in the sun and remain long after the animals have moved on.

Various species and subspecies of *Coelophysis* can be found throughout Pangaea, finding success in a wide range of habitats and locations.

produce the chemical urea as a by-product of protein metabolism. Urea is poisonous but it is water soluble, so only if it is diluted considerably can it be stored in a bladder for a length of time before being voided. Both groups, therefore, excrete large quantities of water with their urine. Because this water must be replaced regularly, these animals are at risk during an extended drought.

Archosaurs such as dinosaurs, crocodiles and pterosaurs, and lizards, as well as a few other animals, produce uric acid instead of urea. Uric acid is neither as poisonous nor as soluble as urea, so it can be stored less hazardously and voided nearly dry, as a paste. Since little water is lost in the process, less water must be replaced—a neat trick that helps these animals survive the dry times.

The longer droughts also affect young animals still in the egg. Most reptile embryos, such as those of the rauisuchians, phytosaurs, and aetosaurs, rely on a yolk that contains a good deal of protein. Dinosaur embryos subsist on a more fatty yolk. Fat metabolism releases more water as a by-product than protein metabolism does. So, dinosaur eggs survive prolonged desiccation better than reptile eggs do. The upshot: The longer and deeper droughts toward the end of the Late Triassic are favoring the survival of the dinosaurs and other archosaurs over others such as therapsids and early mammals.

After many hundreds of the longer climate cycles, the planet's fauna and flora have changed so drastically that now an entirely new period has begun—the Jurassic. The earlier disappearance of animals like the dicynodonts was only a harbinger of the greater extinctions toward the end of the Triassic. The severe climatic extremes have taken their toll on plants and animals across Pangaea. The valleys have witnessed the extinction of the fierce rauisuchians, the docile aetosaurs, the fish-eating phytosaurs, and the incredibly ugly metoposaurs. Now, in the Early Jurassic, crocodiles, pterosaurs, and dinosaurs like the coelophysians and the fabrosaurids have inherited the supercontinent, finally earning them their title of archosaur—the "ruling" reptiles.

The valley looks, in the Early Jurassic, much the same as it did when the Triassic was winding down. Although it is still widening and deepening, sediments are washing in at a rate that has pretty much kept the valley floor at a constant level. Lakes abound, and the area has a parklike look and feel to it. The weather is still severely cyclical, but the wildlife has adjusted.

In contrast to the river basin flood plains, several kinds of coelophysians reside in the valley. Although they vary slightly in size and diet, they are all opportunists. One species spends most of its time in the foothills of the mountains, a hundred or so miles northwest. These lightly built, bipedal, upland dinosaurs usually appear in the valley only when a severe dry spell drives them in. Then, they work their way down the hollows cut in the escarpment and seek out the wetlands around the lakes. Here they mingle freely with other coelophysian species, feeding heavily on the fish gathered in the small pools left by the drying and shrinking lakes. At times, thousands of their footprints lie baking hard into the muddy, former lake bottoms, in the hot Jurassic sun.

When the rains resume, the smaller, upland coelophysians migrate back up the clefts to their normal range, while the lowland species gravitates toward the wooded and scrubby areas that is its normal haunt. Congregating in loose groups of mixed sexes and ages, they make life a challenge for the smaller animals of this ecosystem: the lizardlike reptiles, the small, sleek, long-legged crocodiles, amphibians, and the mammal-like trithelodonts —small, plant-eating therapsids. Much of their prey depends on camouflage or a quick burst of speed to escape predators, so for coelophysians, hunting in small groups has advantages. A small group on the prowl covers more ground than an individual and flushes out prey more easily. Better yet, one member of the band might drive prey into the waiting jaws of another. Not only does this technique work more often than not, it is random enough so that over time all the members of the band benefit. Dinosaurs are the first to use this hunting method regularly.

Other former basin residents doing well in the Jurassic valley are the fabrosaurids. At about half the size of coelophysians, they do their best to avoid the hunting parties, depending on their acute hearing more than their sense of smell to detect predators and find food. With large eyes that are sensitive to the slightest movement, these herbivorous dinosaurs scan far and wide, constantly on the alert. Their fine-tuned senses are suited for life in the ecotone, the area where the scrub transitions into forest. While foraging in flocks, at least one fabrosaurid will keep its head raised above the vegetation to watch for any danger. The forest is always close at hand for cover and, with a great deal of chirping and frantic dashing about, the flock can quickly scatter among its dark shadows.

Fabrosaurids range up and down the valley, and even into the highlands. They use their flat, leaf-shaped teeth and the scissorslike motion of their jaws to cut up vegetation of all types. Grasping their food between tiny forepaws, they chew for a few seconds, then stop and look around nervously while swallowing. They also use their narrow snouts and paws to root around the valley floor, occasionally taking eggs, insects, or carrion.

Ripple marks and dinosaur footprints large and small line the shores of a rift lake. Most shoreline prints are made by predatory dinosaurs. In their search for something to eat, they spend a lot of time near the lakeshore environments of the region, and the amount of prints they leave can give a misleading indication of their true numbers in their habitat.

The many lakes in the greater rift system vary from bodies of fresh water that support extensive wildlife communities to mineralized aggregates so caustic that they are literally devoid of life. Often, soda and mineral deposits will form on the lakes' perimeters, as can be seen on this one.

The deep droughts stress the archosaurs and other animals living in the valley, hardening them, winnowing out those unsuited to harsh climatic extremes. Toward the end of a wet period, most of the plants go dormant. Some lose their leaves or needles; others can get by and keep their foliage. All, though, sustain themselves through the inevitable dry times by drawing on moisture and nutrients stored in their stems and roots.

Like the plants, some animals spend the wet seasons building up reserves, in the form of fatty tissues, and deal with the dry periods by drawing upon these reserves. Others modify their feeding habits instead. Some, like coelophysians, switch to a fish diet and some fabrosaurids shift from a diet of shoots and leaves to one of roots and seeds. Some small tritheledonts estivate, retreating to their burrows and sleeping through the drought.

Perhaps the hardest hit are those animals that depend on the lakes and streams for their existence—the fish. By far the dominant fish are *Semionotus*, whose many brightly colored species vary in size from a few inches to over a foot long. They subsist mostly on tiny arthropods such as insect larvae, water fleas, and clamshrimp—curious little creatures encased in a chitinous bivalved shell just a quarter inch across. These abundant crustaceans feed on the ever-present algae. When times are good, at the height of the wet season, hundreds of millions of clamshrimp feed millions of *Semionotus*, which feed the thousands of pterosaurs, as well as practically every other carnivorous animal in the region.

As many as a dozen species of *Semionotus* might occupy one body of water. Close by the shore, these showy fish exhibit every hue imaginable as they go about their business: feeding, fighting, breeding, biting, or just hanging suspended in the murky green water, slowly drifting, or swiftly disappearing in a cloud of silt. The many species fill the different niches found in each lake. Some feed at the surface, some in midwater, while others are strictly bottom feeders. Some are found only among the lakeshores' weed-choked marshes, others only in its open waters. Some swim through the turquoise water singly, others in huge shoals.

BELOW
The semionotids are a widespread group of fish, found throughout lakes and wetlands of Pangaea, including lakes and ponds in Arizona. In the eastern rift lakes though, they seem to have become particularly successful, radiating into dozens of species that occupy every available lake niche. Often, species are separated into biozones only a few feet apart. One may favor a water depth of no more than three feet; another a depth a few feet deeper. Though living in close proximity neither species interacts with the other.

Rift lakes vary from those shallow enough to change size and shape significantly over a few days or weeks, to those substantial enough to remain more or less unchanged over thousands of years. The long climate cycles, the topography of the valley's floor, and the increased geothermal activity characteristic of the rift system produce a range of lake types. They can vary from deeper, cooler, freshwater lakes, which provide relatively stable habitats for a wide range of plant and wildlife in and around them, to shallower, warmer, slightly soapy-feeling soda lakes, which can support a surprising amount of biological activity, though less varied than the sweetwater lakes and bodies of water so hot and caustic they burn the skin of anything attempting to enter them.

Several million years further on and about a hundred miles north and east of the valley lies another valley—a mirrored twin, as the escarpment here is on the eastern side. This is a cooler and wetter time and place. The trees here are larger and the plants are more varied and abundant, as is the wildlife. Prosauropod dinosaurs, the first truly herbivorous dinosaurs, have finally come into their own. Although they have been around since the Late Triassic, they have never before been abundant or an important part of any habitat in the rift system; competition from other animals, and the dry climate and lack of vegetation kept their numbers down.

Now things have changed. The present climate favors new types of vegetation—and, therefore, greater numbers and types of prosauropods. These plant-eaters spend much of their time on all fours, but if the need arises, they can extend their feeding range considerably by hauling at least half of their twenty-foot length up on their hind limbs. This simple ability makes them the first high-browsing animals on the planet. Hundreds of thousands of pounds of green biomass, until now inaccessible and unexploited, is now theirs for the taking. And take it they do. Once up on its hind legs, a prosauropod grasps branches with a curved claw on each forelimb, drawing them down so it can strip the leaves and needles off with its coarsely serrated, peglike teeth. It fills its cheeks and drops back to all fours. The food is diced with

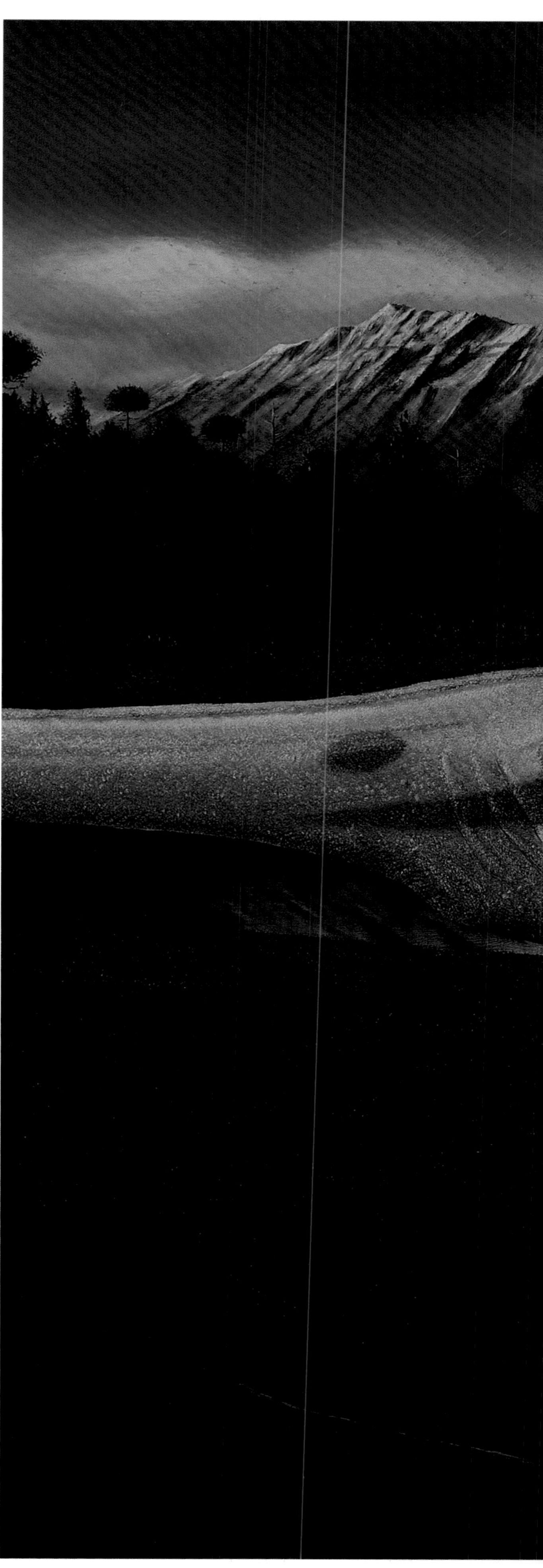

The prosauropods are among the largest animals of the rift ecosystem. Some, like these *Ammosaurus*, can reach twenty feet in length. Descended from a line of theropods, they have reverted to a largely quadrupedal stance and adopted a herbivorous diet. Their increasing size and longer necks have allowed them a higher browsing ability than any other plant-eaters ever. Their jaws are designed to bite off vegetation, but not to chew. Food is swallowed largely unprocessed. To aid in digestion, the animals swallow small pebbles and rocks; sent along with food to the animals' gizzard, these rocks, called gastroliths, essentially do the chewing for the animal.

strong jaws, then sent to the gizzard. Here it is further broken down by small rocks called gastroliths. The prosauropod is a study in eating efficiency. Each move is deliberate. No motion is wasted. While one mouthful is being swallowed, the animal's head is moving toward the next. A step is taken only when all the plant material within reach has been consumed.

Feeding solely on plant material requires a specially adapted digestive system. Leaves, scales, needles, twigs, and cones—the most plentiful food available—are all notoriously lacking in nutrition. The prosauropods must ingest enormous amounts if anything at all is to be gleaned from their gluttony. Fortunately, they have a large stomach, extra-long intestines, and the right population of intestinal microbes. A prosauropod eats steadily for up to six or eight hours, rests or sleeps for three or four, then starts eating again. This can, and does, go on all day and all night. This animal cannot afford to let its stomach go empty for long. Because its diet is so difficult to digest properly, its digestive tract must be kept full to ensure a constant flow of nutrients and calories. As a result of this incessant eating, prosauropod dinosaurs defecate constantly. Throughout the valley, the pungent smell of their droppings identifies them instantly and unmistakably, even when they are out of sight.

Two distinct prosauropods now live in the valley: *Ammosaurus* and *Anchisaurus*. The former often graze along stream channels, lakeshores, and the marshes around them, while the latter prefer the higher, drier scrublands. During wet periods, both tend to congregate in loose associations that might, in a sense, be considered herds. If two of these groups meet at a watering spot or in a clearing, they intermingle freely and are just as likely to remain a larger unit for a while or to break up into smaller groups, for no apparent reason. They seem to take very little notice of each other's company.

Only when threatened by a predator does one of these otherwise slow-moving, methodical animals demonstrate surprising speed and agility. A prosauropod under attack has several options. Its heavily clawed front and hind limbs can inflict substantial amounts of damage on a careless predator, and its tail can strike out and raise a stinging welt on an assailant, break its leg, or, in some cases, even knock it down. However, unless cornered, most prosauropods just head for the nearest cover—fast. Built low to the ground, these herbivores can move quickly through low scrub, thick brush, or dense thickets—all of which usually discourage even the most persistent predators. Still, a thousand pounds or so of meat on the hoof is difficult for any predator to ignore. The prosauropod's most dangerous threat is the largest hunter in the valley, *Dilophosaurus*. These carnivorous dinosaurs are, without a doubt, at the top of the food chain here, as they are up and down most of the other rift valleys. All other wildlife is at risk from attack, as these bipedal hunters, easily twice the size of a coelophysian, are quite capable of catching and eating just about anything they encounter, including ammosaurs and anchisaurs.

Typically, a dilophosaur will stalk a group of prosauropods from the dark shadows of the forest, trying to get as close as possible without being detected, before attacking. The hunter makes a quick dash from cover and, as the herbivores scatter or stand their ground, tries to cut a smaller juvenile from the group and keep it in the open by maneuvering to stay between it and the safety of the forest. While the intended victim watches closely, nervously snorting and pawing the ground, the dilophosaur approaches cautiously, avoiding the herbivore's tail and short, stoutly clawed front legs. Lifting its own long tail high, as a counterbalance, the hunter tries to snap down with its sharp, slender, front teeth, gouging and tearing at its victim's shoulder or haunch, rather than biting down and holding on.

Once the prosauropod is wounded sufficiently, blood loss and shock slow its reactions. The dilophosaur can be patient now. It waits until the wounded animal can barely move any longer, then moves in to feed, holding the prey down with the talons on its front and rear legs while cutting out pieces of flesh with the bladelike teeth at the back of its jaw. When prosauropods are not available, dilophosaurs are also adept at running down and capturing smaller game such as fabrosaurids, driving other, smaller predators from their kills, and scavenging. On occasion, they even take to the lakes in search of

Diplurus, a coelacanth fish that can reach lengths of up to two feet.

Toward the end of the wet season, female dilophosaurs excavate nests some distance from the lakes, fill them with eggs, and cover them over with mounds of vegetation to protect them in the dry times to come. Since most animals here tend to stay close to the lakes during the dry seasons, the clutches are fairly safe from being plundered while they incubate. After hatching at the start of the next wet season, the young dilophosaurs gather in loose bands. While foraging, the hatchlings keep to the underbrush and shadows as much as possible to avoid becoming prey themselves. They are so well camouflaged that it is often impossible to get a true estimate of their numbers. At first, they hunt worms and insect larvae by pawing through the loose soil or tearing at the rotting logs that litter the valley floor. As they grow, they slowly work their way up the food chain by preying on some of the smaller reptiles and the offspring of other dinosaurs.

With the advent of the next dry season, the diminutive predators that still remain spend a lot of time at the lakeshores. Here they can find the ever-present insects, and they can also wade into the shallows after fish. During these dry times, however, there is never really enough to go around and the young animals' ranks are thinned further by starvation and predation. Nine out of ten are lost in the first year alone—not the least of them falling to the enemy within. Many hatchlings and young dilophosaurs are killed and eaten by adults, much as happens with their cousins, the coelophysians.

In about a year, at the beginning of the next wet season, the survivors, now in much smaller bands, spend the first few weeks raiding unguarded reptile nests for eggs and newly hatched young. At first, their frames fill out quickly as their new fat- and protein-rich diet

It seems rather unusual that an animal as formidable as *Dilophosaurus*, which relies on visual communication to the extent that it does, should have evolved a display structure as delicate as its nasal crests. But, that is what it has. As a result, the animals go to considerable effort to avoid damaging these structures. A lot of the behavior the animals display toward each other consists of bobbing and weaving, and generally trying to make themselves look more impressive than they really are. However, they are not above actual physical violence.

PRECEDING PAGES
Dilophosaurus occupies the top of the food chain in the rift region. Approaching twenty feet in length, they are related to *Coelophysis* but are easily twice their size. The paired, slight nasal ridges of *Coelophysis*, a display structure, have developed into large paired crests in *Dilophosaurus*. Colorful and highly noticeable, they are used in territorial and courtship displays.

goes to work. Then the young dinosaurs hit an unprecedented burst of growth; by the middle of the season, at the age of one and a half, they are almost fully grown. Now they prey on larger animals like fabrosaurids.

At the same time, something affects their behavior. They no longer tolerate the company of their own kind. Squabbling and fighting, fierce at times, break up the groups. The dilophosaurs are becoming sexually mature. Their already rapid growth accelerates once again. Thin, bony ridges start to sprout along the snouts of the young males and soon become a pair of bright yellowish orange arches running almost the entire length of their long, delicate heads. In their second year, these young adults scatter widely through the rift system valleys and begin to assert territorial behaviors.

Second-year males trying to establish new territories are generally unsuccessful. Forced out of prime areas by older, larger males, many do not establish territories of their own until at least their third year, and some even later. Most wander about the valleys, biding their time. Anytime in the middle of the rainy season that two adult male dilophosaurs pass near each other and seem to be ignoring one another, at least one is sure to be in its second year. Two full-grown adult males meeting at this time will certainly face off, as prime territories are actively sought after and vigorously defended.

Stylized fighting between adult dilophosaur males ranks as one of the most outlandish spectacles the valley has to offer. As the two males slowly approach each other, each moves its head up and down every so often. Then they perform a lateral display. First, one male turns to its right or left so that the other can get a good look at its head crests. Then the other male turns in the same direction to display *its* head crests. While keeping a wary eye on each other, they start to walk, slowly and tentatively, parallel to each other, throwing in quick head bobs now and then. This can go on for quite some time before one turns and charges, forelimbs spread wide and jaws agape, emitting a deep, loud hiss. The other male can respond by fleeing and ending the confrontation, or by replying in kind.

If the second male charges back, it usually stops short of actually making contact, instead turning and repeating the contest. The boldly patterned crests adorning the dilophosaurs' heads are ornate but delicate structures, and the animals go to great lengths to avoid damaging them. Displays and charges like these are usually enough to identify the dominant male without any further problems, but occasionally there is bloodshed. If the displays and false charges fail, the two animals finally make contact and, in a blur of teeth, limbs, claws, and tails, try to bite or kick each other until one breaks off and surrenders the field. These brief, but intense, confrontations are short, noisy, spectacular, and—fortunately for the animals involved—rare.

Displays and threats aside, a male dilophosaur faces the same challenges in securing mates as virtually all the other males in the valley. First, he must locate a potential mate; then, determine that his intended partner is in fact female and mature; next, get in close enough to get her undivided attention; and, finally, make her as interested in mating as he is. Courtship displays, unlike the bold, colorful, and exaggerated territorial displays, must be more subdued so that they will not be interpreted as threatening behavior.

A prospective mate entering the established territory of a male dilophosaur is greeted as if it were an intruding male—a slow approach followed by a rapid turn to one side to display the head crests. Only the response of the female identifies its gender. Where another male would turn in the same direction and parallel the first male's path, a female will, by standing still and not turning its body, change the male's path into a circle centered around itself. The female follows the displaying male with its head, careful not to show its crests, even though they are much less colorful than those of the male. One or two circuits around the stationary female will usually satisfy the male that it has a partner, so the circling stops and they mate.

The female does not select a mate simply because it is large or strong, or has colorful head crests. In effect, the female selects the male's territory. Any territory bountiful enough to sustain a healthy adult male will also provide for the female and its offspring. But not every territory,

no matter how adequate it may seem, remains available for long.

Shortly after the onset of the dry season comes a spectacular phenomenon, upon which the forests of the Early Jurassic have become dependent—wildfire. Started by sporadic lightning strikes, these fires flare up somewhere along the length of the valley almost every day. At times, the bright, cloudless skies fill with a hazy, acrid smoke, tinted with oranges and yellows, often blocking the sun entirely and throwing the landscape into a dim twilight. At night, the horizon glows with an eerie light. Many smaller fires can burn into one another and become huge fire complexes. When the wind rises, it can push these flames through the dried scrub in the open meadows almost as fast as a dinosaur can run, pausing only momentarily to consume thickets of trees. On occasion, glowing cinders and fiery brands that are blown ahead start smaller fires beyond the flame front, giving the fire a ragged edge as it spreads in fits and starts.

Some fires smolder along, their speed measured in feet per hour, with no flames, just a glow visible here and there within the litter, amid choking, thick, gray smoke. Others, hotter, spread along the valley floor at a brisk pace, with a flame front perhaps a foot high, leaving a mosaic of burned patches, killing some trees, scorching and charring others, leaving still others untouched. A rare few, the crown fires, burn very hot and advance swiftly. The terrible brightness of the yellow-orange flames, the pungent, biting smell and taste of the shifting and swirling smoke, and the sound of the rushing air as it is sucked into the inferno are punctuated by

Fire is an important and necessary component in many healthy ecosystems. Many plants actually require periodic burns as part of their reproductive cycles, evolving seeds that only open when exposed to great heat. In the rift valleys, fires are the result of lightning strikes and lava flows. While wrecking havoc on some animals, others take advantage of them. Ever the opportunists, *Coelophysis* have learned to patrol the edges of the flames, picking off prey that the fires have forced out. This *Coelophysis* has snared a trithelodont, a small, herbivorous therapsid.

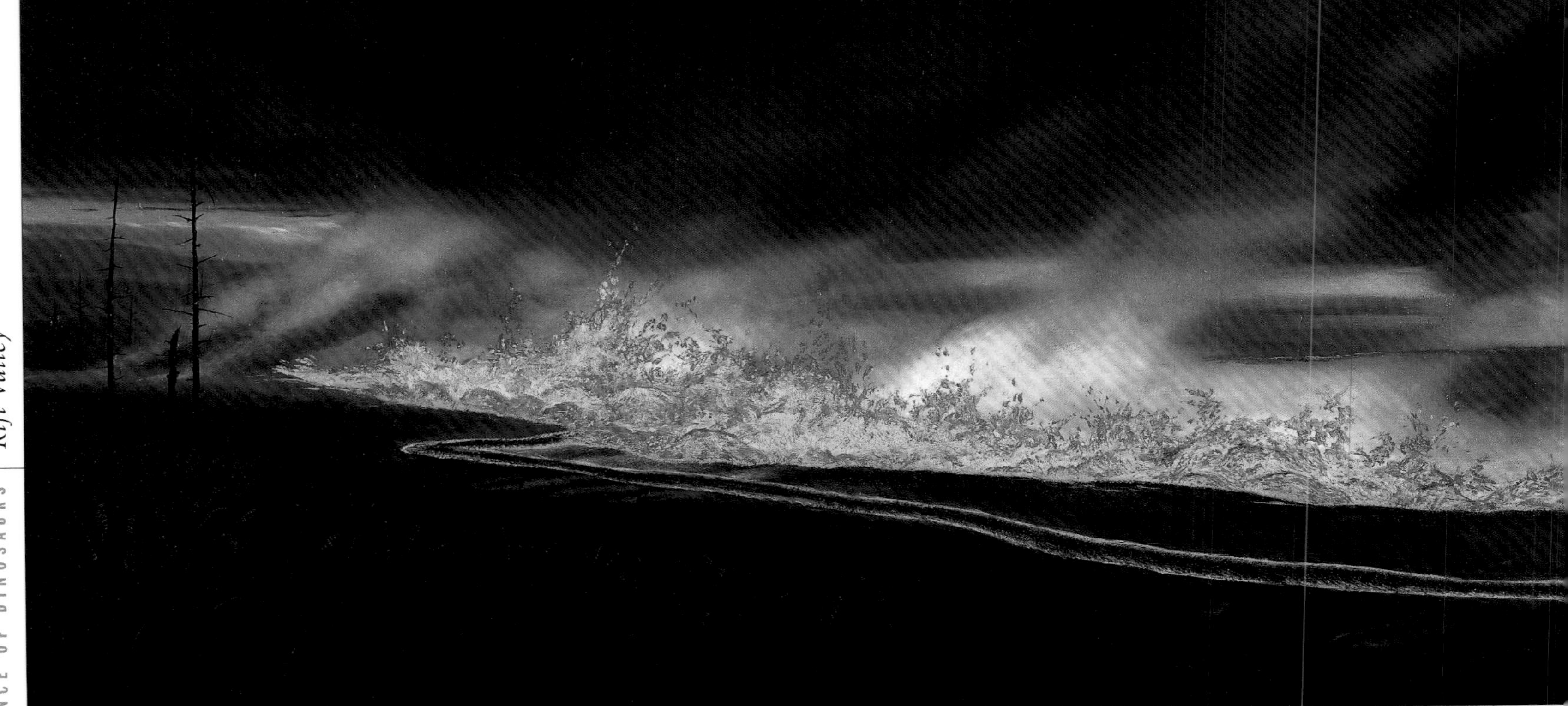

An increasing aspect of life in the rift system is venting, where lava wells up from fractures in the widening crust and spills out into the valleys. As Pangaea continues to test its fracture zones, lava flows will continue to be a factor of life for the plants and animals of this ecosystem.

the roar of the flames and the sound of exploding trees. Often fires burn just along the surface of the valley floor. Since soil is an excellent insulator, the heat does little damage to the plants and animals buried just below the surface. The first plants to recover are usually the ferns, which send up new fronds, often within a few days and even without rain, from rhizomes beneath the surface.

Animals confronted with a fire do not panic readily. The larger ones like the dilophosaurs and the anchisaurs can comfortably avoid the flame front or move along ahead of it. Others wait it out in their burrows. Pterosaurs simply fly away, and the ammosaurs take to the water. Some predators, like the coelophysians, are actually attracted by smoke. Ever the opportunists, they pick their way along the flame front, snatching and grasping at smaller animals routed out by the fire, or they move into recently burned areas to hunt those that survived the passage of the flames and are left without protective cover. Some herbivores are attracted to the fire's by-products: They gnaw on charred wood. A natural antacid, the charcoal seems to neutralize the toxins produced by some of the plants the herbivores eat. Ironically, the dry spells that lead to the fires actually kill many more animals than the flames and smoke do.

The fires also encourage and accelerate growth. When the heavy rains resume, the seeds of trees protected from the fire inside cones or buried in the soil start to germinate and grow rapidly in the nutrient-rich ash. Nutrients that wash out of the ash and into the streams and lakes feed the algae, which in turn feed the clamshrimp, in turn feeding the fish.

The forces that have been rending Pangaea are still at work, and the valleys up and down the rift system continue to widen with each spasm of Earth's crust. Tectonic forces cause deep clefts to penetrate miles into the planet's interior. Convection currents draw trapped heat closer to the surface, turning the rock red hot, melting it and forcing it through the cracks toward the surface. At times, the molten rock cools enough to thicken and crystallize while still underground.

Now, still in the earliest stages of the Jurassic, after a prolonged and exceptionally violent series of earthquakes, long fractures in the crust of the supercontinent have filled with red-hot magma, which is exploding through the crust, sending jets of incandescent lava fountaining hundreds of feet into the air. Once the path of the magma is established, millions of cubic feet of lava spill forth along the fault lines.

Day by day, the huge mass of melted rock produced by these fountains rolls relentlessly across the valley floor. Small fires and great plumes of blinding smoke mark the leading edge of the dark flow, as its glowing margin slowly engulfs the forests and fern prairies. Now and again, a series of violent local explosions and vast quantities of steam mark where the inexorable flow has entered a lake. For a while, the waters of the lake stem the relentless onslaught as the lava solidifies and sinks into cool, deep waters. But eventually, even the largest, deepest lakes succumb and drown. Months later, when the eruptions have covered most of the valley with rock several hundred feet thick, the fountains gradually cease.

The once lush and green vale is now a desolate, lifeless stretch of dark, ropy lava, with tendrils of steam slowly curling up from fissures and cracks. The valley has been dealt a hard blow, but it is not knocked out. Most of the larger wildlife had plenty of time to escape. Many found their way into other valleys where, although spared the lava ordeal, they will suffer because the influx of these hundreds of animals upsets the delicate ecological balance of their new homes. Most of the plants and aquatic animals in the valley have been wiped out, but isolated pockets of wildlife hang on along the edges where the lava did not reach. They will restock and restore the area.

Generally, forest fires disrupt life for a few years or so, but usually not much longer. Cataclysms of this magnitude are a different story. After such complete devastation by a disaster that eliminates even the soil, an ecosystem can take many years to recover fully. In those areas, the plants take on the task of creating new soil. A few hardy pioneer plants, usually lichens and ferns, get a foothold in cracks and fissures where windblown dust and sand have accumulated. Then their roots attack the lava rock, breaking it into smaller pieces; when the plants die, their organic remains combine with these rock particles to produce more soil. Newer, larger plants move in and repeat the process until a substantial soil layer develops on what was barren rock.

In most places this process takes a long time, but not in these Jurassic valleys. When the next wet season rolls around, the torrents of water entering the valley dump millions of tons of silt and sand from the surrounding highlands. In only a few years, much of the lava rock will sport enough soil to support large patches of fern and scrub—more than enough to entice some of the refugee wildlife back to the valley. As those animals feed and their droppings further enrich the soil, the pace of restoration will pick up.

As the breakup of Pangaea continues, the many valleys throughout the great rift system of northeastern North America continue to widen, continuing to profoundly affect the plant and animal life within its boundaries. The devastation has stressed and tested its inhabitants to extremes—so much so, that in its aftermath a relatively obscure, minor group of Triassic archosaurs, the dinosaurs, have been thrust to the forefront as the supercontinent was torn asunder in the Early Jurassic. Small and secretive at first, they are now beginning to fill the niches, vacated at the end of the Triassic, with forms just as well, if not better, suited for the present conditions. The evolutionary momentum established by these active, adaptable animals now seems unstoppable.

Recovery from a lava flow can take time, but eventually life does manage to work its way back. Often, the first pioneers in a cooled lava flow are ferns, as this *Dictyophyllum* growing from a crack in what is now rock shows.

4 Plains Dominion

200–220 Million Years Ago

CHAPTER FOUR

PLAINS DOMINION

Sauropods Actively Shape Their World

PRECEDING PAGES
A narrow band of thirsty conifers hugs a small river on the Morrison Plain, while just a short distance away, the plant growth sharply dwindles down to scrub. The Morrison Plain covers thousands of square miles of interior North America. Though at times harsh, this land is home to some of the largest animals ever to have lived.

OPPOSITE
Allosaurs are the most common large predator of the Morrison Plain. They can reach forty feet in length and several tons in weight and often travel and hunt in groups.

Throughout the Jurassic, the rift valleys of central Pangaea lengthened, widened, deepened, and merged. Seawater had flooded areas once dominated by lakes and wetlands. The great supercontinent, which had existed for one hundred million years, was no more. As Pangaea's two main fragments—Laurasia in the north and Gondwana in the south—moved apart, a long, narrow expanse of water filled the gap. This narrow strait, the beginning of the Atlantic Ocean, extended from Mexico east toward Florida, then northeast along the coast of North America, where it became lost in the maze of large islands and shallow seas forming Europe.

Now, toward the end of the Jurassic, the Atlantic has widened to about a thousand miles. A northern shallow seaway that covered western North America, called the Sundance Sea, has slowly retreated into Canada. The retreat has left a large and virtually featureless alluvial landscape covering hundreds of thousands of square miles from south to north, called the Morrison Plain.

Forty-five million years have passed since the lava flows ravaged the rift valleys of central Pangaea. North America has migrated far enough north that the prevailing winds now come primarily from the west, putting the Morrison Plain in the rain shadow of the mountains. In the southern part of the Plain, the climate is relatively dry and hot. Seasonally intermittent streams running from the higher ground to the west bring in just enough water to tease the environment, but the threat of drought is constant. If a stream finds a place to stop and pool, the lakes it forms are usually salty, and the life in and around them is sparse. The only relief from the heat comes in the form of tropical storms that sweep up out of the southeast from late summer into early winter.

Far to the south, hot, dry air masses born over equatorial Gondwana move in over the ever-widening, warm Atlantic Ocean, sucking up millions of tons of water and carrying it westward and north into the Plain, then releasing it. Each torrential downpour can last for days. The ground saturates quickly and, at times, sheet floods cover the land several inches deep from horizon to horizon. All too soon, the storms and the floods move off to the north, where the vast majority of the Morrison Plain wildlife anxiously awaits the waters they bring.

Toward the northern portion of the Plain, the climate is somewhat dry, almost semiarid in places, but the higher water table here makes for more permanent, wetter, and greener settings of fern, scrub, and trees along river courses or near lakes. Among the thick vegetation close by permanent water, it is easy to recall the forests of the rift valley and the woodlands, but where the wooded areas of those places extended for many miles, the vegetation here dwindles appreciably in height, abundance, and diversity only a few hundred yards from the life-giving waters. Farther away from the water, bare patches of ground appear, spreading until they eventually dominate the distant landscape.

Any animal that takes a brief excursion even farther from the water finds a much different, quite harsh view. Since there is virtually no cover this far from permanent water, the horizon is visible for a full three hundred and sixty degrees. The twisted limbs and trunks of long-dead, skeletonized trees lie along long-gone streams. The plants are stunted, and few and far between, with only handfuls of meager leaves pathetically held out to the sun.

Animal signs include an occasional line of footprints baked into the hardened mud, a random burrow, or a cluster of large white bones, half buried and slowly being recycled. The surfaces of scattered dry streambeds and water holes—none of which has seen permanent water for years—are broken into huge mosaics by deep mud cracks. On the rare occasions that it gets wet, the fine soil sticks to the feet of anything passing by, from dinosaurs to beetles. When dry, the soil can be picked up by the slightest wind and blown into eyes and noses, or swirled into dust devils that drift eerily across the Plain.

Since the water is not evenly distributed, neither are the plants or animals. The water table is closer to the surface here than in the south, so many streams continue to flow through the dry season. Because of the gentle slope of the terrain, many of these watercourses meander slowly and widely before coalescing into rivers and working their way toward the remnants of the Sundance Sea. Their banks are liberally coated with low-growing herbaceous plants and a few woody ones. Larger rivers are flanked by larger woody trees, providing a sinuous, dark green corridor for their passage. In some spots, permanent, spring-fed, sweetwater lakes and shallow, semi-permanent water holes abound. These oases contain enough water to support lungfish, frogs, turtles, dinosaurs, crocodiles, pterosaurs, and mammals and enough trees and other plants to surround them with a living palisade. Often, just a few feet of difference in topography marks the difference between dusty bare ground, green fern-covered glades, thick scrub, heavily wooded thicket, or forest.

The scattered coniferous forests of the Morrison Plain are not as thickly wooded nor as extensive as those of the woodlands or the rift valley. In most places, sunlight streams down through the diffuse canopy, supporting a dense understory of young gymnosperms, tree ferns, cycads, and cycadeoids. The closer the forest is to permanent water, the greater the occurrence of giant tree ferns, which have grown abundantly along forest margins since the Paleozoic Era.

Most of the wooded areas of the Plain are still dominated by a large variety of trees. Mostly gymnosperms, like conifers and ginkgoes, these trees are generally slow growing and drought resistant. Their thick, straight, unbranched trunks extend for thirty or forty feet overhead before the first naked, dead limbs appear. The forest floor is thickly covered with dead needles and as devoid of vegetation as in the woodlands. The temperature can be several degrees cooler at ground level and the change in humidity and insect life is palpable. Here, the breeze whispers only through the branches high above. In the more well-lit and moist areas lies a dense ground cover of lycopods, ferns, and seedlings. Stepping on or bruising the leaves and stems of this undergrowth releases a mixture of aromatic scents.

The wooded river channels, forested lake margins, and fern glades always look their best in early winter, when the heavy rains and flooding have passed. Inevitably, the first wildlife seen or heard are *Comodactylus*—pterosaurs—wheeling far overhead, the graceful curve of their wings silhouetted against the bright blue sky. These long-tailed rhamphorynchoids loom three times larger than the *Eudimorphodon* of the veiled woodlands. They patrol high above the rivers and larger water holes in search of fish and an occasional small crocodile or young turtle, which they catch and swallow on the wing, without missing a beat.

Half the size of *Comodactylus*, the short-tailed pterosaur *Mesadactylus* follows the herds of large herbivores, often perching on their backs, feeding on the tiny creatures stirred up by the passage of the larger animals. These pterodactyloids first appeared during the Early Jurassic and they tend to be a little less choosy in their tastes than the predominantly fish-eating rhamphorynchoids, a difference that can be quite advantageous. Whether long or short tailed, there always seem to be one or two aloft, and their faint, clipped cries constantly fill the air high above the Plain.

By mid-winter, other sounds resonate across the Plain, deep and rumbling, reminiscent of distant thunder, as if the air itself were shuddering. The sounds are produced by animals, though, not weather. These extremely long wavelengths, called infrasound, can travel across miles of empty plains or densely wooded areas with equal ease, and with no interference or loss in a jumble of echoes. They therefore make it possible for the animals that produce them to communicate over long distances.

The sounds are made by sauropod dinosaurs. Restricted primarily to the lower latitudes, sauropods are distant relatives of the prosauropods of the Late Triassic and Early Jurassic. They are, without question, the largest animals ever to walk the planet, pushing one hundred fifty feet in length and one hundred tons in weight. Their effects on the environment, in the form of footprints, droppings, and damaged vegetation, are evident long before the animals themselves are. They are the first animals large enough to shape their environment, and the impact they have on the Plain is enormous.

At a stately, unhurried gait of about a mile an hour, it can take a minute and a half for one to pass. First its relatively tiny head passes by, slowly turning from side to side, its eyes constantly monitoring the location of the members of its group, other groups, food, water, and any signs of danger. The head can be up to a yard long in some species, set on an exceedingly long, slender neck. As the animal slowly passes by, its neck gets wider and wider until it suddenly flares out into an incredibly huge body supported by four immense, creased, pillarlike legs. With every step, the sauropod drives air through its immense lungs and through air sacs distributed throughout its body. Each large foot, even though it stands far behind the animal's eyes, is placed exactly where it is wanted. Fallen logs, slick muddy patches, and the occasional turtle are all avoided; there are no slips, stumbles, or missteps. Finally, its seemingly endless tail glides back and forth, the wavelike motion becoming more exaggerated until the end snaps smartly back and forth overhead.

Then there are the noises—several hundred cubic feet of air sucked in and expelled through a pair of wide nostrils like a gust in a high gale, punctuated by low-level grunts and rumbles. The round, padded feet with their short claws press heavily into the moist soil driving out both air and moisture with a gurgling hiss, leaving an impression almost three feet across. Even the tip of the tail whistles faintly as it swings in from one direction only to be whipped back suddenly in the other. All these sounds mix with the calls of dozens of pterosaur outriders and the buzzing of the ever-present insect hordes. By the time the animal has passed, a medley of faint odors washes in: hot and humid breath, the occasional whiff of fresh manure mixed with crushed vegetation and churned-up soil, and the unmistakable smell of the huge animal itself.

For four or five months of the year, the seasonal rains saturate the northern portion of the Morrison Plain, and the flooding is more pronounced and prolonged than it is farther south. Sauropods have a marked preference for drier land, since they tend to bog down in wet ground, so in groups of three or four up to as many as a dozen, the giant herbivores migrate south, following the courses of the larger rivers and feeding as they go.

For most of the year the southern plain lacks enough vegetation to fuel these massive animals. Only smaller wildlife like camptosaurs and stegosaurs can flourish there year round. While the heavy downpours are making the northern plain inhospitable for sauropods, those same rains are improving conditions farther south. Several weeks after the rains cease, the southern plain again becomes too dry to support the vegetation the giant herbivores require. By mid-spring, when the soil in the north is firm enough, the sauropods return to harvest the vegetation that is now growing there in much more abundance.

In some years the great storms are late, or light, or do not come at all. Driven by instinct, the great herbivores start their journey into the southern plain anyway. If the rains come late, or in less quantity than usual, the sauropods suffer. The toll among the adults may not be too severe, but the egg clutches will be small, the hatchling rate low, and the mortality rate among the young high. If the storms do not come at all, disaster awaits. Dozens of sauropods converge at the remnants of the larger lakes, water holes, and river channels, jostling for whatever water is there, no matter how foul or silty. As the moisture evaporates or is drunk, the shoving becomes more violent. Smaller sauropods are relegated to the muddy outskirts and start to die. Once the water is gone, even the largest animals weaken, collapse, and finally succumb. The stench emanating from hundreds of tons of decaying sauropod can travel for miles downwind. Usually a bloated carcass is the most popular draw in nature, but in the depths of a drought the smell of water is a stronger magnet by far, and the carcasses remain virtually untouched by any of the meat-eaters.

Even during years of normal rainfall, sauropod dinosaurs rarely spend more than several days in any one area. They cannot. A group of a dozen can represent over a half million pounds of flesh demanding to be fed. Sauropods are often a natural disaster in themselves. Even though their droppings might benefit the local fauna, their impact on the vegetation can be as devastating as any fire or flood. What scrub and trees they do not eat outright they may leave so trampled or damaged that disease, insects, or other herbivores finish them off. So the animals are always on the move, stopping only to feed, drink, rest, or wallow. A few hours of sleep is all they get, taking turns in deep sleep so that at least one is conscious all night.

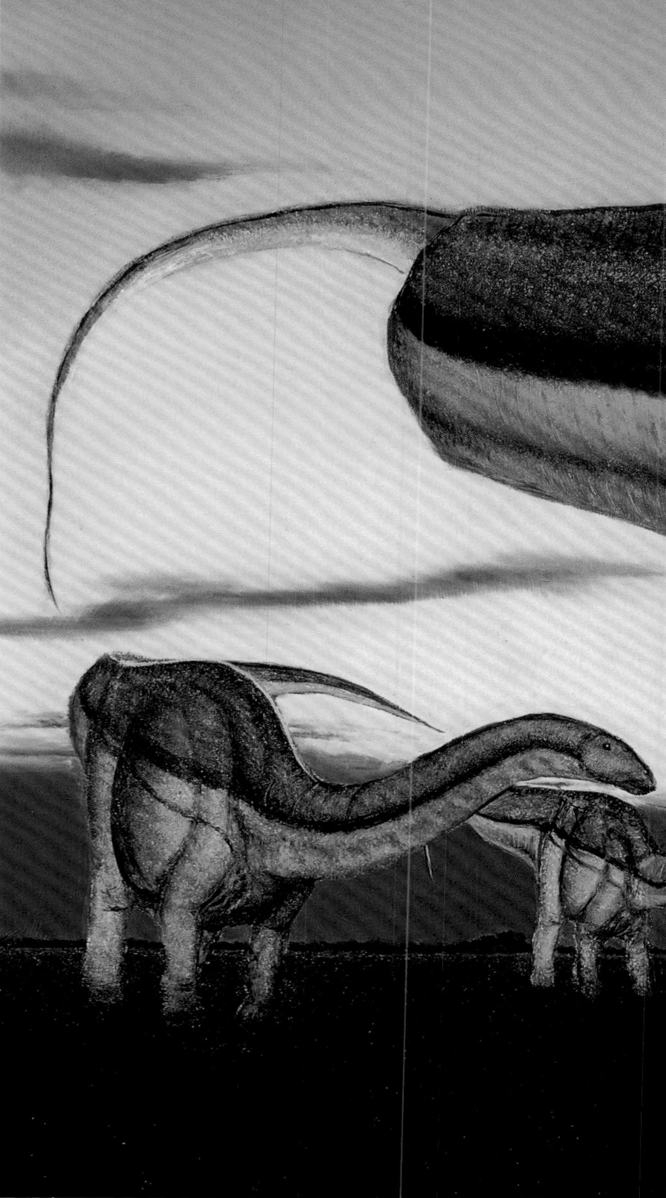

Often, while on the move in response to the change of the seasons, the three types of sauropods here move *en échelon* along a watercourse, neatly keeping out of each other's way. Despite their close resemblance, camarasaurids, diplodocids, and brachiosaurids can be distinguished, even at a distance, by their overall shape, posture, coloration, and feeding habits. Members of these families have each assumed one of three forms, depending on whether they are low, middle, or high browsers.

A herd of *Apatosaurus* travels across a storm-threatened Plain. *Apatosaurus* can reach seventy feet in length and weigh in between twenty to thirty tons. The afternoon thunderstorms that frequently roll across the land are a welcome relief to the animals from the often hot, dry weather of the Plain.

Camarasaurids, easily the most common sauropods on the Plain, hold their necks at the horizontal or slightly above it, while the less common diplodocids keep theirs much closer to the ground. From a distance, a camarasaurid's neck seems to end rather abruptly, with just a hint of a swelling at its end, which is in fact its short-muzzled head; whereas a diplodocid's elongated head and protruding muzzle give its neck a graceful, tapered ending. Neither has anything like the elegant near-vertical attitude of the neck, or the long forelegs and exaggerated high forehead that distinguish the brachiosaurids.

The reason for these differences becomes apparent when the animals feed. The low-slung heads and necks of diplodocids like *Diplodocus* and *Apatosaurus* allow them to stand in one spot and, simply by moving their necks and heads from side to side, use their small, slender teeth and long tongues to grasp clumps of ferns and seedlings. These they either tear off or pull from the ground. Without moving their bulks an inch, they have access to hundreds of pounds of vegetation. In heavily wooded areas, where ground cover may not be as abundant, diplodocids can reach back and up, shift their weight onto their hind legs and tails, and lift their forelegs to assume a tripodal stance. In this pose they can reach more than fifty feet into the canopy and delicately pluck at the epiphytic growth. Specialized blood vessels prevent changes in blood pressure that might cause them to black out while rearing up or dropping back down.

Farthest out from the water, where the plants are low-growing and shrubby but still abundant, stand the diplodocids. They slowly graze on the low brushy scrub and fern prairie, moving forward a step or two only when there is nothing left to eat within their reach. A bit nearer the river, where the vegetation is less scattered and not quite so low or thin, are the camarasaurids. Camarasaurids use their large spoon-shaped teeth to attack the foliage of tree ferns and separate the tougher leaves of medium-sized conifers and ginkgoes from their owners. If the need arises, camarasaurids can also assume a tripodal posture and can actually walk in this stance.

Close to the larger rivers, where the trees grow taller, brachiosaurids browse in the upper story, constantly feeding and always on the move. As large as some of the trees themselves, they often lose interest in a particular tree within a short time and rarely defoliate it, giving the slow-growing conifers and ginkgoes time to recover, sometimes leaving a distinctive browse line. Rearing up on their hindquarters is not in a brachiosaurid's repertoire, but it does not need to be. When an animal's head rides more than forty feet off the ground, the leaves, needles, cones, and seeds of all but the tallest trees are accessible.

An adult sauropod can spend as much as eighteen hours a day feeding. As the animal approaches a stand of trees it moves purposefully, staring intently as if it were already choosing which clusters of branches and needles to eat. Its jaws open wide and engulf an entire cluster. Its mouth closes almost completely, then its head draws back, raking the branches through its teeth to strip off as many needles, cones, and green twigs as possible, yet careful not to tear loose too much of the older, more woody portions. This mass of plant parts is then rolled around in the mouth a bit and swallowed. Lacking a battery of flat teeth, sauropods cannot chew to grind their food, but they do mix it thoroughly with large amounts of saliva. Swallowing dry food is a problem for any animal, but when it has a thirty-foot-long neck, lubrication is critical. Since they produce gallons of saliva, rare is the scene of a majestic sauropod not drooling.

The groups of sauropods ranging throughout the southern plain consist primarily of fully grown individuals. Although groups of subadults occur, juveniles less than a year old are rarely seen in their company. They simply cannot keep up with the pace set by the larger animals. For at least the first year of their lives, the young sauropods seldom venture far from the wetter portions of the Plain.

Although sauropods feed differently, their egg-laying behavior is basically the same. There are no real nests as such. Groups of females deposit their eggs without ceremony on firm ground near permanently well-watered tracts such as riverbanks, lakes, or marshes, just as the early winter rains subside and most danger of flooding is past. After selecting a suitable site,

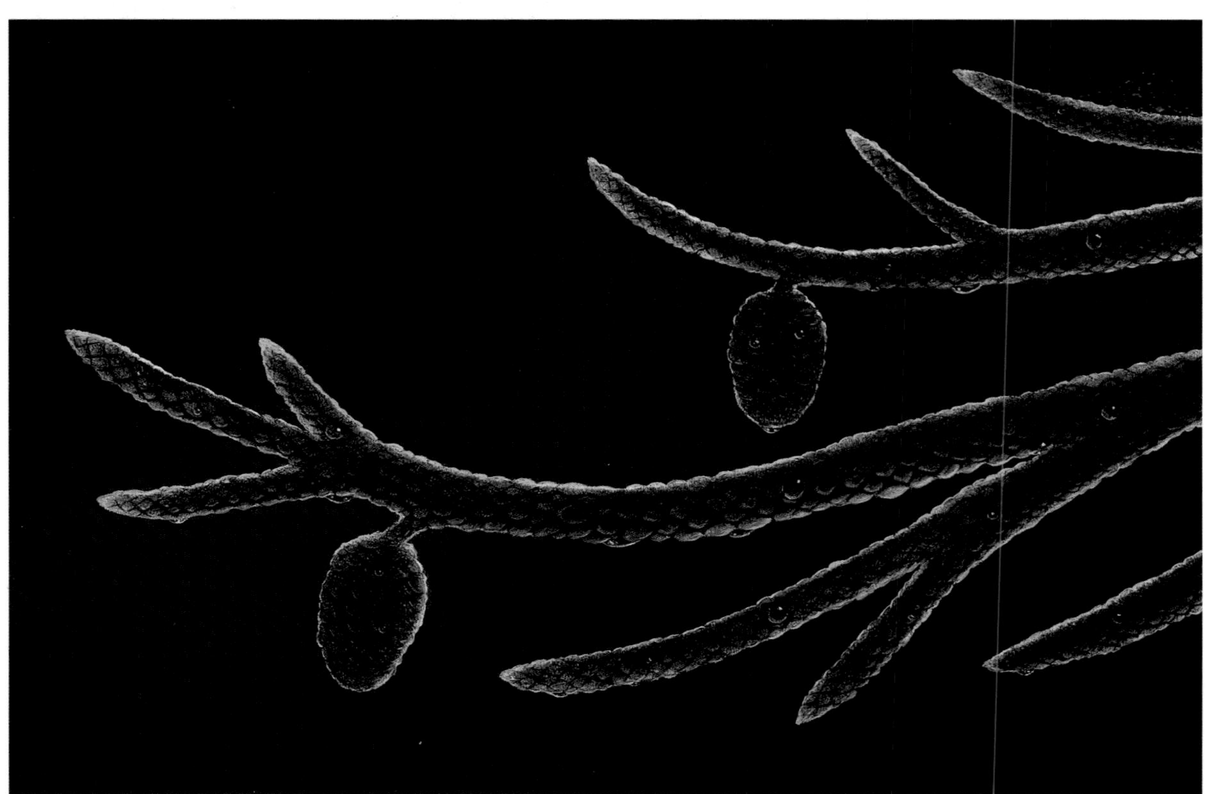

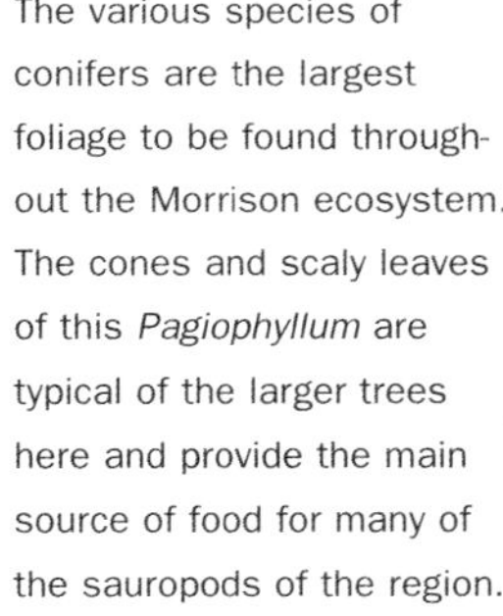

The various species of conifers are the largest foliage to be found throughout the Morrison ecosystem. The cones and scaly leaves of this *Pagiophyllum* are typical of the larger trees here and provide the main source of food for many of the sauropods of the region.

a gravid female flexes its hind legs slightly and, half-crouching, deposits a half-dozen round eggs directly on the ground. Then it straightens up, takes a step or two, crouches again, deposits another half-dozen eggs, and continues until the entire clutch of some two dozen eggs—each eight inches in diameter—is deposited.

Soon afterward, the adults move on. The disparity in size between a hatchling and an adult sauropod is the greatest of any land animal in the history of the planet. For the first months of their lives, the small hatchlings cannot keep up with the herds. It is equally impossible for the adults to guard the nests, nurturing or protecting the young dinosaurs. So many adults lingering in one place, waiting for the eggs to incubate, would decimate the local flora. The plants would not recover in time for the next year's visit and the site would have to be abandoned.

Some sauropods depend on prey swamping; that is, they choose nesting sites where there are simply not enough predators to seriously deplete the thousands of eggs laid. For every egg devoured by a marauding predator, many are not; for every hatchling snatched, many survive. Of the hundreds upon hundreds of hatchlings that wander into the bush and forests, enough survive to return to complete the cycle in ten or twelve years. The perfectly proportioned little sauropods' growth is relatively rapid at first, then slows as they approach sexual maturity and the relative safety of adulthood and grow large enough to take up with a group.

Like the prosauropod dinosaurs before them, the sauropods are life-bound to hunger. Their specialized digestive systems are still rather inefficient and their waste contains a lot of undigested material. Sauropod dinosaurs produce enormous amounts of dung each day, accompanied by large amounts of intestinal gas. This prodigious pungent material might appear to be the ultimate form of natural pollution, but a host of animals on the Plain, and most of the plants, benefit from this waste.

At times the dung seems to be gone before it has had a chance to cool. Within moments of it being deposited, hundreds upon hundreds of insects descend on the steaming, aromatic mounds. Flies are on it in seconds; beetles form little balls of it and roll them away; ants feed on the undigested plant remains or carry it off so that their larvae can. The availability of so many protein-rich insect packets is irresistible to small omnivorous dinosaurs like young *Ornitholestes* and *Coelurus*, to insect-eating birds and pterosaurs, and to the smaller mammals. Small herbivorous dinosaurs and other mammals like docodonts and multituberculates paw through the waste in search of cones and seeds that have escaped the giant herbivore's gastric mill. The few seeds these thorough scavengers miss have now had their seed coats softened and cleansed of any parasitic molds by their passage through the sauropod's gut. They have been dispersed by the movements of the animal and buried in a wealth of fertilizer, increasing their chances of successful germination several fold.

Although, as dinosaurs, sauropods excrete little water with their urine, substantial quantities are still lost by evaporation through their several thousand square feet of skin and lungs; therefore, no opportunity to drink is missed. When sauropod dinosaurs arrive at a water hole or riverbank, all other wildlife gives way.

For camarasaurids and diplodocids, drinking takes no real effort, but a brachiosaurid faces more difficulty. Because of the extreme length of their forelegs, the heads of these sauropods must come down well below their shoulders to make contact with the water. A brachiosaurid must first genuflect at the elbow, which flexes inward, and then bring its chest down to contact its folded forelimbs. Only then can it lower its great neck like a boom and immerse its head to drink.

Water is not the only reason sauropods lower their heads into streams. Since they can not chew their food, they swallow bits of stream gravel—gastroliths—that collect in their gizzard. There they help mix and mash the tough plant parts sauropods eat. These stones are not collected at random. Most camarasaurids, for example, are attracted to dark-colored pebbles and will swallow hard sandstone as well as softer limestone or shale, while many diplodocids are less fussy about color and concentrate more on rounded igneous and metamorphic pebbles and various quartzes. River gravel is not at all common on the Plain, so sauropods must occasionally travel great distances to collect these necessary bits of rock. The animals get quite testy when they need to replenish their gastroliths, and a neighbor trying to muscle in on a promising stash will be dealt with in no uncertain terms.

Salt, another mineral that the giants need, occurs more commonly. Scattered throughout the southern plain are wide, shallow salt lakes. Although they might be devoid of life, the salts that crystallize out of them are critical to sustaining the wildlife of the Plain. Sauropods also use their single-clawed forefeet to scratch at termite mounds. Then they lick up the scrapings, which are rich in minerals, brought to the surface by the industrious insects. They also ingest clay, which contains minerals that can bind with the somewhat toxic substances found in many plants, allowing the dinosaurs to feed on them with impunity.

Many of the Plain's topographic features and habitats are destroyed by, created by, and maintained by sauropods. They contribute more to both the modification and the maintenance of their environment than any other animal of the Mesozoic. Wallows in particular are a popular gathering place. Sauropods find that a nice thick veneer of therapeutic Morrison Plain mud prevents overheating, suffocates ectoparasites, frustrates biting insects, and removes dead skin. Some of the larger wallows can cover many acres and, occasionally, up to a hundred sauropods may indulge at these spas at once. The colossal animals first kneel, then lie down and roll over onto their sides, flexing their necks and tails as far as they can while keeping them in contact with the sticky, viscous mud. Then, they roll onto the other side. Once they are coated, they get back onto all fours and, with a shake of the head to clear their eyes and ears, make room for the next animal. As the mud dries, it flakes off or the animal rubs it off on a suitable tree trunk or one of the large termite mounds that dot the area. Several hundred pounds of soil leave the wallow with each sauropod, so wallows that get used quite regularly are widened and deepened so much that a significant amount of water can collect in them, transforming them into shallow water holes.

Smaller than the sauropods, but much stranger looking, are the stegosaurs. At twenty-five feet in length, and topping the scales at one or two tons, the several species on the Plain neatly fill the niche of low-browsing, mid-sized herbivore. Stegosaurs are easily identified at a distance by their rounded, humplike silhouette. At one end their narrow, low-slung head terminates in an equally narrow, toothless, horn-covered beak. Just behind their short, thick neck are the short but powerful forelimbs with their broad, stubby-toed feet. Then comes the long, graceful curve of the back, arching up to heights in excess of twelve feet. It is topped off with a majestic double row of diamond-shaped, skin-covered, bony plates, making the animal appear almost fifteen feet tall.

Starting just behind the head, each plate is slightly larger than the one before until, just above the animal's hips and long rear legs, the plates gradually shrink and stop just short of the tip of the tail. These distinctively pigmented plates make a stegosaur appear larger and more threatening. Depending on the species, the tail is equipped with any number of pairs of long, horn-covered, nasty-looking spines.

Loners by nature, these normally docile animals come together only at watering places or to breed. They live in the more open reaches of the Plain, where other stegosaurs, potential predators, or anything else can be spotted at a distance. Their isolated lifestyle prevents over-browsing of the limited vegetation, made up primarily of ferns, various types of scrub conifers, and cycads—one of the animal's favorites. Stegosaurs crave the cones and seeds secreted deep within the rosette of palmlike leaves growing from the top of the plant because they are rich in starch and oils. Small bony scutes embedded in the thick skin of the underside of the stegosaur's stout neck protect it from the prickly leaf tips as it deftly plucks seeds and cones from each cycad's crown.

At early morning and in the late evening, they wend their way along well-worn trails to local sources of fresh water where, invariably, there are other stegosaurs. The animals usually just eye each other cautiously, keep their distance, and drink without incident. Each has a home range that can overlap those of other stegosaurs and vary greatly in extent, depending on food, water resources, and the stegosaur population density. In a prolonged or exceptionally deep dry spell, these home ranges overlap more and more as the dinosaurs reluctantly move into more densely populated, wetter places—where tempers are tested and conflicts can occur.

If confronted, a stegosaur backs up and turns sideways, presenting its antagonist with a good view of its impressive, plate-topped profile. This is almost always accompanied by a slow lowering of the head and rapid twitching of the spike-tipped tail, drawing attention away from the stegosaur's more vulnerable front end. If the threat persists, the agitated animal will start to move its forelegs from side to side, pivoting around its hind legs to make the movements of the tail even more exaggerated. Other stegosaurs and most carnivorous dinosaurs usually back off. But a predator driven to extremes might press an attack. The outcome of such desperate attacks is difficult to call. The attacker must inflict enough damage to kill the stegosaur almost outright. The stegosaur need only inflict enough injury to cripple or dissuade its attacker. The Plain offers prey that is more abundant and much easier to take down than an agitated adult stegosaur, so confrontations are not common.

Attacks on other herbivorous dinosaurs, like the bipedal, unarmored ornithopods, are

One of the most bizarrely adorned animals ever to walk the land, stegosaurs are low-browsing loners. While their appearance demands that they be noticed, they are quite capable of defending themselves if the attention they attract is the wrong kind.

usually more one sided and often end on a different note. These small to medium-sized dinosaurs, such as *Camptosaurus*, the smaller *Dryosaurus*, and the even smaller *Othnielia*, are easier to take down than the larger or more well-protected herbivores.

These herbivores have evolved a novel method of processing their food: They can chew. This preprocessing means that these ornithopod dinosaurs do not have mass-increasing systems of gastric mills and fermentation vats like the sauropods and can therefore carry on as smaller, swifter, more agile animals such as *Othnielia*. Reaching lengths of four or five feet, othnielians congregate in loose groups, or flocks, of up to a hundred and drift from one patch of vegetation to the next, always moving, always feeding. They closely inspect every square foot of their feeding area for small seed- and spore-producing ferns, as well as the leaves, seeds, and cones of low-growing conifers and the fleshy seed coats of the cycads and cycadeoids. During the heat of the day, especially during the drier periods, the small ornithopods retreat to the cool darkness of the deep woods to rest. Unable to perspire, and not in the habit of wallowing, they keep cool by dumping excess heat into their blood and then into their lungs, expelling it by panting. They do not stay in one place for long, no matter how hot it is. Even while eating, ornithopods are constantly on the move. Each individual's alertness protects the entire group.

If a predator comes hunting these diminutive dinosaurs, almost everything is in the ornithopods' favor. The eyes of othnielians are large and keen. They can sense even the slightest movements. The animal will focus and freeze, intently studying whatever attracted its attention. Even the blinking of an eyelid can send first one, then an entire group of these hypsilophodontids bolting. Fast and agile, they can move rapidly over terrain where other wildlife would find it difficult to walk; however, these bursts of speed do not last long. As soon as a clump of scrub, a small rise, or another barrier is between them and whatever spooked them, they will stop, regroup, and, if all is well, resume their interrupted activity. The only way to catch one is to get it while it is in the open—moving from one wooded patch to another, going for water, or fleeing the safety of the bush chased by something else. Even while being pursued, most of the small othnielians are reluctant to be driven from their own territory, which they know intimately. Encountering low branches and fallen logs while running helter-skelter through a strange area could be just as dangerous as a confrontation with a predator. During the drier season, the flocks break up into smaller groups or disband entirely.

In contrast to their stay-at-home relatives, the hypsilophodontids, *Dryosaurs* do not even try to eke out an existence when the rains cease. They simply leave. Up to thirteen feet in length, with long, powerful legs and strong arms, these bipedal herbivores are often seen in small groups in the company of the diplodocid sauropods. As the great sauropods move to firmer, then greener pastures during the year, a retinue of dryosaurs follows. Easily distinguished from hypsilophodontids by their larger size, dryosaurs also have a broader, squared-off snout and lack the sharp upper front teeth of their cousins; instead, their mouths have horny beaks on both top and bottom. As their diplodocid companions slowly pull mouthfuls of fern fronds and bracken from the soft soil, they often pull up the plants' thick, ropelike stems. That is when the dryosaurs move in. Using their strong forelimbs, they scrabble and dig at the exposed rhizomes. Staying close to the sauropods during their annual trek and allowing them to do most of the work provides many dryosaurs with an almost limitless supply of their favorite food with a minimum of effort.

Rather than lead secretive lives or seek the protection of large associates, the ornithopod *Camptosaurus* survives by size. These animals are almost twenty-five feet long and weigh a ton or more. Although resembling dryosaurs in many respects, camptosaurs are larger and much more robust. These bipeds use their long snouts and short but flexible necks to pluck seeds, cones, and clusters of needles and leaves from a variety of trees and shrubs. Like many animals, camptosaurs have certain mineral requirements. They will eat certain soils and clays, visit soda lake

shores, and scratch at termite mounds for what they need, but they also have another source—the bones of other dinosaurs. A bleached skeleton, beyond the interest of scavengers, will still pique the interest of ornithopods, who will interrupt their activity to gnaw on these monolithic masses of bone.

Whether chewing on plant material or gnawing on a bone, camptosaurs often assume a four-legged stance, resting the weight of their upper bodies on their strong wrists and hands. In this position, they move slowly from cycad to fern to conifer, selecting, nipping, and chewing, almost all day. Before moving any great distance or running, they push themselves back onto their hind limbs and proceed as bipeds. Unlike their dryosaur relatives, camptosaurs are often seen in the same areas as, and sometimes in the company of, stegosaurs, each apparently indifferent to the other.

Just as there is a great range of herbivores, from the majestic sauropods to the diminutive hypsilophodontids, there is a similar range of carnivores to eat them, from the fearsome *Ceratosaurus* to the much smaller but no less nasty *Ornitholestes.* All the dinosaur predators of the Morrison Plain are members of the most ancient lineage of all dinosaurs, the slender, long-legged, bipedal, and carnivorous theropods. Large, bladelike, serrated teeth and sharp, curved

Stegosaurs are particularly fond of cycad fruit. The pebbled armor that lines the animals' throat region is an effective protection against the sharp, spiny cycad leaves that would otherwise stand between the stegosaur and its favorite food.

claws on strong forelimbs make these animals the perfect hunters to take down almost any of the herbivores.

Ceratosaurs—one-and-a-half-ton, twenty-foot-long predators—do not stalk or hunt from ambush. When a hunting ceratosaur spots a herd of camptosaurs or dryosaurs, it walks toward them directly, holding itself erect, as if it wants to be seen. Sooner or later one of the grazing herbivores will spot the theropod, stop feeding, and grunt loudly. At this signal, the entire herd will look around to identify the threat. As the ceratosaur gets closer, the herd will break and run away, as a group. The predator gives chase, scanning the herd for any hesitation or faltering. Since ceratosaurs usually chase only those animals they think they can catch, they may test many groups before finding an individual whose flight reactions are less than optimal.

With a system of air sacs similar to that of the sauropods, theropod dinosaurs are built not only for speed but for endurance. The more the animals exert themselves, the more they are cooled internally. A determined theropod such as a ceratosaur can pursue a camptosaur for a considerable time, using a steady, loping gait—not quite a walk, yet not quite a run. Since it does not become overheated or winded by this exertion, the ceratosaur still has the energy to attack and kill its exhausted victim when it catches up to it. Ceratosaurs use every weapon at their disposal to dispatch their victim as quickly as possible, because other predators may come poaching. Powered by strong muscles, the claws on the hunter's hands and feet drive deeply into the ornithopod to get a firm grip. Ceratosaurs sport huge, flattened, bladelike teeth that can bite deep, cutting through skin and muscle in search of the arteries. When blood loss or shock cause the prey to collapse, the theropod directs its attention to the herbivore's underside, where the skin is particularly thin, especially where the thigh meets the belly. Once the carcass is open, the ceratosaur pulls out the internal organs first. The heart, lungs, liver, and other organs are especially nutritious and can be removed and eaten quickly. Then the animal uses its forelimbs and legs to brace the disemboweled prey as it strips the skin and meat from its haunches and flanks. The neck, head, and tail are generally left until last. Often the ceratosaur's meal is interrupted by the arrival of a marauding band of another theropod, *Allosaurus*, before it can partake of these less desirable parts.

Much more common than the solitary and nomadic ceratosaurs, allosaurs roam the Plain in familial hunting bands of up to a dozen or more animals. Most are related by blood and organized in a loose hierarchy based on size, age, sex, facial features, and behavior. Allosaurs carry a pair of tall triangular hornlets in front of and above each eye which run into long, slightly smaller, horn ridges that extend down the top of the snout almost to the tip. Their size and the intensity of their color help establish each animal's place in the band. Older, larger allosaurs have bolder, larger head adornments; they dominate other band members and command the best spots at kills, water holes, or resting areas. If an allosaur cannot make its dominant position understood by simply lowering its head and displaying its impressive facial features, it can also use them to deliver a painful head blow to remind a subordinate of its place.

Allosaurs are more territorial than ceratosaurs and are not above driving off an intruding predator and usurping its meal. This is why most other hunters on the Plain kill and eat as fast as they can. Even a ceratosaur will give way to a group of a half-dozen hungry allosaurs, albeit with a great deal of hissing, head shaking, snarling, agitated tail-twitching, and ground pawing. Bullying other predators is effective and efficient, but it seldom produces enough food to satisfy all the members of an allosaur band. So, when the urge builds, the allosaurs hunt. With more numerous but smaller teeth than their distant ceratosaur cousins, allosaurs work communally, relying on many wounds inflicted by many individuals.

Five or six allosaurs on the stalk, with their heads thrust forward and down, eyes alert and scanning, nostrils flaring, clawed hands opening and closing, feet set to the ground toe first, quietly, tails outstretched with their tips twitching—the palpable tension is infectious. All permanent residents of an allosaur band's terri-

OPPOSITE
An *Ornitholestes* prowls around a possible mammal burrow for something to eat. One of the smaller dinosaurian predators of the Morrison, they subsist on small mammals, lizards and other small reptiles, and the leftover remains of large animals.

PRECEDING PAGES
Several medium-sized allosaurs gnaw at the forelimbs of a sauropod during a rainstorm. A large sauropod carcass will keep many allosaurs fed for at least a week, but only the largest among them will get the first crack at the choicest parts.

tory fall prey to these animals at one time or another. Even carrion is devoured with gusto. Small prey like hypsilophodontids are simply run down by smaller allosaurs, caught under foot with hooflike claws, and dismembered. Somewhat larger prey, like a dryosaur, is rushed from ambush.

Allosaurs attack large groups of prey such as camptosaur herds *en masse*. The herbivores that first see the attack coming run away. Others, alerted by this abrupt departure, start running too. Since they do not know where the attackers are, they often blunder right into the allosaurs. Each allosaur is on its own here in the general melee. The attacks are brief, noisy spectacles, blurred by dust clouds, interspersed with the shadowy forms of predator and prey running this way and that in a free-for-all. After the terror of such an attack, the herbivores run off a few hundred yards, stop and look back, grunting and calling in consternation, and seeking reassurance from the others in the herd. Within minutes, they quiet down, regroup, and soon are going about their usual business.

Really large prey like stegosaurs and subadult sauropods require allosaurs to use still another technique. Typically, these larger herbivores stand their ground and defy the hunters. Attacks on these larger animals must be exercises in attrition and can last for days. As the allosaurs approach, individuals spread out to get more room to maneuver, often encircling the prey. Each animal looks for any weakness, then exploits it by quickly advancing and attacking with tooth or claw, trying to inflict as much injury as it can and get out before it gets injured itself. Meanwhile, the prey tries to intimidate the theropods by grunting, hissing, stamping its feet, rearing up on its hind legs to strike out with its forefeet, charging head down, or wielding its whiplike or spiked tail as a weapon. Although this may appear to be a standoff, the predators are in complete control. Rather than discouraging its attackers, all its defensive posturing and behavior simply wears the herbivore down. Eventually, fatigue and blood loss take their toll. Even the largest of the Plain's herbivores can fall under the persistent attack of a band of determined allosaurs. Although the smaller teeth of allosaurs seem much less formidable than the ceratosaurs' large ones, their communal behavior more than compensates for their reduced firepower.

A very large carcass, such as that of a sauropod, offers plenty to go around, so all the allosaurs can feed at their leisure. The feast can continue for days, interrupted only for sleeping or drinking. Fully gorged allosaurs often fall asleep next to the kill, so they can keep an eye on it and resume feasting as soon as they are able. During these intermissions, resident *Ornitholestes* and *Coelurus*, both of them much smaller theropods, and even a wandering ceratosaur may slip in for a bite. At a fresh kill, othnielians sometimes dart in and out between the feeding carnivorous dinosaurs. They are after the gallons of partially digested vegetation in the crop and stomach of the large herbivores. As the allosaurs start to leave the kill, the smaller theropods rush in from all sides and fall upon the leftovers. It is not unusual to find more than one hundred scavenging dinosaurs of all sizes and types, covered in blood and gore, climbing in and around, over and even through the carcass, pulling and tearing at bits of flesh, and fighting among themselves.

Although nowhere near as large as their allosaur and ceratosaur cousins, ornitholestians and coelurans are no less formidable. Both travel widely throughout the Plain, alone or in small family groups, using their large eyes to forage and hunt both day and night. A coeluran, at eight feet in length, is slightly larger and, with longer legs, faster as well. A long, downward-curved neck and grasping hands snatch at and capture lizards, mammals, and the hatchlings of other dinosaurs. A hunting coeluran is a study in patience: walking through brush and undergrowth with its tail extended fully rearward, arms in close to the body, and head low and forward, alert to the slightest noises and the tiniest flicker of motion. At the right sound or hint of movement, the slender dinosaur freezes, for minutes at a time, waiting for a repetition. Then it attacks in a whirlwind, head and arms simultaneously thrust into the tangle of twigs and branches that caught its attention. On occasion, because they are so intent on locating prey stirred up by the passage of a stegosaur or a sauropod, they wander a bit too close to their benefactor. The larger animals do not care to have a theropod agitating their pterosaur sentinels, so all it takes is a turn of the head and a loud snort to send the startled coeluran scurrying on its way.

Sporting a nasal horn like the larger ceratosaurs, ornitholestians are small-game predators that are also adept at fishing. Often they spend several hours a day standing in shallow water, enveloped in the deep shade along the banks of a stream or beside a water hole or lake, especially when dry weather shrinks the water hole, concentrating the fish in a smaller area. Here, they will wait patiently for a fish to swim into the range of their grasping hands and jaws. Sharply pointed, conical teeth in the front of the diminutive hunter's short, powerful jaws catch and hold the slippery prey as they quickly lift it from the water and swallow it. Ornitholestians also use their slender forelimbs and long, thin fingers to dig up furry mammals from their burrows and dispatch them as quickly as the fish.

The mammals of the Morrison Plain remain small, retiring, and nocturnal, avoiding all contact with larger animals by sleeping the day away in their burrows. This strategy has worked well and the mammals have flourished, slowly evolving, diversifying their diets, improving their method of reproduction, and thereby consolidating their place in the Mesozoic.

Just as the largest terrestrial vertebrates on the Plain use sound to keep in touch, so do the smallest. Mammals use the other extreme—ultrasound—to communicate. They also communicate with smell, releasing pheromones and other scents to encourage bonding and to mark territory. Foraging mammals follow regular routes, constantly feeding, repeatedly searching every nook and cranny. They know every inch of their territory, so they can escape danger quickly, even during the darkest moonless night.

Although the territories of different types of mammals overlap, confrontations or conflicts are rare. Right now the Morrison Plain is home to an entire bestiary of these furry, warm-blooded little creatures. The omnivorous docodonts scamper through the darkness in short, fast spurts, poking their long, narrow, bewhiskered snouts under every twig and leaf. Closer to the wetlands are the more discriminating triconodonts. True carnivores, they feast on a smorgasbord of mussels and snails, amphibian eggs and tadpoles, worms, maggots, and grubs. Multituberculates have the distinction of being the first predominantly herbivorous mammals. Inhabiting a broad range, these vegetarians use their piercing, shearing, and crushing teeth to feed on roots, seeds, and herbaceous stems, but they are not above taking an occasional worm, grub, or slug.

Egg layers all, these mammals restrict the range of their foraging and stay close to their burrows, either to warm their eggs or to nurse their young. One group has eliminated at least part of this restriction by giving live birth. Some time ago, the eggs of some mammals were retained within the mother's body. Those eggs did not have to be protected and the female was free to nourish herself until the young were born. These mammals—pantotheres—have refined this practice by eliminating the eggshell, permitting direct nutritional contact between mother and young before birth. Pantotheres are born quite small and immature, only a quarter of an inch long. The tiny pink babies worm their way blindly along the mother's belly until they reach one of a pair of skin folds running down her underside. Within these folds are milk glands. Each newborn bites down on a tuft of fur, which acts as a wick to deliver the life-giving milk, rich in fats, proteins, sugars, and minerals. Female pantotheres can lead a troop of young on a feeding foray while carrying the next brood in their belly folds and pregnant with a third.

Scurrying about in the night, the mammals of the Morrison Plain have managed to eke out a life in the shadows of the giants of the day. Less than glamorous, almost an afterthought, these denizens of the dark nonetheless are doing quite well. Theirs is the domain of the small, of the hidden. Theirs is the dominion of the meek.

CHAPTER FIVE

WANDERING SHORES

Coastal Wildlife of the Niobrara Sea

PRECEDING PAGES
The barrier islands that line the Niobrara seaway's eastern shores make for some of the most beautiful scenes to be found anywhere in the world. These islands, formed by wind, waves, and currents, are prized by wildlife. On the beach, salt-loving plants take root, while in the sky, two *Nyctosaurus*, medium-sized pterosaurs, wheel above a lagoon that separates the island from East America, just visible on the horizon.

OPPOSITE
A male Pteranodon preens in the midday sun. Pteranodon are the largest pterosaurs of the Niobrara, with some having a wingspan of twenty-five feet. They spend several hours a day keeping their fur clean and aerodynamically sound. As heavily dependent on their ability to fly as they are, neatness counts.

Sixty-five million years have passed. Changes in climate, continents, and life itself have swept the globe and ushered in a new period, the Cretaceous. Of all the changes to the planet, it is the extensive global flooding that is most noticeable and profound.

Worldwide, sea levels have risen almost six hundred feet in the past twenty million years, and water now covers four-fifths of the globe—the highest level since life first came ashore. The shallow seas that have inundated the land have allowed warm, tropical waters to flow to the northern polar region, tempering its potentially frigid climate. Some continents have shifted to a maritime climate, moderating both temperature and rainfall. An increase in volcanic activity in the Pacific Ocean has fueled a greenhouse effect, further warming the planet. Plants like the gymnosperms and the new angiosperms now grow everywhere, and a balmy early summer reigns year round across most of the planet. Never before in Earth's history have conditions across the globe been more favorable for animals living on land. Continental wildlife communities, newly isolated by the risen waters, have evolved unimpeded. Marine wildlife communities now have the run of the expanded waters and margins of new island habitats. The result is a riot of different forms occupying every available ecological niche across the land, sea, and air.

In North America, a new, warm, shallow body of water, the Niobrara Sea, effectively separates the continent into two landmasses known as East and West America. The seaway's shape has changed repeatedly as the surrounding shores have advanced and retreated.

Far across the gentle swells of the Niobrara Sea, almost a thousand miles east of the plant-choked deltas, lies the subcontinent of East America. Wide stretches of sparkling sandy beaches dominate its coasts. The shorelines here are an intricate maze of inlets, bays, estuaries, and lagoons, interfingered with innumerable spits, bars, and offshore barrier islands. First forming in the north off the gently sloping coastline, the barrier islands move gradually to the south, sometimes rejoining the mainland, sometimes splitting into smaller islands, often disappearing altogether.

Animals are irresistibly drawn to these islands. Their shores offer a measure of protective isolation to pterosaurs, birds, and seagoing reptiles, who all seek out their sandy beaches to rest, feed, and rear their young in comparative safety.

On the northernmost of these barrier islands, well within the Arctic Circle, the first hint of winter's end is marked not by a change in temperature but by a change of light—or, more precisely, the reappearance of light. The star-studded, inky blackness that has enveloped this region for the last two months begins to be broken by the bluish purple glow of early morning. Dawn this far north, though, is slow to break and morning is weeks away.

The stillness of the cool air is interrupted only by the gentle sound of the Niobrara lapping on the shoreline and the occasional breeze from over the water. In about a month, the first glimmer of sunlight will begin to shine through the mist hanging on the southern horizon.

This first light reveals how the storms of winter have changed the islands. Sand bars that appeared a few years ago have been pushed south by the currents and have grown to form separate, smaller islands. New sand bars and shoals just to the north are already taking their place. These barrier islands are little more than elongated strips of sand piled a few feet above the high-water line. Except for scattered clumps of vegetation hunched in the lee of the low dunes, there are no native inhabitants. With no shelter, and little in the way of food or fresh water, no animals have made these isolated islands their permanent home. Nor have any large animals chosen to spend the winter here. But the return of the sun invites a host of wildlife, both large and small, to return. They find that the sand bars and shoals they know have merged to form a small island. Practically all shoreline, it now stretches close to a mile long and several hundred feet wide.

A few hundred yards offshore, it is not long before the stillness of the sea is broken by a disturbance in the water. Soon, in the cool of the early morning, a dark head atop a long neck will break the surface. It belongs to an *Elasmosaurus*, a type of plesiosaur. A familiar sight of early spring in the far north, these marine creatures are one of the larger seagoing reptiles of the Niobrara, often more than forty feet long and weighing several tons. It is what makes up those forty-odd feet that creates an unforgettable sight: More than half of their length is in their necks. Topped off by small heads that double as toothy fish traps, they look strangely out of place in this marine world of streamlined swimmers. Yet they have adapted without incident, thriving on the abundant fish and squid that live in the cool waters.

Superbly suited for life at or near the surface, elasmosaurs feed in one of two ways. Rising quickly from the depths, snaking their necks through the water, they can shoot their heads up to twenty feet out into a school of small fish or squid. Or, by lifting their heads high above the surface, they can drop down onto their unsuspecting prey. Long, needle-sharp teeth pierce their slippery victims and seldom allow an escape. With a quick jerk of the head, the reptile flips its slippery prey up to dislodge it from its sharp teeth, then catches it in mid-air. A few adjustments, and the fish is poised to go down the long neck headfirst, so the fins and scales can't injure the lining of the elasmosaur's throat. The ability to toss and catch fish seems to be instinctive, and they rarely miss or lose a meal to thieves.

Like other marine reptiles, elasmosaurs make much better time while swimming completely submerged—where is always the chance of an unexpected meal. They usually remain on the surface breathing deeply for several moments before diving. Thirty or so breaths saturate their blood and tissues with enough oxygen to let them remain submerged for up to half an hour.

OPPOSITE
A *Hydrotherosaurus* has made an unusual catch. It is a coelocanth, a lobe-finned fish, that has probably strayed from more eastern waters. *Hydrotherosaurus* belongs to a group called elasmosaurs. They patrol these waters regularly in search of fish. They have also evolved a fish-trap mouth with teeth so long that they stick out the sides of their mouths even when they are closed. A short compact body, four large paddles, and a short tail round their forty-foot length.

Nursing an infected wound, a female *Elasmosaurus* hauls herself onto a beach in the far north to lay her eggs. The wound is probably the result of a shark or mosasaur attack—elasmosaurs are solitary animals, and mostly leave each other alone. They have a habit of napping while basking at the surface of the sea, and, in the long shadows of the early morning light of the spring breeding season, are sometimes subject to attack from below by very large predators looking for an unwary meal.

Elasmosaurs have a strong preference for the north when it comes time to lay their eggs. The females make an effort to nest on the very same beaches where they themselves were born.

Then they exhale deeply, to lose as much buoyancy as possible, before heading down. Elasmosaurs, like all plesiosaurs, use their four large, paddle-like limbs to move stealthily through the clear sea. Alternating front and rear rhythmically up and down, they can "fly" through the water. Although not especially quick, elasmosaurs can still move at a steady clip, making rapid twists and turns, and even backing up, either in pursuit of prey or to avoid predators.

Every year at this time, the attention of female elasmosaurs focuses on the northern Niobrara, which becomes a scene of activity that few stretches of beach anywhere can match. From their entire range, hundreds of egg-laden females manage to appear within a few days of each other, governed by some internal clock. This is the one time of the year when they all head for land, to take advantage of the extended daylight and warmth, which hastens the development and hatching of their eggs. They time their arrival for the highest tide, when the moon is full, and often manage to lay their eggs on the same beaches where they themselves were hatched.

They normally start approaching just before sunrise, while the moon is still above the horizon. Like an invading armada, scores of the giant reptiles head for the beach, enter the surf zone, thrust themselves out of the foam, and laboriously pull themselves onto the sand with a loud, grating hiss. Every once in a while one of the leviathans will stop momentarily and, with a shake of its head, snort a great spray of salty water from its nostrils. Some marine reptiles absorb large amounts of salt, which can kill them if allowed to build up. Special glands in their heads remove the excess salt from their blood and dump it into their nasal passages, where it is unceremoniously expelled.

Just short of the dune fields, the giants stop to catch their breath. Then, largely ignoring each other, they use their rear paddles to dig nest holes. As they dig, their great, long necks swing their heads back periodically to inspect their progress. Within an hour or so, just after full sunrise, they finish the holes and fill them with wet, white, oval eggs. After the last egg is laid, each animal moves forward off the nest and uses its rear flippers to cover it. Then, without even a glance to confirm that the nest is completely filled or the eggs completely covered, the huge reptiles turn and move arduously back down the beach to meet the water as it rushes up.

Although their chests are braced by a considerable amount of bone, elasmosaurs spend very little time on land, and breathing there is difficult for them. Their wheezing and puffing mingle with the sounds of the surf as they head for home. As the waves swirl around their necks and torsos, each female is finally lifted free of the sand. Supported by the water, breathing now comes easier. Soon the water is deep enough for them to submerge completely. As the bottom falls gently away, the elasmosaurs, weightless again, descend with it, using steady, powerful strokes.

Several weeks later, patches of the white sand start bubbling up. Here and there, wet, black, sand-covered faces emerge to blink at the bright Arctic sky. Soon others appear, then more, until the entire length of the beach is alive with tiny faces and dark forms skittering about. Miniature versions of the adults, except for their oversized heads and relatively short necks, the hatchlings scamper down the sandy incline in short, frantic bursts of motion, instinctively heading toward the water in long, ragged ranks.

They move quickly because the most difficult moment of their lives is at hand and they are on their own, a magnet for aerial predators, both birds and pterosaurs. The scrambling hatchlings and hungry predators swooping down to snatch them up form a dizzying swirl of blurred motion, punctuated by small bursts of sand as young elasmosaurs are plucked from the beach. For those that survive the gauntlet, ahead lies an uncertain life at sea, where only a handful will

Its lifeless body floating at the surface, the now dead elasmosaur attracts the attention of the scavengers in the area: small fish, ammonites, and a large shark on the lookout for an easy meal. The elasmosaur's body initially sank to the bottom of the sea. After a week or so, gases brought on by decomposition caused the carcass to refloat itself. The shark, after slowly circling several times, advances and attacks—tearing out large chunks of meat.

A few minutes after this scene took place, the shark bit down deeply as before, but this time bit into the elasmosaur's bloated body cavity. With a strangled, gulping noise, several cubic feet of gas erupted from the wound. As the gas continued to bubble from the gaping hole, buoyancy was lost, and the lifeless elasmosaur began its final descent into the darkness below.

survive to adulthood. Of those that do, some may eventually make their way back to these very shores, continuing a cycle that is generations old.

Weeks after the adult elasmosaurs have left, the daylight is lengthening. The once cool mornings are growing warmer. From its inauspicious beginnings a few years ago, a long, sandy islet a few miles to the south now parallels the coast for more than a mile. Most of its length supports a mix of salt-tolerant plants, but near its southern end, hundreds of low beige mounds dot the beach. They stretch from the high-water mark to the crests of the higher dunes. Each is perhaps five feet across at the base and a foot and a half high, with a shallow depression at the top. About a foot apart at their bases, the mounds cover the beach for several hundred yards, giving it a pockmarked, lunar appearance.

These mounds are nests. They have been deserted for the past eight months. Wind, rain, and the occasional winter storm have eroded them somewhat, but soon they will be restored. The builders are *Hesperornis*, seabirds. When these birds reappear, they are not distant specks high in the cloudless sky, but dark shapes moving swiftly through the clear, blue-tinted water. Their black heads break the surface just long enough to draw a breath, then quickly disappear again. As they approach the shore, their heads

A newly hatched *Elasmosaurus* scampers across the sand on its way to the water. Miniature versions of the adults, they sport shorter necks and oversized heads. Even at this early age the animal's sharp, needle-like teeth can be seen protruding from its closed mouth, making for a mindless, toothy smile.

stay up, turning quickly from side to side to check their bearings. With vigorous kicks of their powerful legs, they match their speed with that of the curling waves and ride the combers up onto the beach.

They swim to the island because they cannot fly. Instead of standing upright and walking out of the spent waves, the hesperornithids lie prone in the wet sand and frog-kick their legs to get onto the upper beach. They plow through the sand because they cannot stand. Their legs spread out sideways, as do their lobed feet, and cannot be brought under their bodies to support them. On shore they make for an ungainly lot, looking as if they need a push to get them on their way.

Unlike the giant marine reptiles, the birds stay and form large nesting colonies. The females are the first to arrive. In nest ownership, the rule is first come, first served, although many will take the same nest they used the previous season. Minor squabbling over nest ownership is generally resolved without injuries. The females seek out nests in the center of the colony first. Those too close to the water are under threat from high tides and storm surges. Those too far from the water entail a long, arduous journey back and forth when feeding. And there is always the threat of attack from a predator that has wandered out to the island, or harassment from the ever-present hordes of the toothed bird, *Ichthyornis*, and the medium-sized pterosaurs, *Nyctosaurus*.

While the last of the females are still arriving, the first of the males begin approaching. Once they get up onto the beach, they fan out to seek mates. Along the way, they pick up a bit of shell, seaweed, or some other token to offer to prospective mates.

The male and female are almost impossible to tell apart, even for them, so they rely more on behavior than appearance to choose a mate. Each suitor crawls up the side of a sand mound and extends the offering to the nest's resident. If this offering is ignored, it has been offered to a female who is not yet ready to mate or has mated already. If the proffered gift is accepted, the female adds it to the mound, then thrusts its head and bill into the air, exposing the white patch on its throat. The male does the same. This process—offer, accep-

Floating on the surface of the Niobrara Sea, an adult *Hesperornis* demonstrates why these birds are so well suited to a life in the water. Having the smallest remnant of wings makes flight an impossibility, and because their legs are so far back on their bodies, the same is true for walking. Aside from some time on the shore during the breeding season, all their life is spent at sea.

tance, mutual throat display—is repeated many times by the pair over the next few days and effectively bonds the two birds for the season.

Each nest is a mixture of sand, feathers, seaweed, excrement, and bits of shell and is surprisingly durable. Females crawl up the sides of their nests, repeatedly bulldozing the sand with their chests. Droppings, judiciously applied to the edges of the nest and dried by the sun, help prevent its collapse. When a female is satisfied with the size and slope of the mound, she sits in the center and redefines the shape and size of the central depression.

After this brief courtship, mating takes place. Soon thereafter, each female lays its eggs and the incubation period begins. Twice a day during this period, once in the morning and again in the late afternoon, the male crawls down to the shore, swims out through the surf, and fishes for both of them. In the water, the hesperornithids are in their element. The froglike kick that looks so ungainly and ineffective on land becomes a quick, powerful, efficient swimming stroke. Superb swimmers, the males stay close to the surface as they travel out to the fishing grounds, raising their heads to breathe every few seconds. When they arrive, they inhale deeply and, with their heads and bills extended, dive down to depths in excess of a hundred feet. As they descend, they trail streams of bubbles—air that was trapped in their feathers to help them float and provide insulation.

At the proper depth, each bird slowly stops its descent and drifts, unmoving, with its head bent back in an S-shaped curve. Powerful eye muscles alter the shape of its lenses, enabling the bird to focus just as well underwater as it does above. When a fish approaches, the hesperornithid pursues its prey with powerful strokes of its legs, and when close enough, extends its neck and reaches out quickly with a toothed bill to snatch at it. Hesperornithids hunt in groups, ensuring enough confusion and disorientation on the part of the fish to increase the chances of a successful catch.

If successful, the bird must surface quickly in order to swallow the prey. Waiting there are the ever-present, ever-hungry *Ichthyornis* and *Nyctosaurus*—the all-purpose scavenger-thieves of the Niobrara. If the hesperornithid does not have the fish securely by the head, it must quickly get it into that position and swallow it before it is torn from its grasp by one of the many birds or pterosaurs that wheel about the skies looking for an easy meal. In any case, whether the fish is swallowed or stolen, each hesperornithid must

make several dives, some lasting over two minutes, in order to fill its gullet.

Then each male starts back to its mate. With its gullet full and its feathers now thoroughly soaked, each bird begins to porpoise vigorously at the surface. This thrashing about introduces air back into its plumage and restores some buoyancy, so it doesn't have to work so hard on the journey home.

The six-foot length of an adult hesperornithid puts off a number of potential predators lurking in the depths. But not all of them—there are marine reptiles, sharks, and even fish large and aggressive enough to attack hesperornithids successfully. Some of these hunters enter this part of the Niobrara at this time of year specifically to feed on the large, temporary concentration of these essentially defenseless nesting birds.

Back on the island, after struggling up the beach, each male raises its head in greeting to its mate. The female raises its head in reply and starts to tap the male's bill with its own. This makes the male regurgitate some of its load of partially digested fish so that the female can feed. Afterward, the male usually lies on the sunward side of the mound's slope in order to dry its feathers, while noisy aerial filchers circle looking for leftover scraps. After drying off, the male preens itself to restore the overlapping pattern of its feathers and remove bits of seaweed and sand.

This is a quiet time in the colony, when the adults can afford the indulgences that come with being expectant parents. Couples spend

time doing a little house cleaning and grooming each other, which reinforces the pair bond, and occasionally grab a nap in the pleasant spring weather. It is over all too soon at the end of the month. As the chicks begin to hatch, the parents alternate between fishing and protecting the young. As each successive egg hatches, the fishing trips become more frequent. The number of chicks determines the number of trips that must be made each day. The number of fish caught and returned to the nest, in turn, determines the number of offspring that will survive. Normally, only one or two chicks per nest, usually the oldest and largest, will survive. In a particularly good year, more may survive, but sometimes none. And if the fish shoals are too far out, too deep, or too few, the adults keep what they catch for themselves, letting the chicks die, and mate again later if conditions improve.

Once free of their eggs, the featherless chicks have no protection from the harmful ultraviolet rays of the sun. An adult bird must, therefore, be on hand to shield the chicks from the sun. At this latitude, the sun never rises very high in the sky, so a long shadow is guaranteed. However, the adults' dark plumage, which camouflages them so well while fishing at depths of a hundred feet, becomes a real problem on the hot beach, so the large birds pant continuously in order to avoid overheating. During the heat of the day, the setting parents lie on their mounds, mouths agape, with throats pulsing rapidly, trying their best to keep cool.

Soon the chicks have grown a coat of soft, light gray down, which protects them from the

Pterosaurs and seabirds often spend the night on the closest island to them. As dawn breaks, they begin to stir. Awakened by the first light, active fliers such as birds and small pterosaurs have already taken to the air to begin their morning activities. Large *Pteranodon* remain still, sitting quietly and preening. They await the full sun and the thermal updrafts so vital to the flight of these consummate soarers.

A *Hesperornis* nest in the middle of the rookery quickly becomes the target of Ichthyornids, the all-purpose scavengers of the Niobrara. An unguarded nest is usually the result of an adult bird being lost on a fishing trip. The remaining parent, needing to feed, will eventually abandon the nest. Patrolling Ichthyornids soon zero in on unattended eggs and chicks. Although the presence of these smaller-toothed birds quickly elicits a noisy protest, none of the neighboring Hesperornids will abandon their own nests to drive off the interlopers. By swiftly making short order of anything in the rookery left unattended, Ichthyornids and other scavengers actually perform a vital service by keeping the nesting area relatively clean.

sun's heat—a good thing, since it has become more difficult for all the rapidly growing chicks to fit in the shade provided by the adult birds. Not long after, the fast-growing young are each eating almost as much as their parents. Now that the surviving chicks are large enough to be left unattended, both parents go to sea to hunt simultaneously, making four or five trips a day to feed their demanding brood. The chicks no longer all fit in the nest, and many noisy confrontations take place with neighbors.

By the height of the Arctic summer, the colony appears to be in total confusion. The noise of constantly chattering birds can be almost deafening. And when the weather gets hot, the combined smell of droppings and partially digested fish remains fills the air. Colonies that have been used for many years build up deep layers of guano, adding to the mess. The chaotic beach, packed with stressed parents and impatient, adventurous chicks, all barely managing to get around by heaving their bodies through the sand and constantly harassed by the persistent ichthyornans and pterosaurs, stands in stark contrast to the placid waters of the Niobrara.

It is a scene that is not destined to last very long. In a few short weeks, black feathers replace the chicks' gray down. They continuously leave their nests and make their way down to the water's edge to meet their returning parents. But even persistent bill tapping by the chicks now produces only an occasional fish meal. By summer's end, the young make their way past the breakers out into the open sea and do not return to the beach to be fed. The adults also stop returning. Neither fledgling nor adult will make landfall again until next season. With nothing to scavenge or steal, the ichthyornans and nyctosaurs also leave the rookery for different areas of the Niobrara. All that remains are the silent, empty mounds left to the elements in the growing shadows of the Arctic fall. The shores are deserted once again.

As the years come and go, the hesperornithids still nest in the Niobrara, but no longer on the same beaches. The sands that made those shores have drifted hundreds of miles southward and now make up an island several miles long and almost a half mile wide, still just off the mainland, still composed of fine white particles, still drifting south, one grain at a time. The hesperornithids and elasmosaurs, preferring cooler areas for child-rearing, have abandoned these shores.

Winter here in the central Niobrara is less a study in contrasts than in the far north. There is no season of darkness, and only an occasional winter storm quiets the inhabitants. The island plays host to a variety of wildlife—birds, pterosaurs, and the occasional marine reptile. Some visit to sleep or rest, making it a stopover on a migration route. Others stake out a claim for a few weeks and try out the local waters for the fishing. Aside from those animals that wind up as another's dinner, most of the wildlife tends to go about its business with little notice of the neighbors. Territorial and reproductive battles, which had once seemed so important, give way to day-to-day existence, before these animals move on.

In late winter, the mornings tend to be bright, with just a few wispy clouds in the sky. By midmorning they usually burn off and the sun shines down on a scene of incredible beauty. An azure sky, met at the horizon by turquoise waters and just a hint of a sea-scented breeze, lends a peaceful feel. Just a few days after the last shorebird has left, out in the distance to the west, small white arcs begin to appear just above the horizon. After a time individual forms can be made out, stretched out horizontally above the sea. Eventually, they reveal themselves as flocks of large, winged *Pteranodon*—handsome, crested pterosaurs, some sporting wingspans of over twenty-five feet. Closer in to shore, their true size becomes apparent. In addition to their huge wingspan, a large male carries a crest that may extend three feet over its head. Add a bill of almost equal length, and a six-foot-long head is not uncommon. Several species of *Pteranodon* inhabit the Niobrara, each with its own uniquely styled headgear.

Watching them slowly riding the thermals above the island is almost hypnotizing. By dras-

Triumphantly displaying its catch, a six-foot-long *Hesperornis* rises to the surface in a lagoon separating an island from the mainland. Awkward on land and incapable of flying, their true home is in the water. Few animals can match their fishing skills. Snaring this fish dinner was made easier by the bird's replaceable, pointed teeth and its ability to focus its eyes underwater.

tically increasing their size, lightening their bones—so that in some places they are a fiftieth of an inch thick—and perfecting their soaring technique, pteranodons have become some of the most elegant and graceful animals ever to take to the air. Because of their ultralightweight design, they can remain aloft at incredibly slow speeds. So little effort seems to be required to keep them in the air that they seem to float. The scene of these giants hanging nearly motionless in the bright blue sky above the turquoise waters of the Niobrara, keeping just the right distance apart, and occasionally whistling to each other, approaches the sublime.

Over the next few days, flocks of pteranodon begin gliding in gracefully over the brilliant white sand. As the huge pterosaurs arrive, this serene image stands in stark contrast to the reality emerging on the shores. They are here to breed, and time is short. The first on the scene are always the males. Some left this island almost five years ago, then only about two-thirds grown. They have spent their time at sea, riding the winds, skimming the surface for fish, and maturing, with only the rarest of landfalls, so this is their first time back. Others have been here before, two years ago.

After setting down, they instinctively seek higher ground. High ground here means a series of long, low hills running down the center of the island. Although only a few tens of feet above sea level, these dunes are high enough to suit their purposes. The areas they use are usually easy to pick out. Because they are reused every year, the plants that cover them are very sparse, when compared with the denser ground cover on dunes not used for nesting.

Males who arrive after the dune crests have been claimed must fight their way to the top by fencing, a form of combat no less earnest for being so ritualized. The adversaries face each other, flourishing their long beaks and head-crests. Each combatant then alternately raises and lowers its head, displaying its long beak and crest while shaking its six-foot-long head from side to side, pausing only long enough to observe its opponent. After a few moments of this display activity, the fighting begins. The

Two male *Pteranodon* prepare to square off in a confrontation over courtship territory (above). On the small islands on which they breed, prime nesting space is at a premium. The combat, called fencing, will determine which males get the best stretch of beach, and thus be able to attract the most females in their harem. Facing off, each male judges his opponent's strength by posture and crest size. The two combatants knock bills (opposite) and try to topple their opponent. Winners get the choicest locations on the island—usually the highest ground. Losers sometimes have to wait until the following year to get another chance at mating.

combatants smack the sides of their beaks together in an attempt to turn their opponent's head or perhaps even knock him off balance. Each animal clacks its bill and calls out for added effect. Sometimes with their beaks raised, sometimes with their beaks lowered, the pair's bills strike each other with loud cracks. Up and down the beach, the sharp reports of the blows resound from daybreak until sunset, mingling with their calls, the cries of the shorebirds and the other pterosaurs, and the rush of the nearby surf. The males continue fencing until one or the other breaks off, by stepping back. This gesture identifies it as the loser, and it retires to a less desirable territory. The winner then engages the attention of another male, in a more desirable location, and the combat begins again.

Males who arrive too early have too many battles to fight in order to maintain their places on the dune's crest. Those who arrive too late may not have enough time to work their way to the dunes which, by then, are buried deep within the colony. Because each territorial dispute is settled soon after each male arrives, once they are all on the island there is very little further squabbling. Except for the occasional border skirmish, life within the colony soon settles down. Each male passes the time by slowly walking around the edges of its domain, marking its territory by posturing and vocalizing at its boundary until the females show up.

About half the size of the males, and with only a hint of a crest, the females also take several days to arrive. On approach they slowly circle, as if taking in the entire colony from the air before landing. On the ground, they move through the outlying territories toward the dunes. As they waddle through and across the unseen but very real territorial boundaries, the males pull themselves up to their full height and shake their heads from side to side. Although this display is an important factor used by females in choosing a mate, it is not the only one. The size of a male's territory also matters to the females, and its location is key.

Over the next few days, the polygamous males will form harems of up to a half a dozen females. The delicate truces among neighboring males are disrupted repeatedly as the females parade through the colony. There may even be some additional fencing and redrawing of territorial boundaries, until the females have selected their mates. As expected, the males who hold the more protected dune tops attract more females. Those down on the beach are chosen by only one or two females, if they're lucky. Since females outnumber males two to one, practically all of the males are chosen by at least one female. Bachelorhood is thrust upon only some younger males returning to the island for the first time, and a few older ones returning for the last.

Life is harder for male pteranodons than for females. They take more than twice as long as females to reach sexual maturity, so they have twice as long to suffer the perils that might befall pteranodons at sea, like storms, predators, and disease. Battle injuries also contribute. Although pteranodons never fight to the death, a misdirected blow might strike the animal on its wing. A proper blow might knock one down, and its wing, extended to regain balance, might touch the ground too hard or be stepped on by another. Their extremely thin, hollow wing bones do not stand up well to such abuse and often break—a death sentence to animals as dependent on flight as these.

Pteranodon nests are called scrapes because of the way they are formed. The females scoop them out of the sand shortly after they select their mates. They simply set their chests down on the sand and shift their bodies from side to side until a shallow depression a few feet across is formed. The nests, such as they are, are created in less than a minute, but the sight of one is enough to stimulate courtship display behavior in the male.

When it sees the nest, the male lowers its beak to its chest, displays its crest, and slowly shakes it from side to side several times. Then it quickly raises its beak and emits a long drawn-out call. This sequence is repeated over and over until the female falls in with it, repeating the head rocking and sky calling. Once their visual and vocal displays become synchronous, mating follows. The calls, coming from so many animals at once, combine into one continuous sound, piercing the calm Niobrara seascape.

A few weeks later there is first one, then another slightly mottled egg lying in each nest,

OPPOSITE

In the waning sunlight of a late afternoon, and adult male *Pteranodon* banks as it comes off the Niobrara after a day spent fishing. *Pteranodon* are some of the most elegant, graceful animals ever to have taken to the air. Although they are capable of short periods of powered flight, they can cover hundreds of miles a day by soaring.

A newly-hatched *Pteranodon* chick sits beneath its mother's body. *Pteranodon* time their eggs to hatch several days apart, an advantage the larger chick will use if food becomes scarce. Most often only one chick will survive to adulthood. At this early age the greatest danger to the chick is being stepped on or smothered by their much larger parent—twenty percent of the young die in this manner. Adults often eat remaining eggshell fragments in order to keep the nesting area clean and probably as an additional source of calcium.

blending in nicely with its speckled sandy floor. With eggs laid, there is no longer a reason for border clashes between males. In fact, they are no longer needed at the colony, as they take no part in guarding the nest or feeding the chicks. The sight of eggs triggers a response that effectively sees all the males gone from the colony within a few days. For the next two years, they will spend their time away from the island at sea—alone, sometimes aloft, turning slowly in large lazy circles, sometimes alighting on the surface to fish or rest.

The females are much less territorial, so the departure of the males has something of a calming effect on the entire colony. Some noisy confrontations still occur when nearby nests are too closely approached, but they are nothing compared with the commotion caused by two adult males trying to reestablish a territorial boundary. Each female can now concentrate on its chicks' well-being. And that now depends on their ability to feed them—but first they must feed themselves.

Upon awakening at first light, each pteranodon preens, making its fur as streamlined and aerodynamically sound as possible. It may spend several hours a day preening, usually just before or after a flight. Once satisfied that its coat is in order, the pterasaur extends its large wings to their fullest and holds them motionless. Although this appears to be nothing more than an early morning stretch, it is an important part of the daily ritual. Wing stretching is really a test to determine the temperature of the air over the beach. As the sun beats down on the white sand, much of the heat energy radiates back into the air above it, forming a column of warmed air, a thermal. When these plumes of hot, rising air form over the beaches and drift out over the water, they provide a means by which the pteranodons can cover large distances without expending a lot of energy.

One by one, the pteranodons amble toward the water, with outstretched wings.

Occasionally making a slight increase in their step, they become airborne with hardly any need to flap their large wings. Each easily lifts from the sand through the combined effects of the gentle sea breeze, its own forward motion, and the warm rising air. Soaring out off the island, then banking sharply to stay over the hot sand, each is constantly aware of the air traffic and adjusts its flight accordingly. Moving silently over the beach, lifted higher and higher by the warmed air mass, these white-winged giants soon fill the sky. As each *Pteranodon* reaches the northern end of the island, it wheels about to stay above the beach and remain within the forming thermal plume.

The pteranodons turn again at the southern end of the island and continue to soar along the beach, only northward now, gaining altitude all the while. The few remaining females on the beach appear even smaller, while the shallow nests fade from view as the rising sun washes out the shadows. Below, a steady stream of pteranodons also rise almost without effort in the heated air. The most perfect soaring animals ever to have flown are off to fish.

Heading out into the open waters to the west, their journey does not last long. They are going to feed on the vast shoals of *Apsopelix*, a herring-like fish about a foot long, which enter these waters each year to satisfy their own reproductive urges. Upon reaching the shoals of fish, each pterosaur folds its wings back slightly and descends to the surface.

At this hour of the day, the fish are near the surface, feeding on tiny crustaceans that have risen from the depths to feed on algae. Because pteranodons' eyes are sensitive to red light, they can see the fish clearly through the blue reflection of the sky on the water. Coming in just above the gently rolling waves, each *Pteranodon* reaches down with its long, toothless beak and expertly snatches its prey out of the water. A small crest on the end of its beak helps it recover when its head drops after making contact with a fish. Once its head is horizontal again, the fish is swallowed—a perfect skimmer. Several successful passes and a full gullet will soon have a *Pteranodon* ready to return.

With a crop full of fish, a *Pteranodon* can weigh up to twenty percent more than it did on the trip out, so for the flight home, adjustments must be made. The forward edges of the wings are raised slightly to increase lift, and their heads are carried a little farther back from their filled bellies in order to move their centers of gravity more rearward. Then, each begins a slow, steady, up-and-down movement of its great wings.

When the coast comes into sight, each *Pteranodon* increases the rhythm of the powerful strokes to create the additional lift needed to reach the rookery. Once above the beach, small flaps of skin that stretch along the leading edges of a pterosaur's wings from its wrists to its shoulders adjust the airflow over the wings, so the animal can bring its airspeed down to almost zero before settling onto the sand with a bounce. Several weeks and many fishing trips later, the first eggs start to hatch. Female pteranodons do not attempt to help their chicks in any way. It sometimes takes two or three days for young pteranodons to fully break free of their eggs. Ungainly and wet, the beige, dappled, crestless chicks, which will one day grace the Cretaceous skies, push themselves free of their eggs and their entangling membranes, finally emerging onto the warm sand totally exhausted. The females generally pick up the larger pieces of eggshell and eat

Dinnertime for a *Pteranodon* chick. Adult females feed their young a half-digested stew of fish by regurgitation. It looks uncomfortable, but neither adult nor chick seems harmed by this technique. *Pteranodon* also use their throat pouches to pant in the hot sun—flapping them in the breeze and extending them to radiate heat.

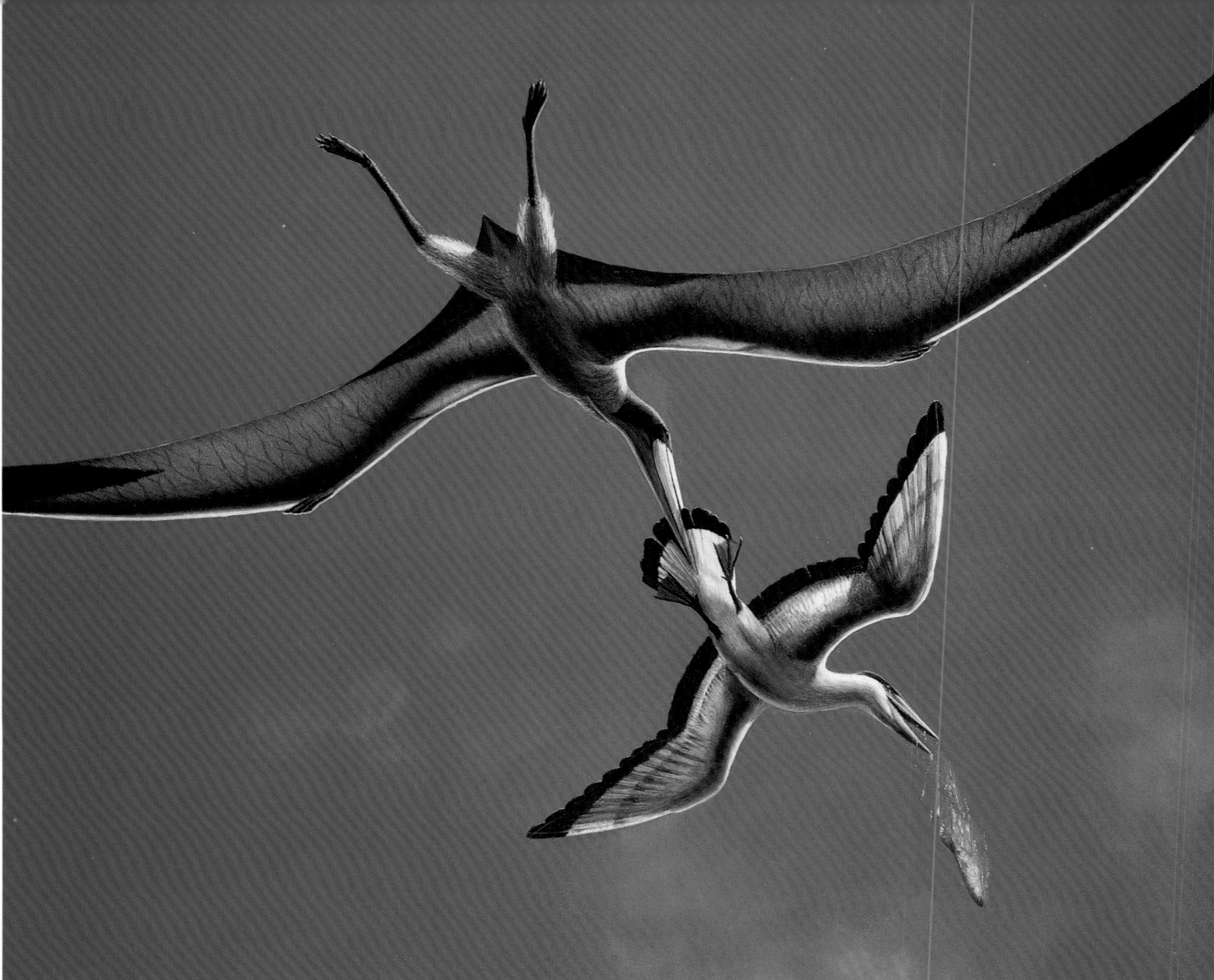

Included among the other pterosaurs of the Niobrara is *Nyctosaurus*, shown here doing what they do best: soaring in the Niobrara breeze (opposite) and stealing food (above). With an eight-foot wingspan, they are about one-third the size of *Pteranodon*, but are much faster and more maneuverable. Flocks of dozens can be seen floating on the winds for hours on end. With their wings outstretched and using their legs to steer, they have learned that they can make a living by harassing other pterosaurs and birds into giving up their catch of fish or squid. Often they fly up from the rear and grab at a leg or tail, forcing the victim into a stall and not letting go until a meal is coughed up, as this *Nyctosaurus* has done to this *Ichthyornis*.

them. This helps keep the ever-present scavengers and insects away from the vulnerable chicks, and also provides a source of minerals.

Once it has gained some strength, a newborn chick clumsily makes its way to its mother's head and taps at its bill. In response, the female instinctively regurgitates some fish onto the sand near the nest. At first the young pterosaur pecks tentatively at the smaller bits of partially digested fish. Then, after grasping a piece in its beak, it tilts its head back and swallows. Evidently stimulated by the sensation of food in its stomach, it immediately seeks out other pieces and swallows them rapidly. Later, young pteranodons learn to thrust their pointed beaks directly down their mother's throat to retrieve the fish themselves. This minimizes waste and keeps the nest area clean and free from pests.

By the time they are just a few days old, the young pterosaur chicks are alert and active and their movements much more coordinated. It is now that the second egg in the nest usually hatches, and even before the younger chick is free of its egg, the older sibling is poking at it with its long, pointed beak, establishing a pecking order that will last for the rest of the newborn chick's life. Once free, the new hatchling generally crawls to the edge of the nest depression and faces outward. This is the only position that does not incur the wrath of the older sibling. In this submissive posture the smaller chick does not pose a threat to the larger chick's food and so will be left alone. Receiving no help from the mother, both chicks are on their own at feeding time.

The competition between *Pteranodon* chicks is usually intense, but when the chicks are of different sexes and the older is the female, the intensity increases. The female must take an upper hand as soon as possible or face the possibility that its faster-growing male sibling will overtake it and win out. In any case, each successive meal is consumed by the older chick with greater speed than the last, leaving less time and less fish for the now stunted and weakened younger one. Normally, there is only enough food to raise one chick successfully. The second egg and chick are only insurance, to cover the possible loss of the first. Breeding every other year requires that each breeding season be a successful one, and the length of time each fishing trip takes usually means that the mother can supply only enough fish to feed one chick.

By the time it is a few weeks old, the surviving chick's short, soft, white fur has thickened nicely and it is now able to move about freely in its two-foot-wide territory. The rookery now has a feel of a hesperornithid colony—a noisy, smelly mixture of begging juveniles, annoying scavengers, and agitated adults. The air is filled with ichthyornids and pterosaurs all going about their business. But, day after day, the bright sky is still clear of clouds, the thermals still form, and the fish still rise to feed. For a *Pteranodon*, it does not get any better than this.

A quick survey of the rookery reveals that most of the nests contain a female and the one surviving chick of her clutch. A few, those with an exceptional provider, contain two chicks. Some nests by now are clearly abandoned. If a *Pteranodon* fails to return from a fishing foray, her chick will perish. The young pterosaur's instinctive urge to stay within the confines of its nest, coupled with the general indifference of the neighboring females, combine to guarantee the chick's death.

Soon, all along the beaches of the island, every breeze has chicks stepping to the edges of their nests, facing the wind, instinctively extending their narrow wings and moving them up and down. They are growing up and are very impatient. By the equinox, although not nearly fully grown, the young pterosaurs are ready to fly. The chicks begin to spend more time facing into the sea breeze. Here they instinctively go through the motions of flight while still on the ground. Spreading its wings, each makes adjustments in its body, head, and wings as the breezes gently change direction and intensity.

As the days progress, more and more of them take tentative, short flights along the beach, and soon some of the more skillful and adventurous are actually launching themselves into the air. During these practice flights, some find themselves forced down onto the surface of the water, where they fall victim to sharks and large marine lizards called mosasaurs, which patrol these waters. Both predators have learned that, at this time of year, this is a place rich in potential prey.

Early autumn sees the fledgling chicks riding the thermals and catching fish on their own. About three-quarters the size of an adult, the female fledglings must wait two years for sexual

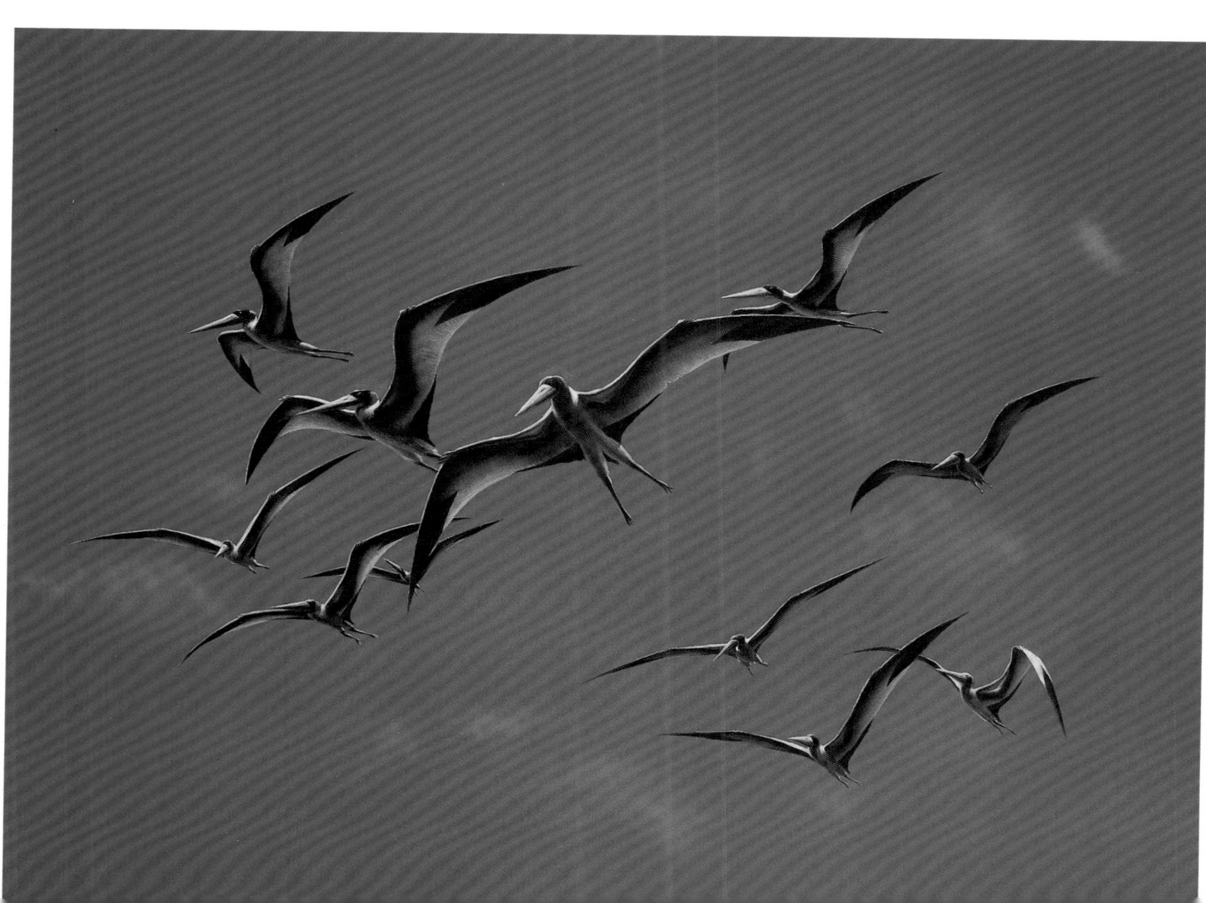

maturity. Males must wait four to five years, when the full development of their crests and coloration marks this event to the other pteranodons. During this time they remain mostly at sea, eating, sleeping, and growing without having to make landfall at all.

Late autumn finds the rookery devoid of the giant pterosaurs. The prevailing winds have changed direction. The rainy season has begun. The skies cloud up, the days shorten, the sand no longer bakes under the relentless sun, and the thermals no longer form. The shoals of fish have moved out of the area, following other urges. And next year a different group of pteranodons will return and repeat this biennial cycle.

While the pteranodons are at sea, the currents move the sands that formed their island and its shores. Other islands and other shores are assembled and reassembled, over and over, as the sand is transported southward.

Generations later, the sands have coalesced into a new strip of land almost three miles long

Thirty feet of *Tylosaurus* breaks the surface of the Niobrara. Equipped with a hinged lower jaw that allows the animal to bolt down huge chunks of meat, tylosaurs will basically eat anything smaller than themselves that they can swallow. While being fierce predators, they exhibit a certain degree of sophistication. Mature individuals have a fairly well-defined sense of their territories, where they learn the habits of their prey. When challenged by members of their own species, either for territory or courtship rights, they go at each other with a ferocity not usually seen. Many tylosaurs can be seen with scrapes and bruises, and even with damaged snouts from ramming incidents. Few survive to an old age unscratched.

and half a mile wide, hugging the southwestern coast of East America. Too far south for the pteranodons to nest on now, these shores are used by sea turtles and then, only when it comes time for them to breed. When they come to the island, as the elasmosaurs did far to the north a long time ago, it is again only the females, and they stay only a short while. But since their breeding season is still months away, these surprisingly graceful swimmers remain far out to sea, some feeding on plants, some on jellyfish, and others on whatever they can pluck from the seabed.

With similar paddle-like limbs, but with very un-turtle-like long bodies, giant mosasaurs also prowl these waters for food. Unlike their distant turtle cousins, who use their paddles for propulsion, these dark, sleek lizards use the side-to-side movement of their broad, muscular tails to undulate through the water, using their paddles only for steering and braking. They move with a rhythmic grace that belies their capabilities as incredibly savage predators.

Although a few species have adapted to a life near the bottom, feeding on the shellfish

that abound in certain areas, most mosasaurs are speedy, powerful, near-shore predators. Their heavy jaws are equipped with sharp, slightly curved, replaceable conical teeth and an extra joint to increase their gape and biting force. Although they're not agile enough to catch the smaller fish of the Niobrara, they do pursue larger ray-finned fish, sharks, squid and other swimming mollusks, seabirds, pterosaurs, turtles, and even other mosasaurs—in short, anything smaller than themselves.

At the top of their food chains, mosasaurs such as *Tylosaurus* demonstrate their superiority at every opportunity. Mosasaurs often appear as just a head, barely breaking the surface of the water long enough for it to exhale, inhale, and then silently submerge, leaving hardly a ripple. So highly adapted to life in the sea are they that they are no longer capable of venturing onto land even to lay eggs on some sandy beach. Instead, the female keeps the eggs in her body until the embryo has developed, and the offspring is expelled alive.

About a foot long when they are born, young tylosaurs spend the first year or so in the relative safety of the numerous lagoons and estuaries far to the southwest of the vast inland sea. Using primarily their sense of sight, they feed, grow, and generally avoid being eaten until they reach a length of three or four feet. At this stage, they leave the waters that have served as their nurseries and head north and east to enter the Niobrara. In the open sea, hearing becomes more important, as the tylosaurs learn to differentiate among the underwater noises that constantly assail all marine inhabitants. Tylosaurs can identify and deal with most of the other animals with which they share their watery environment on the basis of sound alone. Because sound travels underwater much farther than light and much faster than it does in the air, these marine lizards have plenty of time to anticipate and prepare for the arrival of potential prey or a threat.

Mosasaurs are solitary animals and tolerate each other's presence only during a brief courtship and mating period. Confrontations between fully grown animals are generally avoided by the use of a paddles-down, exaggerated swimming motion that communicates a threat to any mosasaur seeking to enter another's territory. More often than not, this threatening display is sufficient to avoid a conflict. But, on occasion, serious fighting is the only way to resolve a dispute. When this happens, the adversaries go at each other with a ferocity not often seen between animals of the same species. At first, each animal maneuvers for position. Then when the opportunity presents itself, one will go directly for the other's head and clamp down as hard as it can. So vicious are these attacks that usually only one is required to determine a winner. If not killed outright, the loser often dies later of its wounds. Beached tylosaurs commonly sport wounds and battle scars, broken bones and paddles, and smashed-in snouts. Few live to a ripe old age unscathed. Prime hunting areas in the Niobrara are highly prized and not given up without a fight.

The juvenile tylosaurs roam widely, with no set pattern, feeding primarily on fish and ammonites. Distant relatives of the squid and octopus, both coiled and straight-shelled ammonites are often just visible under the surface of the water as dark shapes rocking gently with the waves and moving slowly along in groups. These swimming cephalopod mollusks live in chambered shells similar to those of snails, ranging from several inches to several feet in diameter, and the Cretaceous seas are filled with them.

If a hunting tylosaur makes contact with a school of ammonites, it will generally circle it at least once, widely, then dive. When it is directly under the mollusks, it will swim up into them, gnashing its great jaws and teeth this way and that, trying to injure as many of the cephalopods as it can. The attack scatters the school in all directions, leaving only the injured swimming erratically through flecks of broken shell slowly fluttering to the bottom. These crippled mollusks now have the tylosaur's undivided attention. It grasps each one by its tentacled head and shakes it violently, sending much of the damaged shell flying, so that the animal inside can be swallowed—a messy but effective technique.

The tylosaurs are also there when the hesperornithids congregate to form their nesting

OPPOSITE

Flight or an ink cloud are the only options available when a mosasaur attacks a school of ammonites. Mosasaurs feed on fish, turtles, ammonites, birds, and even other mosasaurs; in short, anything they can fit into their mouths and swallow.

ABOVE
Fleeing a mosasaur that has just snapped off a paddle, a young *Archelon* leaves a trail of blood as it heads toward the depths and hopefully safety. If it survives, the young three-foot-long sea turtle will reach twelve feet in length, a size it arrives at slowly on its diet of jellyfish.

OPPOSITE
Death of an island. A submerged sand bar is all that is left of a Niobrara barrier island after the passage of a tropical storm. Once a haven for wildlife, the drifting sands of the island are now left to settle into the depths of the deeper waters of the Atlantic Ocean.

colonies. Although the water is the birds' true element, they are no match for a hunting mosasaur. Many clutches of hesperornithid chicks starve to death because one or both parents have fallen prey to a tylosaur.

Farther south, the tylosaurs cruise the shores of the barrier islands to prey on the fledging pteranodons who alight on the surface of the water because of fatigue, inexperience, or just plain poor judgment. Silhouetted against the bright sky, the young pterosaurs make an easy target for the deadly reptiles as they swim directly up toward their unsuspecting prey. Often a *Pteranodon* sitting on the surface too long, smoothly riding the gentle swells up and down, suddenly disappears in a brief flurry of splashes.

Still farther south, the tylosaurs meet to wreak havoc on the sea turtles who use these islands for breeding. In standard tylosaur fashion, the turtles are stalked and seized from below and behind. The turtles' shells, elegant frameworks of skin-covered bone, are literally shaken apart by the powerful marine lizards, who swallow the larger bits one piece at a time. Smaller pieces provide a meal for the entourage of small fish that constantly accompany the reptiles.

It is here, in the far south of the Niobrara, that the tylosaurs and the wandering shores of the barrier islands part company. The mosasaurs swim off to the west, across the narrow sea, and swing northward to repeat their cyclical journey. The islands, however, continue their southward migration.

Several hundred decades pass and the currents along the shore have led the sands of the southernmost barrier islands beyond the limit of the subcontinent of East America. Here the southern waters of the Niobrara begin to blend with those of the western Atlantic Ocean. The organisms that secreted the tiny shells that until now had helped replenish the sandy beaches are gone. Now exposed on three sides to erosion from giant sea swells, more pronounced tides, and the full fury of open ocean storms, the islands are quickly being worn away, and lost ground is not being replaced.

The islands' journeys are almost over. During late summer and early autumn, severe tropical storms enter the area from the southeast. Appearing at first as dark, distant, threatening clouds, they move in quickly. Soon the winds pick up, and the now exposed eastern shores of these tiny strips of sand are battered by fifteen-foot-high waves driven by hundred-mile-an-hour winds. The few shorebirds and pterosaurs who were still using them to rest during extended fishing trips or migrations have already left. Lasting not more than a day or so, these storms track northwest to make life more exciting for the animals there.

Once the storm's fury abates, the sun shines clear and bright above the gentle swells of the Atlantic. Some of the wave tops ruffle slightly, hinting at the presence of submerged sand bars. Soon, they will be gone too and the waves will move on, undisturbed once again.

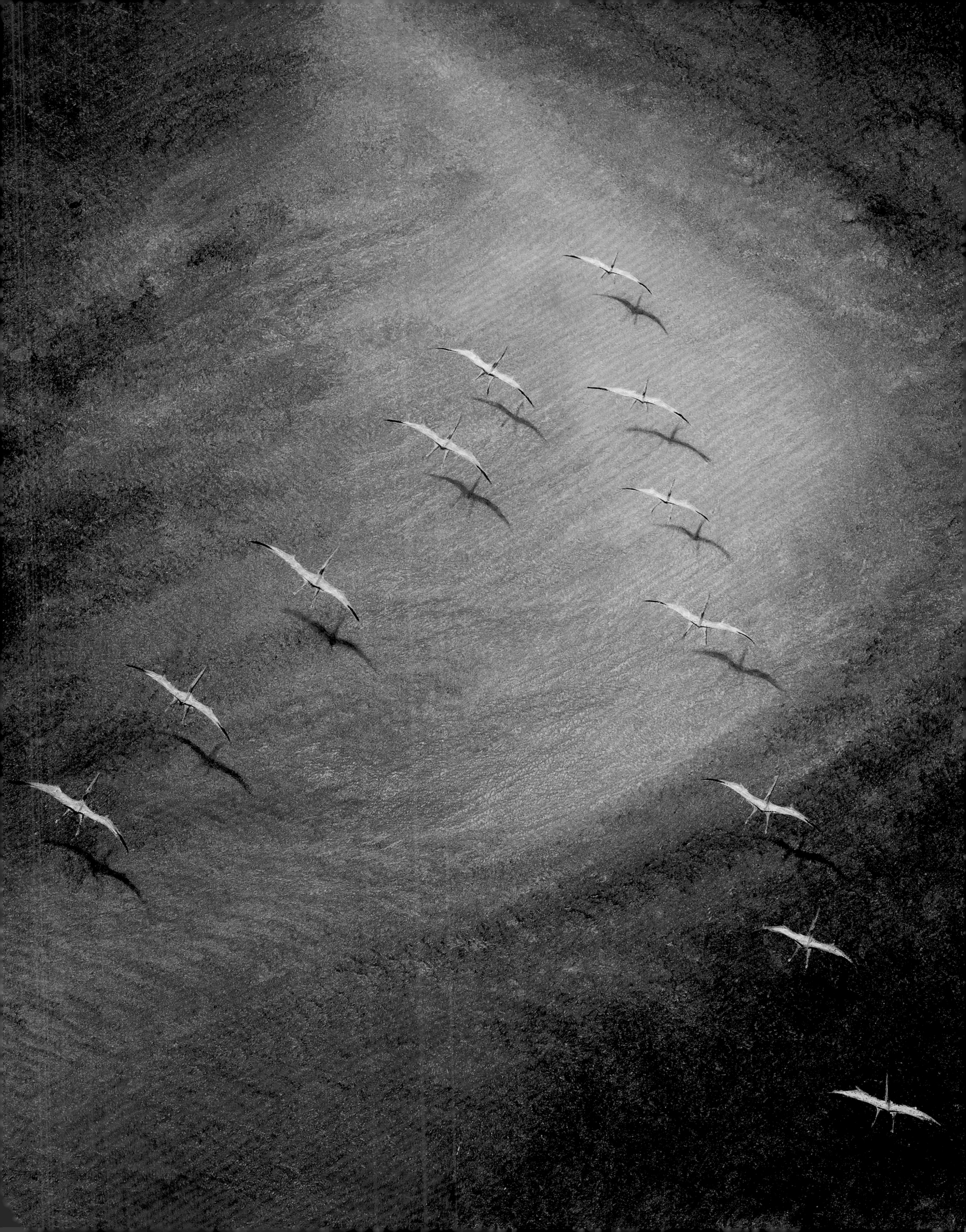

CHAPTER SIX

CORRIDOR

The Great Dinosaur Migrations of Late Cretaceous West America

PRECEDING PAGES
On a continent that doubles as a migratory corridor, the dinosaurs of West America make their presence known even when appearing to be nowhere in sight. As the great herds that live here embark on their yearly treks, paths are worn down, riverbanks are trampled, and eventually every fresh patch of ground will bear witness to their passage.

OPPOSITE
A male *Parasaurolophus* rears up and bellows out in early evening. Many duckbill dinosaurs spend this time of day socializing, either to mark territory, reinforce herd bonds, or, in this case of some males, to gather up their harem for the night. The elegant crest on the animal is hollowed out in a series of complex chambers, allowing a whole range of courtship, territorial, and alarm calls. Notice the tick birds on the animal's back. The vertical skin folds on the dinosaur's shoulders are prime targets for bloodsucking pests. Thus, the birds are not only tolerated, but welcome.

Above the wind and waves, beyond the sandy stretches of beach, the ebb and flow of the Niobrara has shaped and reshaped countless barrier islands. The coasts and character of the lands that border it have changed as well. Fifteen million years have now passed by. During that time, wetlands, islands, and flood plains have played host to a variety of wildlife. Though they differed from each other, many were influenced by a single factor more than any other. An abundance of water, a lack of water, or pronounced seasonal changes are all powerful forces, and often the strength of a single environmental agent sets the pattern for an ecosystem.

Once in a very great while, a system in nature is so special that it merits a category all its own. In a confluence of natural progressions unmatched in the Mesozoic, West America now stretches north to south across the Western Hemisphere as a unique superecosystem, a vast, living corridor. From the Arctic, it extends for several thousand miles, well into the tropics. Bordered on the west by the Pacific Ocean and on the east by the ever-changing Niobrara Sea, it is a long, narrow landmass dominated by a mountain chain running the entire length of its western margin. These are the young Rocky Mountains, still forming and ever so slowly rising higher. On the east coast of the continent lie wetlands, low-lying coastal plains, and large rivers. The climate is warm and humid. Here, groves of willow, palm, and cypress stand beside swamps and marshes. Moving west, the elevation gradually increases. These lowlands, laden with great forests of oak, poplar, ash, and walnut, broken by glades of ferns, honeysuckle, dogwood, and poison ivy, begin to merge into hills and highlands, still crossed by numerous small streams. In these hills, forests of hardwood trees stand alongside groves of evergreen conifers and ginkgoes, all underlain by a carpet of more ferns, holly, and laurel.

Resplendent in its cryptic coloration, an adult bull *Parasaurolophus* stands atop a rise on an early spring morning in Late Cretaceous Alberta. A healthy male *Parasaurolophus* is one of the most attractive large animals ever to appear on Earth, a fact they almost seem to be aware of themselves. Although at first the color pattern of the animal seems bold, it works surprisingly well in blending in with the forested areas that are the favorite habitats of the species. The dark ankle bands are signaling devices and are used during migration.

Finally, the highlands farther west merge into the Rocky Mountains. Punctuated with volcanoes and rocked by earthquakes, this mountain chain shows its youth in its craggy, snow-capped peaks. These mountains create a rain shadow, holding moisture from the Pacific Ocean back from the highlands to the east. The land and air can be quite dry, even though most rivers of the continent have their headwaters here. At the farthest reaches of West America, the mountains drop sharply and soon encounter the waters of the Pacific.

Throughout the continent, rhythms of life are regulated by the tremendous burst of plant growth that takes place in the north each spring. The temperate climate and moderate rainfall create a near-perfect combination for the plants, which lie in an uninterrupted photosynthetic carpet from the Arctic to the tropics. Trees in the far north experience a massive spurt of seasonal growth, followed by a period in fall and winter when they shut down and do not grow at all. Although most of the plants here drop their leaves at the approach of winter, they more than make up for the loss in the spring and summer when the extended daylight sets off an explosion of new growth.

The rich flora, covering a pathway a few hundred miles wide and several thousand miles long, seems a perfect setting for large animals that like to feed on plants and move around a lot. That is exactly the kind of wildlife that makes up the majority of the large animals on the continent. The natural propensity for large, herbivorous dinosaurs to migrate has found a perfect match with the geography of this continent. Waves of migrants follow the waves of greenery that roll across the north lands each

spring. The routes of migration vary slightly from year to year, influenced by external environmental factors and more latent, subtle, internal factors.

In taking advantage of the almost limitless supply of food, the wildlife that visits this region, in turn, sets the tempo of life for every other animal across the continent. Underlying the seemingly aimless mass movements are balanced, structured patterns. Individuals rely on and are influenced by each other and the groups of which they are a part. The groups and herds, in turn, rely on and influence each other. All move with the rhythm of the land, players in a symphony whose cadence is set by plant growth and the seasons. The continent-wide migration functions as a living singularity—an immense, focused organism. In most ecosystems, migration is only part of the mode of life; in this land, here in the Late Cretaceous, it *is* the mode of life.

The pace of life in any ecosystem is set by the largest plant-eating animals. The most numerous large plant-eaters in West America are the hadrosaurids, the duck-billed dinosaurs. Descended from ornithopods of the Early Cretaceous, hadrosaurids are split into two major branches, the hadrosaurines and lambeosaurines. Although both weigh in at two to ten tons and range in length from twenty-five to forty feet, they differ in several important ways, both in their physical makeup and in their social habits. Hadrosaurines are built a bit lighter than lambeosaurines, with slimmer hips and hind limbs. The biggest difference, though, is in their heads. Where lambeosaurines have crests and narrow muzzles, hadrosaurines are crestless and have wide muzzles. Each group is now responding to the botanical revolution that is sweeping the Late Cretaceous. Faster growing, more adaptable, broad-leaved, flowering and fruit-bearing angiosperms are steadily replacing the needle or scale-leafed, cone-bearing gymnosperms and other plant groups as Earth's dominant flora.

The other group of large plant-eaters consists of ceratopsids, the horned dinosaurs. Large ceratopsids are unique to West America. They are imposing animals, with what might be considered an attitude. They never seem content unless they are on the move. No animal on Earth has ever evolved heads the size of theirs, nor more garishly decorated ones. These stout, heavily built, four-legged herbivores bear absolutely huge heads with neck frills in a multitude of shapes and sizes, degrees of ornamentation, and colors. The horns that give them their nickname come in a bewildering array—long, short, sharp, blunt, straight, curved, drooping, or erect. Like the hadrosaurids, ceratopsids come in two basic types: the chasmosaurines, with large neck frills and short nose horns, and the centrosaurines, with short neck frills and long nose horns.

As the angiosperms continue to increase in numbers and diversity, some have begun to enclose their seeds in various types of fleshy fruits. Among the different kinds are berries, and grapes, pictured here. They have become an important food source for migrating animals, which gorge on them in late summer. In addition to providing a quick source of calories, the animals actually *like* to eat them. In the process, they distribute the seeds within them throughout the continent.

Migration is not easy, and animals do not undertake it without good reason. Some animals migrate for food, some for a more favorable climate, and some to reproduce. When needs converge, the urge can prove irresistible. The large plant-eaters of the Late Cretaceous migrate for all three reasons. The botanical revolution that has been sweeping the globe is one that these animals have played a direct role in creating. Since the wave of extinctions at the end of the Jurassic, an age of low browsing has been in full gear. The sauropods have never recovered their full numbers in North America and, in most areas of the continent, the high browsing in which they special-

PRECEDING PAGES
In the lowlands of Montana, bachelor herds of *Parasaurolophus* and *Corythosaurus* gather at a clearing in late winter. As early spring approaches in West America, groups of young male duckbill dinosaurs begin to collect in open areas spread throughout the southern coastal plains of the continent. Soon to experience their first season as breeding adults, they also await to embark on the great migration that gives this land the special character it is known for. Note the browse line on the trees in the distance and the general brown color of the foliage, all hinting at the need for recovery, new growth, that the departure of the herds will allow.

OPPOSITE
A female *Hadrosaurus* and two of her year-old offspring pause for a drink before departing on the journey to the nesting grounds in the highlands. *Hadrosaurus* and other hadrosaurine duckbills are very gregarious by nature, and the young generally spend their early years growing up within the large herds they were born into. Their crested cousins, on the other hand, tend to be loners. Within their first year of life, the young segregate into their own herds, and a scene like this in early spring among lambeosaurines would be very rare.

ized is a thing of the past. Most plant-eating dinosaurs now do most of their foraging, and therefore most of their damage, within ten feet of the ground. The angiosperms, with their faster rate of growth and more efficient method of reproducing, have directly benefited from this low-browsing mode of feeding.

The herbivores feed on a varied diet: the increasing numbers of the new broad-leaved trees, as well as their traditional choices of ferns, cycads, and conifers. They have been able to spread right along with these food sources, as these new plants have expanded their ranges. As a result, West America is populated with a large variety of successful, numerous, and adaptable herbivorous dinosaurs. Throughout the winter, the plains and uplands of the south serve as ideal foraging ground for the large herbivores. They spend their time storing up energy and replenishing their reserves of fat. But the increase in daylight of early spring brings with it a familiar urge, marked by a restlessness among the herds. Many of these animals thrive best in temperate climates, so they leave the increasingly warmer and wetter south, and follow the more moderate temperatures and moisture levels to higher latitudes and higher ground.

As the herds move farther north, the quality and quantity of their food increases. Springtime in the higher latitudes and in the Arctic, with its increased hours of daylight, sees the greatest flush of new plant growth, and the longer growing season in the north means more food is available. Also, the higher the latitude, in the temperate and Arctic regions, the higher the density of calories in plant tissues and the lower the fiber content—factors that help both the adults and their growing offspring. Like all animals in tune with their environment, the herds of plant-eaters now find their greatest need for food timed with its greatest abundance.

The urge to migrate coincides with another powerful force—the need to reproduce. The young benefit from the migration even before they have hatched. Along the southern coastal plains, the soil is poorly drained. Eggs laid in nests dug here face the threat of drowning in heavy rains and the usual spring flooding. Only by leaving this environment altogether can this threat be avoided.

There are downsides to picking up and moving. The annual exodus exacts a heavy toll. Only the fit and able survive the ordeal; those animals best able to find their way, forage for food, travel the distances, and avoid predation are the ones that complete the journey successfully. Within each herd are animals that have made the journey before and know the landmarks, river fords, and water holes, and animals that are making the trip for the first time must learn these things through repetition. Each herd has thousands of noses, eyes, and ears. In its travels, acting as an immense living thing, it is ever alert: feeding, drinking, resting, and moving as a single unit. No time is lost; no motion is wasted. As a result, the migration is sustained by its own inertia. Only those that can complete and repeat it year after year, generation after generation, will survive. Animals with the proper instincts and characteristics pass these traits on to their offspring, which then become successful migrants themselves.

Animals migrate for the very simple reason that, despite the rigors and hardships involved, it is more advantageous for them to migrate than to stay put. It is self-perpetuating, because the migrants are trapped by their own success. The urge to migrate is so ingrained that if the conditions that prompt it were to improve suddenly, the animals would probably still pick up and move. Rarely in Earth's history have so many various elements converged to influence each other on such an enormous scale.

The West American migrations begin with the end of winter. This is a quiet season, when plants and wildlife regroup in preparation for a coming rebirth. In the north lands, the darkness of winter slowly releases its grip on the land through several weeks of ever-brightening twilight. As sunlight begins to return to the Arctic, it reveals a cool, damp land of mostly bare trees and dead leaves. The rainstorms of the winter months have soaked the leaf litter, leaving the damp, dank track of decay—of dead twigs too waterladen to snap, and worms too wet to breathe. The few small animals that choose to spend the winter here either begin to emerge from hibernation or scamper through the brush to glean

the last few specks of available food before the spring renewal. The land is quiet, with temperatures hovering near freezing. It is not a popular place for most wildlife.

In the southern coastal plains, winters tend to be mild and rainy, so most of the larger herds of horned and duck-billed dinosaurs on the continent spend the season here. Both types of dinosaurs share the same general lands but they have their own behaviors and habits. The winter herds browse in different areas, segregated according to age and species. They pass the months browsing in groups, sorting out their status, and braving the occasional chilly storm. Before long though, the increasing daylight of late winter begins to have an effect on them. They become restless, nervous, easily distracted, and agitated.

The more numerous duck-billed animals follow patterns of behavior that soon define their differences as lambeosaurines and hadrosaurines. Though similar in appearance, the two groups descend from ancestors with different social habits. Hadrosaurines gather in the largest groups of animals on the continent; a herd can often number in the hundreds of thousands. Even younger animals travel and reach adulthood within the main herd. These animals tend to prefer the drier, higher, and more open areas of the coastal plains. The basic body types and shapes of the various hadrosaurine species are similar, and it can be difficult to tell the sexes apart. Though by and large they tend to be somewhat less colorful than their lambeosaurine cousins, the hadrosaurines are still impressive animals, making up for what they lack in individual appearance by their sheer numbers.

Lambeosaurines frequent more wooded areas and in winter can be found in the lower coastal plains. The more densely forested habitat is well suited for their smaller social and family groups. They are brighter in color than hadrosaurines and easy to recognize by the elaborate crests that both males and females sport. Differences between the sexes are more pronounced as well: Females usually are less brightly colored than males and are adorned with smaller crests.

Lambeosaurines must rank among the most beautiful animals ever to have walked the planet. The several species of these crested duckbills, variously adorned in coloration that is at once cryptic and striking, have an elegant presence that few animals can match. During the mating season, males especially move about with an air and grace that belies their three-ton weight. Crowned with their bizarre head crests, they can draw more attention just standing still than many animals can in their wildest courtship displays.

The two types of animals also feed differently. Where hadrosaurine ancestors were content to bite off big clumps of foliage, lambeosaurine ancestors were more particular in their choice of vegetation. The lambeosaurines now have muzzles only about half as wide as those of the hadrosaurines. They are also more discriminating in their choice of plant food. To take in enough food, they need to spend more hours of the day eating and fewer hours socializing.

The next largest group of large plant-eating dinosaurs, the ceratopsids, are irritable, ornery animals. They are always watchful and nervous. To be in the company of ceratopsids is to be surrounded by the most alert eyes, ears, and noses on the continent. Although they are outnumbered substantially by the duckbills, they have a powerful presence that quickly asserts itself whenever groups of the two animals meet. There is never any direct fighting, but there is never any question about which animals defer to which. Ceratopsids immediately dominate in any situation when the two groups come together, even when the duck-billed herd is larger and made up of larger animals. Meetings like this often occur at the mud and dust patches in which the animals like to wallow and roll and at water holes and ponds when they come to drink. The horned dinosaurs are always allowed to drink and wallow first, even when they enter the scene after others have arrived.

There are important reasons for this level of respect that go beyond just the obvious—that is, those long, sharp horns. Like the duckbills, they are attractive animals, but the immediate impression is not one of elegance, but of power. Elaborately adorned with imposing frills and menacing horns and scutes, every square inch

OPPOSITE

A six- to eight-foot-long theropod, *Troodon* is one of the most successful animals on the continent. They are intelligent and adaptable and are found throughout a wide range of habitats and locations. They share an affinity with the larger herbivores of West America, nesting near their large rookeries and preying on hatchlings and smaller wildlife that the herds attract. Females construct precise nests about three feet in diameter and arrange their eggs in a spiral, half burying them in the soil, with the blunt end facing up. The clutch of about a dozen eggs is brooded, and the precocial young leave the nest almost immediately after hatching.

of the animals commands respect, and even a small herd of ceratopsids is imposing. Whether long frilled or short frilled, ceratopsids almost always travel in herds, but, like the duckbills, each of the two groups have their preferred habitat. Centrosaurines usually prefer the higher and drier open spaces in larger herds, while the chasmosaurines usually spend their time in the greener lowlands, in somewhat smaller herds.

Late winter on the southern coastal plains has a palpable air of expectant change. It can be seen and felt in the land, the weather, and especially among the wildlife. The landscape looks badly in need of a rest, as the weather and the tenants have taken their toll, leaving it muddy and partly denuded. By the time winter is about to pass into early spring, the region will have played host to the herds of dinosaurs for more than three months. Most of the trees keep their leaves throughout the year. Yet there are still defined growing seasons and, since the next period of leaf growth is not set to occur until spring, the trees and shrubs throughout the south are beginning to show the effects of the dinosaurs' constant munching. Three months of browsing would make a significant impact on any habitat, but because these animals do practically all their feeding within a dozen feet of the ground, they leave a conspicuous browse line throughout the region.

During the summer months, while the migrants are browsing in the north, the land and foliage will recover and appear fresh and inviting again when the animals return in the fall. The extensive pruning of winter stimulates new growth in the plants. There always are year-round residents: Many ornithomimid dinosaurs, small herbivorous and carnivorous dinosaurs, and several armored dinosaurs and large theropods live their entire lives in the coastal plains. But these animals never come close to having the ecological impact of the great herds, and their presence on the land is not nearly as noticeable.

Late winter also sees the onset of the reproductive season. Male duck-billed and horned dinosaurs in the largest herds compete throughout the expanse of the herd itself. In some species, hadrosaurine males earn the right to mate with females based on localized skirmishes and jousting matches. Male ceratopsids literally lock horns in an attempt to establish dominance in the herd. Long ago, the distinct horns of the ceratopsids became a means to earn status in the herd's hierarchy. Now, as the horns have become longer and sharper, ceratopsids must wield these implements of destruction to assert position without permanent damage to themselves and, by extension, their rivals.

Heightening the ceratopsids' display and reinforcing the advantage that horn size bestows, their neck frills have enlarged to varying degrees. Each species has its own pattern of frills, spikes, and horns. In some, the horns are blunt and used to up-end opponents; in others, they are interlocked in a head-to-head pushing, shoving, and thrusting type of wrestling match; and in still others they are simply exaggerated and outlandish visual displays that, accompanied by large neck frills adorned with scallops, hooks, knobs, and spikes, enable contests to be resolved with essentially no contact. In general, the longer-frilled chasmosaurines, with their shorter horns, place a greater emphasis on display, while the shorter-frilled centrosaurines lock their longer horns more often.

Both actual and potential contact make a stunning show. It begins with bluff and bluster. The animals, snorting and grunting, first try to intimidate each other by raising their forepaws up a few feet off the ground in a beak-down display that exposes their frills. Then they come down hard on their upraised forelimbs with a loud thud. The bulls then approach each other, snorting, pawing the ground, heads lowered, horns leveled, and frills elevated for maximum effect. Following the threat displays, most males lock horns and attempt to topple their opponent or get it to back down, or even run off. In eons of this side-to-side posturing and pushing, the animals have developed incredibly powerful muscles in their forelimbs, giving them a slightly bow-legged stance and enabling them to pivot side-to-side exceptionally well.

As a result of all this scrapping, few adult males sport unscarred faces or frills. On occasion, the horns break, and animals sometimes lose an eye as a result of an altercation. Oddly, many males get hurt even before they make contact. Often, they land so hard during the threat displays that they cause stress fractures in their forelimbs. If they are lucky, they can get around with just a moderate degree of pain, but many a male horned dinosaur has fallen to a predator because of lack of speed from a fracture that did not heal properly.

Lambeosaurines approach the rutting season with equally serious intent. The small social units of mixed ages that formed during the winter months begin to disperse, with older juveniles banding together and moving off by themselves. The adults that are left begin to gather by the twenties and thirties, and before long will form harems, each led by an adult male. The process by which the harems form is elaborate, as showy as the animals themselves.

One of the most striking lambeosaurines is *Parasaurolophus.* What sets the species apart is perhaps the most elegant crest ever to evolve in any animal. This hollow adornment not only signals sex and species but also serves as a resonating chamber, amplifying the animal's calls. A bull parasaurolophan becomes a harem leader by a process best described as natural election. It is a process of elimination. The sexually mature adults begin to congregate in groups of a few dozen animals, into a lek—a communal display gathering. These leks are scattered throughout the animals' southern range. They are prime showcases of dinosaur etiquette and regulation. The animals prefer to use the same sites year after year, and the continual use of these areas keeps them free of trees, often for decades.

Leks usually form in early morning on open patches of ground. As the animals assemble, the males gravitate toward the center of the lek and begin to display to each other. The females take up spots on the periphery, to observe the action. As the process gets under way, each male parades up and down, nodding his head so as to best display his distinctly striped face and crest sail. Periodically, each bull stops, stands upright, head pointed skyward, and vocalizes. The piercing call, deep and sonorous, builds slowly as it resonates up through the three-foot crest and then down again toward the

Two female *Parasaurolophus* on the edge of a lek. The female duckbills that gather at the peripheries of a lek have their own way of sorting out status among themselves, though they are much more civil at it than their male counterparts. Although the animal on the left appears to be grooming its forelimb, it may actually be engaged in a displacement behavior. Behaviors such as this, which may involve grooming or scratching, are meant to diffuse the tension one animal experiences when confronted by another animal of greater rank.

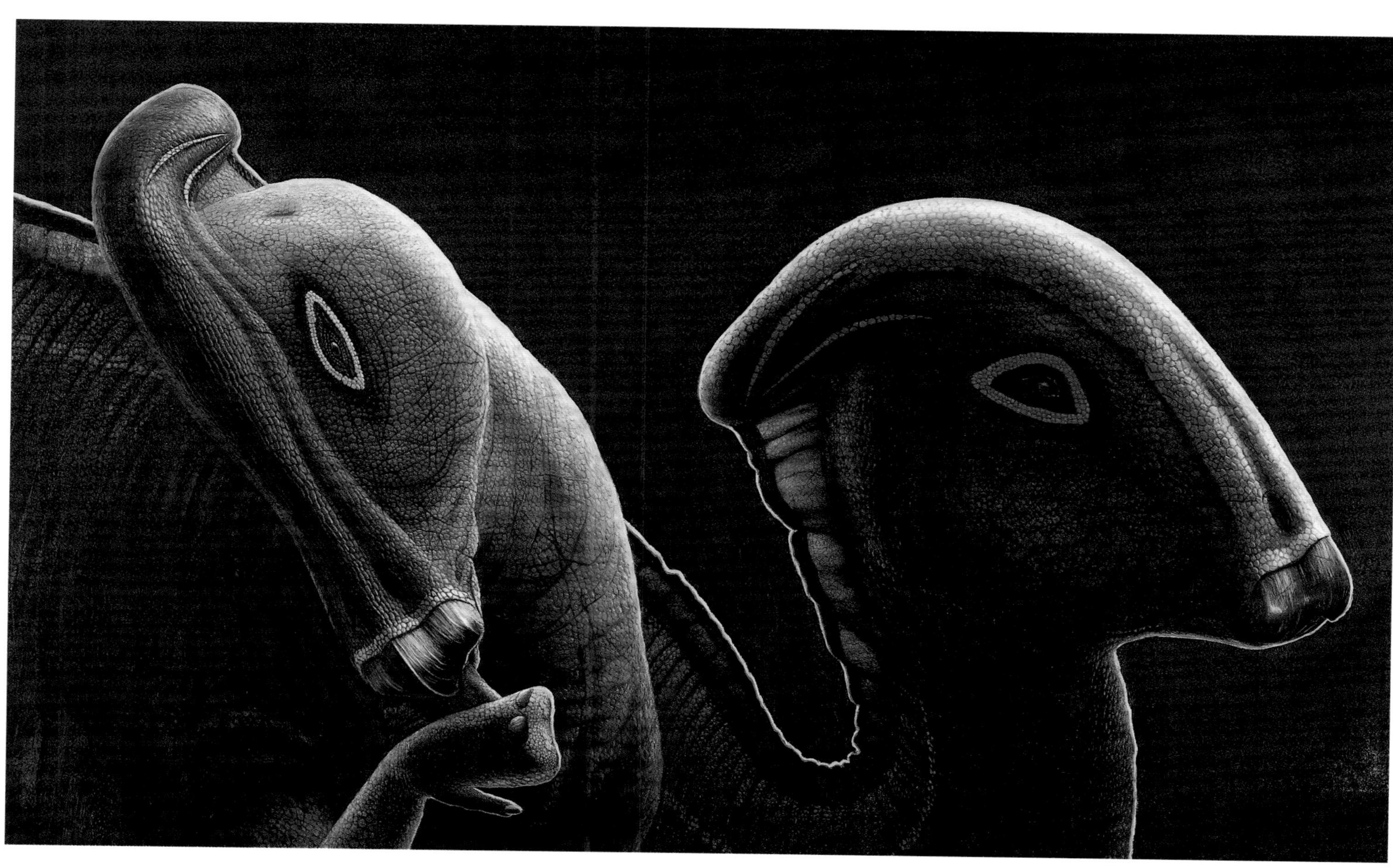

PRECEDING PAGES

Adult *Parasaurolophus* gather at a lek on an early morning in late winter. A lek is a communal display ground and is used by the animals to sort out social hierarchies at the beginning of the breeding season. The males congregate in the inner parts of the lek and proceed to display and fight among themselves, while the females gather around the peripheries to scout out the action. The goal of the males is to capture and hold the center-most territories which give them bragging rights to the females. Ultimately, though, while it is the males that fight to win the rights to the females, it is the females who make the decision of which male to pair up with.

nasal opening. After about ten seconds, the bull breaks off sharply and emits a series of shorter calls. Each male then resumes his strutting and head-bobbing.

These actions are contagious: Once one male starts, it is soon joined by its rivals, and sometimes the low-frequency tones that the several dozen animals can create reverberate for miles. All too often, bluff is not enough, and actual fighting breaks out. Having no dangerous or threatening weapons at their disposal, as the ceratopsids do, parasaurolophans fight by pushing and biting. For the animals involved, though, the stakes are just as real, and two three-ton beasts going at each other put on quite a show. Several dozen bulls calling, displaying, and fighting, confined in a relatively small area, create an absolutely awesome scene. The females certainly seem to think so, because they watch the trials before them intently.

The bulls strive toward one goal, to occupy the center of the lek. The males with the largest crests, most colorful appearances, and most intimidating bluff and bluster win out and seize the center-most areas. Success might seem to guarantee that these particular animals would get their pick of the females; however, though the males do the fighting, it is the females that ultimately make the choice. The females make their decisions based on the outcome of the displays and fights. Any male that can occupy the central territory of the lek will often attract a harem of a half-dozen or so females.

Several species of lambeosaurine use leks as part of their courtship behavior. Because their different crests produce different sounds, any area populated with these animals resounds with a unique concert to welcome the arrival of spring.

As early spring arrives in the southern coastal plains, the usual idle chatter of early evening can be heard throughout the day, a low but steady cacophony of whistles, grunts, hoots, and bellows. Whether they gather at a lek or pair up within a herd, by the time their travels begin, the vast majority of migrating animals on the continent have mated. The eggs that will be laid at the nesting grounds are already beginning to develop. By now, harems have been formed, hierarchies have been established by dominant and subordinate animals alike, and large groups of animals are waiting.

Although the migrating species of dinosaurs all move in the same direction, separate herds of the same species do not all set off at the same time—although most manage to begin moving within a few days of each other. In the cumulative actions of hundreds of groups of animals all moving to their own clocks and the rhythms of their own herds, there emerges a synthesis of fine-tuned elegance. Although it may be impossible to predict the exact time that a herd will begin its journey, it is not at all hard to tell that the moment is getting near. As the time approaches, the constant chattering escalates to a din. It is as if the entire herd releases its anxiety verbally. Every animal gives off the unmistakable feeling of not wanting to be the first one to set off. The signal to move is unseen and unheard. But, finally, with the single step of a solitary leader, the epic journey is on.

The departure of the majority of the dinosaur population of the south proves a boon to those left behind. The small herds of young stay-at-homes make nothing like the environmental dent that their parents made, so the local habitat has time to recover. New areas are now opened, and with less competition for food, there is a large increase in the resources available to the growing but still immature animals. While the adults are away, the young experience a growth spurt that leaves them considerably larger by the time the adults return with the next generation in the fall.

Although many of the large herbivorous dinosaurs from Mexico to Alberta migrate, no one species or group makes the entire five-thousand-mile journey. Rather, each population of lambeosaurines, hadrosaurines, and ceratopsids makes its own migration. Their travels vary in duration, distance, destination, time of departure, and time of arrival. One group's summer nesting ground may be near another's winter feeding ground. At any given time, though, one group or another is on the move. Each moves a set distance, depending on the season, until it reaches the area it finds suitable, then it stops. In some species, groups sometimes merge to form mass herds, filling the land from one horizon to the other, and as each individual in the herd is part of the group's migration, each group is part of the *entire* migration.

Not all the animals of West America migrate. Many stay in their habitats year round—the armored ankylosaurids and nodosaurids, for example. Not nearly as numerous as some of the other herbivores, these equally massive animals are superbly *not* adapted for long journeys. They are content to remain where they are. Large tyrannosaurs also appear comfortably ensconced in their home territories; they would just as soon have the prey come to them. As good as it sounds, migration is not for everyone.

The moment the animals begin moving there is an enormous release of tension. As the signal to move begins to ripple through the herds, the entire landscape of the coastal plains and lowlands is transformed. The first to set off are the ceratopsids. They choose the migratory route to suit their needs, following no set path and varying from year to year, as the huge herbivores seek out meadows and groves in search of food. Being first gives them the choicest vegetation from which to pick, and it quickly becomes apparent why the larger herds of duckbills have chosen to follow these horned dinosaurs. Crossing terrain with a minimum of difficulty, ceratopsids quite effectively cut through dense thickets of bramble and vines, easing the way for the hadrosaurines and lambeosaurines and other dinosaurs.

The ceratopsids' strong horny beaks, fleshy cheek pouches, batteries of self-sharpening shearing teeth, and massive jaw muscles—and the large expanse of bony frill at the rear of the head to anchor them—all speak of their ability to process any and all plant parts. Fronds, stems, fruits, and seeds all go down well with them. Occasionally, in order to get at leaves or fruits that are out of their reach, they will bring down an entire tree, using their massive heads, horns, and forelimbs to push it over.

On the march, confrontations diminish. Other instincts are at work now. The journey ahead is long and hazardous. Only by attempting it in the safety of numbers can success be expected, and to that end, a sense of harmony throughout the herd benefits every animal.

Ceratopsids normally feed four to seven feet off the ground. Much of the foliage the horned dinosaurs expose or push over while trying to get at their food they leave uneaten—open to any animals that follow on their heels. Invariably, those animals turn out to be the herds of hadrosaurines. Their horny, wide muzzles make the hadrosaurines more effective in exploiting the ecological swath that the ceratopsids open up. Their broad mouths pull up large amounts of greenery, and they eagerly eat the low-lying ferns, ground pines, and shrubs that the horned dinosaurs passed over. They use their tongues and muscular cheek pouches to keep the plant material between their large batteries of teeth, finely grinding down the leaves and stems. If the ground cover becomes too sparse, the hadrosaurines rear up on their hind legs and extend their feeding range up to as much as eighteen feet, pulling entire branches of needles and leaves directly from the upright trees.

This is the pattern of the migration—a succession of herds of plant-eating animals, organized by their abilities to attack and best process the foliage ahead of them. The horned dinosaurs open tracts of foliage, where the other animals can avail themselves of the ready fodder. The particular animals that follow the ceratopsids proceed in order of their browsing abilities, which are determined by their teeth and mouth size. The wider their muzzle, the easier it is for them to deal with the plants left by the ceratopsids. The first in line are the widemouthed hadrosaurines. After them, lines of lambeosaurines take their turns—again, based on their feeding hardware and abilities to best deal with the state of the food presented to them.

To maintain their balance while shifting their weight from one foot to another when walking, duck-billed dinosaurs move their heads forward and backward. As the thousands of animals bob their heads, ripples run through the herds. The herds of hadrosaurines flow through the migration corridor like a dark river, with no apparent order or structure. The flood of animals swirls around obstacles, backs up at slight

PRECEDING PAGES

A *Parasaurolophus* nesting colony. Like most duckbill dinosaurs, *Parasaurolophus* nest in large rookeries. The females construct large, circular nests about ten feet in diameter. The nests are spaced apart by the length of the adults and are about three feet high and six feet wide at the top. They are lined with vegetation, filled with up to two dozen eggs, and are then covered with more foliage, which, as it rots, generates heat that incubates the eggs.

When the young hatch out, they are fed a diet of plant food mixed with a substance called crop milk. Produced by the females by sloughing off the inner linings of their crop, this "milk" is a rich first food for the young. It is full of fats, proteins, minerals, calories, and the microorganisms that the young will need for their own digestive tracts. They grow fast on it, almost tripling their length in three weeks. They feed by regurgitation, trough-style from the lower jaw of the female.

The bold white eye and snout rings of the female are imprinting devices, helping the young bond with their mother from the moment they first hatch out.

rises, pours over them in a tumult, and slows down at constrictions, only to spread out again after passing through.

As if the thundering noise their tramping creates was not enough, the calls of tens of thousands of animals in the herd can raise the sound of their passing to an uproar. The low-pitched grunts from their nasal sacs and the incessant lowing from deep within their throats fills the air and keeps them in touch with each other when visibility is poor. Surrounded by these reassuring noises, the buzzing insects, the clouds of dust, and the familiar, pervasive aroma of several thousand other multi-ton herbivores, mixed with the fragrances released by their dung and the trampled and chewed vegetation, each hadrosaurine walks and feeds secure within the safety of the vast herd.

As the great waves of hadrosaurines descend on tracts of foliage, with their less discriminate palates and wide muzzles, they make relatively quick work of the newly available fodder. Although they can gulp down large amounts, the huge numbers of animals still leave enough foliage for those that follow. Often, the last straggling columns of hadrosaurines mingle with the first advancing units of lambeosaurines.

The smaller social units in which the lambeosaurines travel make fewer demands for food than the huge herds of their cousins. Although the lambeosaurines arrive in the wake of the last of the hadrosaurines, when significant amounts of foliage have already been taken by the wide-mouthed duckbills, their narrower snout and jaws are perfectly suited to rummaging through the debris. Patches of ground cover too small to interest a hadrosaurine can be harvested easily by a lambeosaurine. A cycad trunk opened and partially devoured by a ceratopsid cannot be easily handled by the broad mouth and jaws of a hadrosaurine. A lambeosaurine, however, can easily pick out the starch-filled pith and avoid the husk. While ceratopsids and hadrosaurines remove entire branches from trees and wind up eating a lot of wood, lambeosaurines go after smaller clusters of needles on the conifers and eat fewer of the largely indigestible twigs and branches.

Lambeosaurines bear dark ankle bands, which hadrosaurines lack. These dark strips are signaling devices, beacons for the animals in the rear to follow. Ankle bands probably evolved as a response to the social habits of these animals. A signaling device on an animal such as a hadrosaurine, with its strong herding instinct, imparts no great advantage. But to animals like lambeosaurines, which travel in much smaller herds, it comes in very handy during those times of the year when the animals need to be reminded to stay in line and travel together.

After the last of the giant herbivores has moved on, the vegetation throughout the migration pathways will recover. There are enough seeds, rhizomes, tubers, and roots in the ground and enough dung and urine on the ground now to ensure that the plants will grow back. For the most part, the corridor is wide enough so that the migrants need never take the same route two years in a row, giving most of the foliage enough time to come back before the next onslaught.

The migrants continue traveling toward their summer destinations, staying in a given area for only a short period, but their cumulative effect on each habitat lasts year round. During the migration, millions of small, ground-dwelling animals see catastrophe strike. Trees are toppled, burrows collapsed, and territorial boundaries obliterated. Small mammals, snakes, turtles, lizards, and insects do their best to keep out of harm's way while the herds are moving through, and following their passing try to get their lives back in order. Many animals depend for their livelihood on this restoration period. Birds, small pterosaurs, and small theropods follow the great herds, intently watching every footstep the big animals make. Any small creature startled into darting away quickly becomes a meal for these migratory tagalongs.

Many smaller herbivores also find good reason to travel behind the migrants. The wide swath that the horned and duck-billed dinosaurs cut brings great amounts of previously inaccessible vegetation suddenly into reach. As the herds move on, tender leaves, fruits, and berries that were brought down but missed or passed over by the migrants are suddenly available, and many small herbivores waste no time in availing themselves of the newfound bounty. Hypsilophodontids, pods of local, immature lambeosaurines, the dome-headed pachycephalosaurs, and elegant ornithomimids all share in the feast. Often, the migrations provide the only means for many of these animals to supplement or vary their diets at this time of year.

Having survived a rigorous trip and run a gauntlet of predators, river crossings, and earthen obstacles, the wayfarers would seem to deserve a well-earned rest. In many respects, however, the hardest time of the year has yet to come. As the herds enter their nesting regions, the scene resembles that of the mounds that hesperornithids constructed on the Niobrara barrier islands—but on a scale to dwarf any seabird that ever lived. Most of the large herbivores nest in large colonies. Even the lambeosaurines, which travel in the smallest herds, join up at the end of their migrations and nest by the thousands. Many nesting colonies are located near permanent streams or lakes, which provide a ready supply of water, but also maintain stands of vegetation during the dry season. Because of the daily quantities of food and water required by three-ton animals, the landscape can support only a certain number of them. Even so, the central and northern uplands are filled with communal rookeries which often extend beyond the horizon, forming supercolonies that can stretch on for dozens of miles across the highlands. Such areas often look like war zones and, in many respects, they are.

Most large herbivores begin their lives in earthen nests scattered through these huge colonies. Hadrosaurines and lambeosaurines construct large, circular nests about ten feet in diameter and three feet high. Each nest has a bowl-shaped depression in the center about six feet across. The animals start by piling the dirt around them into mounds. They finish them off by using their snouts to scrape and smooth out the centers. All this activity packs the soil down, making the nest more than strong enough to stand up to the purpose for which it was built. Each nest is separated from the next by roughly the length of an adult animal. This leaves enough room for the large herbivores to move to and from their nest without upsetting others or inadvertently destroying unattended nests.

By the time the waves of migrants roll into the nesting colonies that will be their home ground for the next several months, the eggs that the females have been carrying on the trip north are almost ready to be laid. The smaller groups of parasaurolophans, having joined up and made the journey in a larger herd, enter a territory that is familiar to most of them. Once there, each bull secures an area in the nesting ground big enough to house the females in his harem. Most seasons see little in the way of a large-scale turnover in seniority among the bulls, and, as a result, many of the females use nests that they built in previous years.

Having completed any repairs, the females proceed to line the nest with vegetation. Conifer branches, ferns, or whatever is available are used to fill the depressions in the nests. The plant material makes a soft-cushioned lining for the eggs and subsequently for the hatchlings when they emerge; it also traps the heat of the day to keep the eggs warm through the night. After the females have laid their eggs, they gather more foliage and cover the eggs with it. At this early point in the season, there is a lot of fresh, loose plant material spread around the many nests. Since conifers dominate the foliage here, the air around the colonies is redolent of pine.

The nesting colonies are worlds unto themselves, specialized, seasonal, isolated ecosystems. The herds that descend on the upland regions every spring do more than lay their eggs and raise their young. They also provoke the convergence of whole communities of animals that take advantage of the bounty that the herds represent. From the Arctic regions to the mid-latitudes, up and down the highlands, countless eggs are laid by hundreds of thousands of female animals in untold numbers of nests. The vast numbers of nesting adults time their egg-laying so that in six to eight weeks, most of the eggs will have hatched, raising the concept of prey swamping to a new scale.

The journeys of the massive migrants automatically become the focal point for most other animals on the continent. Every footstep becomes a series of opportunities to be harassed, exploited, and preyed upon. As much as the migrations are an integral part of the life cycles of the herding animals, they are equally important to the wildlife that follows them. These camp followers could no more do without the seasonal appearance of the herds than the herds could do without their migrations themselves. Whether the adults are foraging, tending their nests, laying their eggs, feeding their young, defecating, drinking, sleeping, or just milling about, a series of animals ensure that the big herbivores will never be alone.

It is on the outskirts of the colonies, ringing the edges of the outermost nests, that the presence of the camp followers begins to be felt. As varied as the animals are that depend on the herds and colonies, are the ways in which they make use of them. First are the predators. Between the adults and the eggs and nestlings they produce, the huge rookeries represent an enormous food source to any group of meat-eating animals. The predators range from small to incredibly large animals and feed on an equal-

A *Parasaurolophus* hatchling sits within its nest, a few hours after emerging from its egg. Having had time to dry itself off, the young two-foot-long dinosaur will spend the next few months living within and nearby the nest it was born in. The soft, downy coat of the animal protects it from losing heat through its skin and works to keep the animal warm at night and during cooler weather and also those times when the temperature gets too hot. It also blends in quite nicely with the leaf litter and broken eggshell within the nest, serving as camouflage, and, all in all, looks comfortable as well.

At this early age, the young have no hint of the crest of their parents. They are born with a sharp, horny edge to their bill, a sort of egg "tooth," which helps them chip out of their egg. It is a long process and can take almost a week.

The short snout and large eyes of the young are no accident, and elicit a maternal response in the females. By any measure, it works, for the degree of maternal care in these animals is among the highest in any dinosaur.

ly wide range of animals. Not only do they frequent the colonies to prey upon the herds directly, but many also prey upon the animals that the herds attract.

The most noticeable predators are the largest, the tyrannosaurids. Many grow over forty feet in length and several tons in weight. Smaller, but just as interesting, are the troodontids. Averaging less than ten feet in length, these bipedal theropods have numerous small, serrated teeth set into a long head with a narrow snout. Each is equipped with extremely large eyes that can focus forward and provide excellent depth perception. This ability, coupled with their agility, allows them to use the enlarged claws on the inner toe of each foot with telling effect. They are intelligent, adaptable animals and have successfully established themselves in West America, as well as in Asia. Here, they fill the small- to medium-sized predator niche quite nicely, with several species spread among a number of habitats throughout the continent.

The dromaeosaurids—nimble, speedy theropods armed with long, razor-sharp claws on hands and feet—are also a presence on the continent, abiding in localized pockets throughout the highlands. Although they have diminished in size and numbers from their heyday in the Early Cretaceous, they help fill the smaller predatory role with the troodontids. Ornithomimids, such as *Struthiomimus* and *Ornithomimus*, follow and nest near the herds, tagging along with the larger animals. Eating a mixed diet of fruits, leaves, small animals, insects, and occasionally an unattended egg or hatchling, they are largely tolerated and mostly ignored. Other less common, more specialized forms of ornithomimids live in isolated, mountainous regions and have a rather insignificant effect on the ecosystem as a whole.

Keeping in tow with the large herbivores are herds of smaller plant-eating animals. As in the rest of the world, the hypsilophodontids are successfully established on the continent. Herds of *Thescelosaurus* and *Orodromeus* build their nesting colonies right next to the colonies of hadrosaurines and lambeosaurines. They serve as an early warning system for the main colonies and feed their young on the insects that are attracted to the huge rookeries.

After the nests are refurbished and the females lay their eggs, a change of pace comes over the rookeries, as the waiting begins. Spring melts into summer, and the days lengthen to such a degree that, in the higher latitudes, night is at most a fleeting event. Eighteen-, twenty-, even twenty-two-hour days become the norm. The plants surrounding the colonies burst forth in a riot of growth, and the skies shine with a deep blue unknown in the south. Yet even though the sun shines practically nonstop, there is a crispness to the air. For the past several million years of the Late Cretaceous, a gradual cooling trend has become noticeable and nowhere is it more apparent than near the poles, even at the height of summer.

In parasaurolophan colonies, the females leave their nests early each morning to drink and eat. They return several hours later to resume their egg-watching vigil. During these times the importance of good location in the nesting colony becomes clear. While they are gone the nests, particularly at the periphery, are attacked by the troodontids and large varanid lizards that live in the area year round. Although the bulls may be nearby, they tend to stay mostly around their own harems and will do little to discourage a predator from raiding a neighbor's nest. More often than not, the nests most at risk are the ones at the edges of the rookery.

Although many nests are raided and some completely destroyed, most remain unscathed. The nests and their eggs are so abundant that the predators are quite simply swamped. The fact that this food supply is available for only a few weeks a year prevents the resident predator population of lizards and dinosaurs from increasing to a point where they might seriously affect the colony's success. The same is true of the large predators. Although many adult herbivores are brought down near or at the nesting site, not nearly enough are killed to substantially affect the herds. There will be no comparable increase in the number of local large predators either, because the bonanza provided by the migrants is seasonal and short-lived.

Once the long incubation period has ended, faint grunts and chirps resonate from within the eggs in each nest. Soon, the end of an egg cracks and a tiny, wet head appears. Shortly thereafter, one forepaw, then another will emerge from the shell. Finally, an entire juvenile will tumble out of its egg and land among the eggs and bodies of its siblings. In some species, the hatchlings may take several days to emerge. Hadrosaurine and hypsilophodontid young are born with a soft layer of down, which helps regulate their body temperature. Given the unpredictable and often cool weather in the mid-latitude highlands and farther north, it is a real asset. Hatchlings throughout the various colonies all have some form of camouflage coloring to their downy coats, which helps them blend into their nests. As the young grow, the coat also helps them retain much of the energy they get from their food. It is usually shed after the first year but gives them a neat, attractive appearance in the interim.

The first sight of the awkwardly moving young chirping and squirming about the nest in a tangle of tiny limbs, tails, and crestless, hornless heads, with flattened faces and large eyes, sets off a reflexive response in each female. It will at once lower its head toward the hatchlings. The sight of the first large, moving figure over the nest is immediately imprinted upon the hatchlings. They are born almost helpless and they really do need to be looked after. Fortunately, the urge to nurture them is strong in the females, and as a result, hadrosaurines have developed one of the highest degrees of parental care of any dinosaur.

Returning from a foraging trip, a female will approach its young, lower its head, and set its lower bill over the rim of the nest, just at the edge. The bold white rings surrounding its eyes initiate a reflex in the newly hatched juveniles, and they approach and peck at the mouth of their mother. This causes the female to regurgitate a warm, semidigested slurry into a shallow pouch in its throat. The hatchlings then crowd around and feed as if from a trough.

In order to rear their young successfully, females feed them a diet of vegetation supplemented by crop milk. Nesting females produce this "milk" by sloughing off the innermost lining of their crops and regurgitating it as part of the meal. Crop milk is an extremely nutritious first food for the hatchlings. It is rich in fats, proteins, and calories and contains important vitamins and minerals, as well as digestive microorganisms that the hatchlings will need for their own digestive systems. Combined with the female's last meal, crop milk creates a sort of "vegetable soup" that is responsible for the rapid growth and development of the hatchling dinosaurs. The young grow so quickly that they will double their length in three weeks and triple it in eight. The adults' feeding trips quickly escalate to several a day. Smaller trees are soon defoliated, larger ones quickly stripped of leaves up to fifteen feet from the ground, and the adults are forced to forage farther and farther to meet the demands of the growing young.

As they grow, the hatchlings begin to crowd the nest. This forces the adults even farther from the colony, to a point where they are traveling many miles in each direction to feed their charges. During these forays, the adults are subject to attack by the tyrannosaurids and dromaeosaurids that patrol the outer regions of the rookery territories. If an adult—especially a female—does not return from a feeding trip, the effects on its nestlings will be catastrophic. The hatchlings' earlier imprinting of their mother now has both good and bad consequences. If a parent does not return, the hatchlings will remain at the nest until they starve to death. So strong is their loyalty to their nest site that they will not venture from it, and, because no other adult will bother to feed them, they will soon lose strength and die. Even though food may be only a short walk away, they will not leave to eat it, never having learned to associate green growth with food. In their limited experience, food comes from a large, moving, ring-eyed creature that periodically appears, bends its head down, and produces something to eat. They are completely unaware that acres of plants surround them or, more to the point, that those plants represent meals. If the adults survive, the young will have to be taught to associate foliage with food. In the nest, that lesson is still weeks away.

Located on the outskirts of duckbill colonies are the nesting colonies of the hypsilophodontids. The *Orodromeus* and *Thescelosaurus* colonies are arranged so as not to lie in the pathways that the larger dinosaurs use on their foraging trips. Sometimes, however, the edge of a hypsilophodontid colony blends into the outermost edges of a lambeosaurine or hadrosaurine rookery, and the two colonies share real estate.

Most of these smaller dinosaurs live in the highlands year round. The leaves, buds, shoots, berries, and other fruits on which they feed sustain them during the months that the main herds are in the southern lowlands. The hypsilophodontids spend their time in flocks scattered through the woodlands and clearings in the upland areas a little farther west. Although the northernmost populations migrate southward to better lighted regions in winter, as a rule, they have small home ranges. They are creatures of the high country and mingle with the larger herds only during the breeding sea-

PRECEDING PAGES
Dromaeosaurids are a large and successful group of predatory dinosaurs, found in many parts of the world, and ranging from small to large animals. They are all characterized by a compact body, large, dexterous forelimbs, a long, stiffened tail, and an enlarged second toe on the hind limb, which is held off the ground as the animal walks. *Dromaeosaurus*, pictured here, occupies a role as a small predator, feeding on a wide variety of smaller wildlife. Though measuring about six feet in length, it is a solidly built animal.

son, which, not uncoincidentally, is at the same time of the year for both types of animals. When the hypsilophodontids are among the duckbills, however, different relationships are at play. By nesting in such close proximity, each group derives benefits that would be lost if they nested separately. The hypsilophodontids choose to nest so close to the duckbills because the big animals provide a ready source of food for their young. Hypsilophodontid hatchlings have a different diet than their herbivorous parents. They are insectivorous, feeding on the juicy maggots, grubs, and other invertebrates that are attracted to the droppings of the big herbivores. The lambeosaurines and hadrosaurines benefit because they are alerted to danger by the hypsilophodontids on the edges of their territories. Each side tolerates the other, and each group gains from the presence of the other.

Unlike the larger dinosaurs, hypsilophodontid females brood their clutches. Their downy undersides are well suited to this purpose, so they have no need to cover the eggs with vegetation, as the duckbills do. When the young begin to hatch, they emerge a lot faster than the duckbills. They pop off the top of their eggshell, crawl out, and lay in the nest for several hours until they are able to walk. The hatchlings emerge in the morning, which gives their downy coats time to dry off and lets them warm up in the sun. In the cool night, a wet, sluggish hatchling might actually freeze to death.

Within a few hours after birth, the young group together, forming loose crèches, stay near the adults not so much for guidance but for protection. Hypsilophodontids form strong social units, and their herding instinct is one of the strongest in any group of wildlife. Being mobile and rather self-reliant, young hypsilophodontids take to wandering around the confines of their rookery in search of their first meal, and they do not have far to go to find it. When they hatch, they are ready for a diet of insects, and their first meal is literally all around them. They immediately make for the dung left by the herds in the area and begin searching through the droppings. Whole communities of dung beetles and other insects are attracted to the droppings, and they provide a rich supply of food for any animals that take the time to look for them.

Insects are a great food source for any growing animal. In addition, the beetles and grubs in the dung heaps are covered in a complex assortment of intestinal flora, picked up in the droppings that have passed through the digestive tracts of the adults. The young will need these microorganisms for their own digestive systems as they grow and their diet changes to a primarily herbivorous one. The droppings of herbivorous animals also contain seeds, the occasional undigested fruits, and other foodstuffs that often pass through the guts of the big plant-eaters, and the young hypsilophodontids quickly learn to zero in on these tidbits.

The mid-summer sun is a permanent fixture in the higher latitudes. All the little dramas that play out at this time of year flow from the extended hours of daylight. In the regions closer to the North Pole, the sun shines nonstop throughout the day, and even in the lands farther south, nighttime is at most a few hours long. The heat may come and go, but the light is constant. This season of light has a direct impact on the animals, and they adjust their life cycles accordingly. Much of what was hidden under cover of darkness is now thrown into the open light of day. The animals feed, drink, and even sleep in the almost constant daylight. As the height of mid-summer approaches, the nestlings throughout the countryside are growing up. In less than a month's time, they have tripled in length and grown in weight several times more. In the short space of time to follow, they will explode out of their confines across the scenery that surrounds them.

Several varieties of troodontids nest throughout the expanse of the continent. They have an especially strong affinity for the nesting colonies of duckbills and hypsilophodontids, and it is almost a given that if the herbivores are nearby, the carnivorous troodontids will be too. Often, their presence can be told by shed teeth and missing nestlings. They are an important part of the nesting ecosystems. Part of their impact stems from their adaptability. Since their ancestors arrived from Asia, troodontids have adjusted to life on the North

American continent quite nicely. They are successful, alert, opportunistic predators.

Troodontids usually first show up following the migrating herds near the end of their journeys. Elegantly decked out in a camouflaged coat of downy feathers that varies from area to area, they are handsome, efficient-looking animals. They seem to appear out of nowhere, but it is because they winter in the highlands that they are not noticed until mid-spring. They move with a disconcerting grace among the uprooted and toppled trees, the leafless cycads, and the patches of exposed dark soil that have so recently been stripped of their plant cover. With arms held close to their bodies, long, sharply clawed fingers curled into knobby, bony fists and heads held as high as possible on their necks, this small, loosely organized army of camp followers uses sharp vision and acute hearing to detect the slightest motion.

As the bright days of summer draw to a close, the air of expectant change once again descends, this time across the northern latitudes of West America. Throughout the days of endless sunlight over the weeks gone by, the only noticeable change has been in the multitude of broods spreading over the north lands, as the young grew fast and began to spill out of their nests. Now the passing of the equinox highlights the changes to come. Once they begin, they accelerate with breathtaking speed. The days begin to shorten and, coupled with a slight chill in the air and a touch of color in the local foliage, the pace of change quickens to a rush. As the animals prepare for the long trek south, the land offers up a final bounty. New food sources come into season, adding to the diet of twigs, leaves, and branches. Many plants are producing offspring of their own in the form of seeds, and in many cases, these seeds are contained in edible fruits and berries. As these food sources become available, they provide a nutritious and tasty diet for young and old alike. The high sugar content of the bumper crop of fruit helps the adults bulk up, and it gives the young a spurt of growth for the journey to come.

For the young dinosaurs, predigested food supplemented by crop milk has given way to foraged meals. They learn what to eat by imitative behavior and by recovering and eating what the adults drop as they feed, quickly developing a taste for the sweet berries growing on the bushes in the area. Often, they fight over these tasty morsels, and for a meal on the vine, it is first come, first served. Following as the adults forage, the young herbivores have now started to respond to the signaling devices of the adults, such as ankle bands, and have learned the meaning of keeping up with the rest of the troop.

On the trip south, the single-minded focus that prevailed in the springtime is replaced with a more leisurely, ambling gait. On the return trip, the juveniles slow the herds to a point where they will average only about half the speed they did on the way north, so the southward leg takes about twice as long as the trip north. This means that the herds spend more time within the territories of the predator packs.

As the herds of duck-billed and horned dinosaurs make their way to the southern coastal plains, they begin to disperse. The clans of ceratopsids remain pretty much intact. Hadrosaurines remain an unstructured, evenly spread-out herd. The lambeosaurines break up into groups based on sex and age; females seek the company of other females, bulls form bachelor herds, and juveniles group together in flocks of up to a hundred, for safety in numbers. Then, all work their way up the gentle slopes of the foothills to the west. Here they hug the wooded areas, both for the availability of food and the lower chance of attack from the larger predators that cannot pursue prey effectively among the trees. Set apart like this, each group can feed on its own, move at its own pace, and generally not interfere or compete with the others.

For now, the journey is over. Scattered throughout the coastal lowlands, the thousands and thousands of participants reestablish themselves in their home ranges and build reserves for next year, when the great migration again calls itself into existence, silently summoning its individual units. Then, the vast herds will form again, as they have for so very long.

OVERLEAF

Although the horns of ceratopsians are formidable weapons, they are used more often against members of their own species than for defense. Animals such as these two *Chasmosaurus* will lock horns and pivot in a test of strength for any number of reasons. Courtship rites, territorial battles, social status—any and all may bring these irritable powerhouses to blow.

CHAPTER SEVEN

GLENS OF HELL CREEK

The Domain of The Tyrannosaurs

PRECEDING PAGES
Sunlight glistens through a glade of broad-leaved trees in Hell Creek. By this time in the Late Cretaceous, the change-over from the old conifer- and fern- dominated flora is relatively complete, and the woodlands throughout the area are composed primarily of the newer angiosperms.

OPPOSITE
A low sun illuminates the face of a subadult *Tyrannosaurus*. Young tyrannosaurs differ considerably from adults in having a more lightly built skull and muzzle. As the animals mature, they begin to take on the massive construction so characteristic of the adults.

It has been a few million years since the vast herds plodded up and down the seaside corridor of West America in their annual migration, and changes have occurred that have altered the continent and its inhabitants. For one, the continent has grown. Its westward movement has caused it to overtake, collide with, and accrete a number of Pacific islands, adding acreage. This movement has pushed the Rocky Mountains higher, increasing both the number of volcanoes and the intensity of their eruptions. Ashfalls blanket the West American corridor more than ever before.

Because of these changes, as well as a general uplift of central North America during the last four or five million years, the Niobrara Sea is begrudgingly letting go of its hold on mid-America. The waterway has been gradually shrinking and slowly draining off to the north and south. In places, and at times, West and East America have rejoined, uniting lands long separated. Fluctuations in the inland sea have had a profound effect on the wildlife living in it, on it, and along its shores. Each time the sea expanded, the corridor constricted. During this time, terrestrial habitats were destroyed or reduced, and dinosaur diversity dropped. When the Niobrara Sea receded, the West American corridor widened, and new and different types of dinosaurs evolved to exploit the enlarged habitat.

Here, among the countless rivers and streams that cover the Montana Plain, the climate is subtropical, and wildlife is on the rebound, reclaiming land left exposed by the most recent regression of the Niobrara's waters. Peat marshes and coastal swamps of cedar and cypress are taking hold on the former seabed and now dominate the shores of West America. These soggy coastal wetlands are made even more so by seasonal storms that blow in off the receding Niobrara. A bit farther inland, broken only here and there by low hills, lies Hell Creek—a widespread, fertile, almost featureless web of flood plains.

Hell Creek is dominated by vast, largely open plains, interspersed with open broad-leaved angiosperm forests that predominate in the low-lying and wetter areas. Conifers hold their own in scattered groves of cedar, laurel, and redwood trees up and into the higher elevations, while cypresses dominate the coastal swamps. Ginkgoes are rare and cycads rarer still. Most abundant close to watercourses and water holes, the trees of these woodlands are not large by any standards, generally topping off at fifty or sixty feet. They do not form a thick canopy except right along the water's edge. The forest floor, now practically devoid of ferns, abounds with low shrubs, vines, and wildflowers. These often extend beyond the woodlands' margins and out, forming picturesque glades and meadows, dotted after the rains with thousands of tiny points of color.

Smaller angiosperms have entered into a special relationship with certain animals that goes well beyond simply providing food. Until the advent of an entirely new type of reproductive system, almost all land plants had to depend primarily on the wind, and to a much lesser extent on water, to transfer pollen from one plant to another. Angiosperms have now evolved brightly colored, pleasingly scented, sweetly flavored accessories to the standard plant reproductive organs. These flowers allure any number of insect types. Among the wildflowers spread across the Late Cretaceous meadows and heaths hover multitudes of butterflies, bees, and other insects, ensuring their own survival, as well as that of the plants. Driven mainly by hunger, many kinds of Cretaceous insects visit flowers regularly to collect and feed on their nectar, and even on the pollen itself. In the process, pollen grains are delivered efficiently from one plant to another, ensuring fertilization without having to depend on the vagaries of the wind.

Many of these plants also depend on larger animals to disperse their seeds. Each seed contains an embryo plant and food reserves, representing the next generation of plants, so they are often designed to pass unscathed through the digestive track of an herbivore. This type of cooperation and coevolution has played a substantial part in the relatively rapid spread and success of the angiosperms. With the wetlands at the forefront, the forests are expanding eastward by slowly following the retreating waters of the seaway.

These plains, and to a lesser extent the highlands and coastal margins that surround them, are now home to a variety of wildlife. Interspersed among the scattered glens and glades of Hell Creek are lakes and water holes that provide water throughout the year. The larger bodies of water are inhabited by freshwater sharks and rays, paddlefish and garfish. Turtles of every description, dietary preference, and size swim in their waters and bask on their shores alongside alligators and an occasional crocodile. Salamanders, snakes, and lizards, camouflaged in earth tones or flaunting vivid colors warnings of toxins, slither, skitter, and wend their ways through meadows and open woodlands. Stalking all of these creatures are innumerable small, agile theropods and long-legged wading birds. Nearby trees house owls, which feed on any number of small mammals. Animals representing almost every class of vertebrate can be accounted for, going about their business in the year-round, warm, humid climate.

In many terrestrial ecosystems the general pace and overall direction are driven by the herbivores, the animals that spend their lives placidly chewing on the local vegetation, and Hell Creek has its fair share of them. Plants collect and store energy from the sun by reconstituting and concentrating the energy into a form that can be held and released on demand. This energy can also be transferred efficiently and effectively into another animal through predation. These relatively dull-witted, mostly harmless herbivores have become "middlemen," determining by their diets and feeding methods the overall diversity and abundance of the plants and, by their own numbers, availability, and defensive tactics, the number and kinds of predators. This is an extremely important and pivotal role for animals that, when it comes right down to it, do little more than eat, defecate, and procreate.

Several kinds of hadrosaurines and ceratopsids as well as ankylosaurines ply the woods. As always, a cadre of meat-eating animals stands ready to take advantage of the caloric and nutritional bonanza represented by these herbivores. All the major Late Cretaceous theropod dinosaur groups of North America have representatives in Hell Creek. Troodontids, dromaeosaurids, and albertosaurs work daily at culling the herbivore herds and maintaining a balanced ecosystem, but something new has been added. The expanding environment created by the withdrawal of the Niobrara Sea, the near-tropical climate, the spreading forests, and the slowly increasing populations of herbivores of all types and sizes provide an opportunity for the appearance of a new predator.

Now, deep in the Late Cretaceous, one animal has taken the art of hunting and scavenging to levels never before seen—the theropod *Tyrannosaurus.* Although the packs of tyrannosaurs constitute only a very small portion of the entire population of the dinosaurs of Hell Creek and account for only a fraction of the deaths that occur here, they dominate the ecosystem simply by their imposing presence. Even when spotted at a distance, no matter whether they are hunting, patrolling, or simply going for a drink, they bring all activity to a stop, as countless pairs of eyes watch the pack's progress across the open plains. Whether feeding, wallowing, or resting, other animals come to their feet, all eyes, and ears, and noses. For some animals, the sight of a tyrannosaur is but a momentary interruption; for others, it is an adrenaline-rich experience. Responses can vary from a slow blink and an apathetic resumption of activity to an all-out, wild-eyed flight at top speed. No dinosaur in North America, not even the majestic sauropods, have ever had such an impact on the behavior of other animals in their habitat. Any animal that can elicit this range of responses among its neighbors is clearly in control.

One of the largest theropods ever, tyrannosaurs can reach lengths in excess of forty feet and weights of well over six tons. Their jaws, the strongest by far of any dinosaur, are equipped with fifty large, thick, serrated teeth, which are continuously replaced. Their dark eyes can face forward for clear depth perception as well as outward for a wide peripheral view. They peer from beneath eye ridges and brow crests that can vary considerably from individual to individual and are used to establish and maintain rank and status within the hunting group. Although not designed for endurance, their powerful legs can propel these beasts at speeds that practically ensure they can outrun their favorite foods—hadrosaurids and ceratopsids—especially if that potential food is aged, injured, or inexperienced.

By and large, tyrannosaurs avoid the more heavily wooded, wetter areas of Hell Creek and keep to the drier open plains and uplands, where hunting is a bit easier due to the firmer ground and the availability of prey. Despite the reaction of other dinosaurs at the mere sight of them, tyrannosaurs tend to kill only when they have to. Ever the opportunists, these animals will take whatever they find, dead or alive. Normally tyrannosaurs prefer fresh meat, and they can, and eventually will, eat just about any part of any animal. When they hunt, their size means that all of the herbivores in their territory are potential prey. It also means they can steal from others—including other tyrannosaurs.

The hunting groups, or packs, are almost always outgrowths of the tyrannosaurs' method of nesting and of raising of their offspring. These packs vary in size and makeup. Each exists only because its members have chosen to follow one animal's lead when it comes to moving, feeding, drinking, or resting for the night. This boss animal is most often the largest, and

Leaf litter is a simple yet profound component to any ecosystem, and plays an enormous role in the cycle of decay and regeneration of a woodland. Whereas conifer needles and cones, as well as ginkgo and cycad leaves once made up the majority of the leaf litter of the planet's forests, increasingly, sassafras, willow, and poplar leaves, among others, can be found there.

almost invariably a female, as they tend to be somewhat bigger than the males.

Since most pack members are related to the lead animal in some way, the pack is a family unit of sorts. For various reasons, not the least of which is the limited standing room around a kill, these units rarely exceed a half-dozen adult members. If dinnertime squabbles become too frequent or intense because there is not enough food or room to eat it, one or more animals will break away and establish a territory elsewhere. This accounts for any lone tyrannosaurs encountered in Hell Creek. Although the feeding styles and diets of such solitary tyrannosaurs must be modified somewhat—they tend to scavenge a bit more and only hunt smaller prey—they seem to get along fine on their own.

Within the family unit usually only one pair breeds. Because of the care given to the young, tyrannosaur clutches are relatively small. The rest of the adults, if there are any, act as helpers, protecting and providing food for the young as if they were their own. The young hatch completely feathered and are wobbling about in the nest within a few minutes and wandering around within a few hours. For their first weeks, they stay either in the nest or close by it. The reason is simple: Periodically one or more of the adults, usually older siblings, will visit the nest and, at sight of the young, regurgitate a meal onto the ground. The young respond by diving in and over each other to eat whatever comes out. Although these impromptu banquets are always welcomed, young tyrannosaurs are not totally dependent on them. While the adults are away, they scour the area as a group searching for mammals, lizards, young birds, or whatever else they can stir up.

Once they reach a length of five or six feet and are able to keep up with the adults, they leave the nesting area, which by now is alive with flies and reeks of feces and uneaten remains of regurgitated meals. The smaller tyrannosaurs join and stay with the packs, generally keeping their distance from the larger members as they lose their juvenile down coats and coloration and acquire a more adult aspect. Their teeth and jaws are not yet large or strong enough to maintain any kind of rank within the pack except the very lowest and most vulnerable. Also, their rapidly increasing size requires larger meals than those regurgitated at the nest or hunted down on their own. Their best bet for survival now is to hang around the fringes of a pack hunt and nip in at the subsequent communal feast. Their narrower heads and jaws allow them to squeeze in and recover meat that is not readily accessible to the larger pack members.

Young tyrannosaurs undergo other changes as they grow, which transform their more typical theropod jaws and teeth into the more specialized ones of adults. As a juvenile gets older, its muzzle and jaws deepen. It loses a number of teeth and those that remain grow wider, becoming thicker and stronger. The entire face is then reinforced to deliver and absorb the forces to which it will be subjected as the animal matures. This gives the final shape of an adult tyrannosaur's head a much more swollen appearance than that of a juvenile. These changes in anatomy both reflect and allow for changes in diet and hunting style, as the animals are weaned from regurgitated meals to prey provided by the pack, and ultimately to prey they kill or help kill themselves.

Only about half the young tyrannosaurs make it through their first year, and less than a third make it through their second. Many fall prey to their own kind, and not necessarily outside the family unit.

Within a tyrannosaur pack, each animal's behavior is limited by what any larger and more dominant member will tolerate. Any disruption in the makeup of a pack, such as the death or departure of one or more members, is a call for a reorganization. Relationships are challenged, changed, or reinforced, sometimes violently, until order within the pack is restored. Only when a status quo is established does an uneasy peace descend on the group.

Among gregarious animals that share resources or otherwise engage in coordinated activities, subtle signs can be given or received to determine rank. Body posture, head-tilting, vocalizations, direction of gaze, and even scent are used to signal one's standing. These create and ensure an order within the group without the expenditure of energy and the danger of injury inherent in using physical contests to get the same results.

Within a family group several simple devices are used to see to it that each member knows its status and ranking in the hierarchy. Given the strength and death-dealing potential of these animals, great lengths must be taken to resolve problems without coming to serious blows. Adult tyrannosaurs use their brightly and distinctly colored head ridges and brow crests to identify each other, and either confirm their position in the unit or establish a new one. Any animal that wants to move up within the pack's hierarchy generally starts by approaching a more dominant individual and trying to stare it down, face to face, and practically nose to nose. The first to turn away has just declared itself subordinate to the other. If neither backs down, the two animals engage in a closed-mouth, side-to-side head-butting and shoving match. Again, the first to turn away shows itself subordinate to the other. Normally these contests are enough to determine rank and the animals part, secure in the knowledge of their status. Sometimes the contest goes further.

These displays and behaviors are often used successfully against other tyrannosaurs that are not in the family unit. Territorial ownership is never granted or guaranteed. It must be earned. Any time the head displays and staring fail to deter a trespassing tyrannosaur, it will be set upon by the more aggressive members of the family unit. Even entire other packs may be attacked when all else fails, resulting in perhaps the most awesome sight the Cretaceous has to offer—a fight among adult tyrannosaurs.

Once attempts to resolve differences bloodlessly have failed, tyrannosaurs pull out all the stops. No quarter is asked, and none given. When it has escalated to this point, there can be only one outcome—death. The relatively harmless staring and head-butting contests can go on for some time, but these all-out fights are extremely violent and very short lived. The contestants approach, grapple momentarily, and then bite out at each other with a fury and passion unrivaled anywhere or anytime by any other animal. Within moments, one of the combatants manages to get the other's neck or head in its jaws and then holds on for all it is worth. At this point the fight is over. Bites delivered by these powerful animals are so devastating to flesh and bone that a second one is rarely needed. The bitten animal may struggle for a time while still in the other's grasp, but this simply deepens the wounds. The biter will not release its grip until the loser is dead, and more often than not, a cannibalistic feast follows the victory.

Tyrannosaurs do not behave the way they do to establish and maintain territories; instead, their territories result from their behavior. Their appearance, the noises they make, and the smell of their urine, their dung, and even their breath announce that this area has a pack of tyrannosaurs in residence. There is no room for any additional predators and their presence will not be tolerated. One of the reasons tyrannosaurs patrol their territories regularly is to maintain ownership, or at least to renew the lease. Areas not visited and marked often enough will be usurped by others, either neighbors looking to expand or loners looking to establish a territory of their own. Another reason, of course, is to look for any sign of prey. The huge theropods often start stalking after the midday heat, waiting until dusk to initiate attacks, as the waning light of day makes their prey more vulnerable. With pupils fully dilated, the tyrannosaurs' large eyes can collect much more light than those of either ceratopsids or hadrosaurids. The tyrannosaurs' success rate for attacks in the low light of dusk and dawn is usually much higher than at other times. On occasion, they may even hunt by moonlight.

Packs of tyrannosaurs generally move about at an almost leisurely pace, stopping often, seeking any sign—sight, scent, or sound—of any prey. When they spot potential prey, the theropods approach slowly, either clustered in a group or strung out in a skirmish line, heads down and thrust forward, giving the potential prey their undivided attention. At this point, in the half light of dawn or dusk, whether an attack will occur depends almost entirely on the intended victim. A healthy hadrosaurid or ceratopsid has a certain way of carrying itself, a way in which it holds its head and looks around, alert and never really relaxed. Young animals reveal their vulnerability by looking around too often or not enough, very old animals by the pace at which they walk, and injured animals by the way they might favor a limb. If the pack

PRECEDING PAGES

Predator extraordinaire. Size, speed, firepower, finesse; all these and more culminate in *Tyrannosaurus*, the most formidable land predator in Earth's history. Exceptional senses of smell and hearing, stereoscopic vision, a never-ending supply of huge serrated teeth, coupled with an enormously powerful bite, and topped off with a nasty disposition combine to create an animal whose sheer presence commands respect from every other animal it comes in contact with. Superbly efficient predators, they are not above passing over a free meal, as this individual scouting out a leftover *Edmontosaurus* rib cage illustrates.

notices any vulnerable behavior, it will generally follow the lead of the boss animal. If that female decides to attack, they follow; if not, usually they will not bother.

Tyrannosaur attacks on herds of herbivores are confused, violent, nasty affairs. Once struck in the neck or head by the powerful jaws and sharp teeth, the prey's central nervous system seems to shut down entirely. As shock sets in, the herbivore lies where it fell and does nothing while the predators set on it. In reality the tyrannosaur's muscle-packed jaws have driven its strong, sharp teeth deep into the prey's neck, crushing the bones, severing the blood vessels, and rupturing the spine. Often tyrannosaurs will start feeding before the prey animal has even lost consciousness, let alone died.

If the attack somehow goes awry and the prey animal escapes with only injuries, it is probably worse off. The serrations along the edges of tyrannosaur teeth hold meat from previous meals—fetid, rotten scraps that harbor bacteria, giving off a powerful stench that shrouds tyrannosaur heads in a perpetual cloud of flies, but also extending the predator's arsenal. Any wound inflicted by these malodorous, microbe-laden jaws will almost certainly turn septic in a few days, delivering a slow, painful death, and providing the resident tyrannosaur pack with a feast when it discovers the dead or dying animal.

Normally during a hunt, pack members cooperate to a degree. Once the prey is down, any pretense of communal effort is abandoned; however, without some sort of order, some pack member will get seriously injured. Carcass etiquette—pack behavior around a kill—depends on the size of the prey and the number and size of the tyrannosaurs looking for a share. As with most other theropods that hunt and feed in groups, the larger animals generally get first crack at the prime cuts. If there is a big size discrepancy among the pack members, larger individuals eat first, while the smaller ones wait. If all are pretty much the same size, as many will feed as can find room at the carcass. Taking a second or two to brush aside the attempts of smaller pack members to feed may be worth the effort, but prolonged squabbling to dislodge a pack member of comparable size is just not worth the time and risk involved. There is always, of course, the requisite pushing and snapping, and hissing and snarling that make each meal an adventure, but the repasts generally come off without major incident.

A tyrannosaur's lower jaw fits within its upper one, giving the animal a pronounced overbite. This results in a scissorlike cutting motion when its jaws close on flesh. Although the teeth along the front sides of the mouth have sharp, serrated edges, the serrations are widely spaced and only marginally useful for cutting. Instead, they bind the teeth to the flesh, affording a better grip, so when the tyrannosaur pulls its head back with its formidable neck muscles the meat is torn rather than cut from the carcass. This messy but effective technique is useful for pulling large portions from the kill quickly. The tyrannosaur then throws its head back, quickly bolting down masses of flesh that can weigh more than five hundred pounds.

As the available meat dwindles, the carcass is dismembered and the pieces dragged away so individual pack members can continue to feed alone. Now, a still-hungry tyrannosaur can take its time and use the smaller teeth in the very front of its jaws to neatly strip away any flesh lying close to or attached to bone. Sometimes it affects a chewing motion of sorts, using the shorter, thinner teeth toward the rear of each jaw to slice and dice pieces too unwieldy to swallow comfortably. When the meat on the carcass is abundant, the tyrannosaurs will stay in the area and feed again several hours later. The only parts of a carcass tyrannosaurs regularly avoid eating are the large bones and, if the victim is an herbivore, the stomach contents of half-digested vegetation.

Tyrannosaurs are ultimately at the mercy of the herbivores' behavior. A shift in the migratory route of the herds of ceratopsids or hadrosaurids, or a lessening of the total rainfall in a given rainy season could mean starvation for a pack of tyrannosaurs. If the tyrannosaur population in a given year has already been weakened, it might lead to a local extinction. Prey animals have several less dramatic options for dealing with predators. Camouflage is common, especially among smaller animals. When combined with a generally secretive lifestyle, camouflage can be quite effective, especially against predators like tyrannosaurs, which hunt mostly by sight. Then, there is always flight, either straight out at top speed or combined with side-to-side feints and quick turns, relying on inertia to propel the pursuer in the wrong direction. Herding enhances these options, offering prey animals the advantage of hundreds of pairs of eyes and ears constantly on the alert. But the option predators dislike most and are often least capable of dealing with is the counterattack, when prey animals such as ceratopsids or ankylosaurids either stand their ground or charge right back.

Camouflage and flight, in that order, are usually the best ways for hypsilophodontids such as *Thescelosaurus* to avoid predation by tyrannosaurs. Flocks of these timorous, ten- to eleven-foot-long plant-eaters go about their daily lives, on either two legs or four, constantly alert to any signs of danger. Normally too small to interest a pack of tyrannosaurs, they regularly fall prey to a solitary tyrannosaur, or any of the other, smaller theropods that hunt throughout Hell Creek, including subadult tyrannosaurs. If one member of a flock feels threatened, its first instinct is to stop what it is doing, emit a short, sharp chirp, then remain absolutely motionless, depending on coloration and shading patterns to blend it into its surroundings. This behavior signals other members of the flock that there is danger nearby and, one by one, they all quickly freeze, not even turning their heads to look about. Enough of these swift little herbivores will be facing in enough directions so that eyes will be looking in all directions, giving the flock a panoramic view. If the danger passes, each nervous herbivore, one at a time, cautiously resumes its activity. If the threat persists and comes closer, the flock bursts into flight in an instant. This type of response presents many potential targets at once, causing some hesitation on the part of the startled hunter. In the resulting confusion, the fleeing herbivores can pick up a few extra steps and seconds to make good their collective and individual escapes. Even attacks by predator packs can be confounded when presented with so many small targets fleeing in so many directions at once. This strategy, though effective, is not foolproof, and many of the smaller herbivores fall prey to theropods despite this behavior.

The same is true for the ornithomimid dinosaurs, such as *Ornithomimus.* These curious, toothless theropods fill the niche between the relatively smaller and predominantly plant-eating hypsilophodontids and the much larger, entirely herbivorous hadrosaurids. Ranging anywhere from ten to thirteen feet in length, they have long, flexible necks supporting small, narrow heads equipped with sharp ears and large eyes. With these sensors providing information to their relatively large brains, these animals do not miss much. Fleet-footed and adroit, these maneuverable omnivores fall prey to the equally fast and nimble troodontids and dromaeosaurids, but they are generally too quick and elusive for the larger tyrannosaurs. Although ornithomimids can deliver a kick lethal to some of the smaller theropods, flight is their only real defense against the larger ones.

Ornithomimids move about Hell Creek in flocks composed of animals of mixed ages, sizes, and sexes, nipping at buds, fleshy fruit, and flowers, scrabbling through rotting vegetation for fat grubs, rummaging through the underbrush to scare up mammals, overturning logs to look for large millipedes and salamanders, and raiding nests for eggs and hatchlings. They are constantly on the move, feeding all the while. They will peck at almost anything and swallow only when their mouths are full. When they are not searching for food, they can be found taking dust baths. Places where the dust is just the right consistency are visited often by flocks of ornithomimids. Here they lie down and roll around; the dust absorbs excess oils in their down coats and helps rid them of ticks and feather lice.

Hadrosaurids also flee from attacks by theropods, especially from the larger tyrannosaur packs. For the huge herds of these duck-billed dinosaurs, flight is their first and only response to danger. Their endurance, watchful nature, and great numbers are their best defense against predation.

Stalking tyrannosaurs signal their intentions by walking with their necks and heads low and parallel to the ground. This posture usually alerts nearby plant-eaters, such as the hadrosaurids. Any animals along the edges of a herd have at least one eye and one ear facing outward to watch and listen for danger. Those within the herd stay focused on each other. This way danger signals can be transmitted through the herd quite rapidly. Hadrosaurids closest to a hunting or stalking tyrannosaur instinctively start to move away even if they are not the immediate object of the theropod's attention. Each animal increases its vocalizations as it turns aside in an attempt to preserve its personal space within the group; as a result, the entire herd turns slowly away from the threat. Although tyrannosaurs tend to take longer strides than their hadrosaurid prey and can easily outrun them in the short haul, the duckbills' stamina is far greater. Unless caught quickly, a hadrosaurid with a lead can usually outdistance rather than outrun hunting tyrannosaurs. Tyrannosaurs therefore attack suddenly, from cover if possible, and strike hard and quickly.

The herbivores probably best able to cope with tyrannosaur attacks, even from packs, are the ceratopsids. Predators tend to be nervous about sustaining injuries. Even minor skin lesions can become infected and lead to conditions as debilitating as a broken foot or leg. Any prey animal that stands its ground gives its attacker pause. No other animals of Hell Creek are as well suited to this as the ankylosaurids and ceratopsids.

For the relatively slow-moving ankylosaurids outrunning potential danger is out of the question. The largest of the ankylosaurids, *Ankylosaurus* often reach lengths well in excess

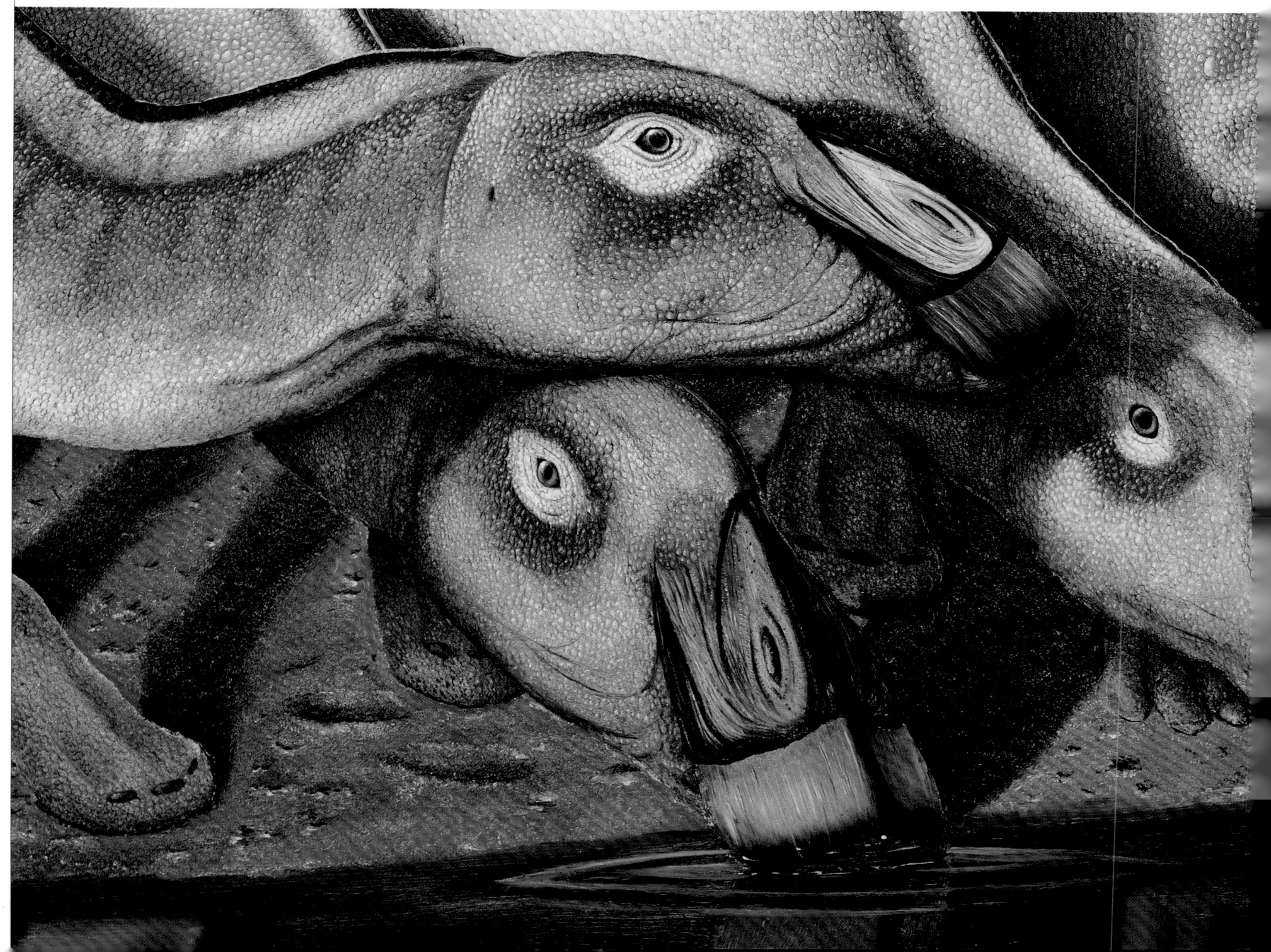

of thirty feet. Although not very abundant, these walking fortresses travel when and where they want throughout Hell Creek, alone or in small groups, with little to fear from tyrannosaur or other theropod attacks. Whenever accosted by large theropods such as tyrannosaurs, these slow but powerful animals lumber around, brandishing the large bony clubs at the ends of their tails. The club, almost a foot and a half across, at one end and the strong jaws, equipped with short but sharp teeth, at the other end make these animals' defense anything but passive—despite appearances. If they should become totally surrounded, or exhausted, or both, ankylosaurs simply squat, presenting a heavily armored, spike-studded, nearly impervious back. The combination of low-slung bodies and massive weights—up to four tons—makes these herbivores impossible for even a tyrannosaur to flip over. As low browsers, ankylosaurs use their relatively broad beaks to crop whatever ground cover is available. Their intestines simmer with microbes that ferment the otherwise largely indigestible plant material. Like all animals that use this fermentation-vat digestion on such a large scale, they produce great quantities of gas in the process.

Quite abundant in Hell Creek and falling somewhere between the faster, unarmored hadrosaurids and the slower, heavily armored ankylosaurids are the ceratopsids. Here is a group of dinosaurs, ranging far and wide throughout the lowlands of the Late Cretaceous, adapted to gather and process relatively low-quality, low-growing vegetation. The plants on which the ceratopsids feed, the angiosperms, can withstand and recover from their onslaught to a degree never possible in the slow-growing gymnosperms, such as conifers. The angiosperms and plant-eating dinosaurs such as the hadro-

Several *Edmontosaurus* and a lone *Triceratops* pause to drink from a stream. Though they are impressive animals in their own right, both are wary living in the domain of the tyrannosaurs. Even an action as simple as drinking water is approached with caution, and at least one animal in the group is always on the lookout for trouble.

saurids and the ceratopsids are altering the biology of North America. Low-growing herbaceous angiosperms counter the decimation wrought by the herds of large herbivores with rapid regrowth and prodigious reproductive rates. The larger, woody angiosperms have taken a different tack, evolving chemical defenses to deter browsing dinosaurs. Some plants secrete bitter, astringent tannins, while others secrete poisonous alkaloids. The damaged plants also release airborne hormones that trigger the production of these same distasteful chemicals in trees that have yet to be attacked. For the herbivores, depending on the way the wind is blowing, moving on does not necessarily ensure a move to better pasture.

Both long-faced chasmosaurines, *Torosaurus* and *Triceratops* share the tapered muzzle, relatively short nose horns, and long brow horns characteristic of this group. At twenty-five feet in length and approaching eight tons in weight, they represent the largest of all ceratopsids. Each animal is accompanied everywhere by a retinue of birds. Some follow along behind the large animals looking for insects and anything else stirred up by their passage, while others actually ride on the backs of the migrants, searching for and eating ticks. These and other parasites are often found in the folds of skin, and especially under the neck frill of the huge animals.

Like so many herbivores in Hell Creek, most of the the impressive-looking chasmosaurines spend much of their lives on the move as members of vast herds; however, unlike the evenly distributed hadrosaurid herds, the herds of many ceratopsids have structure. Clusters of animals are separated by relatively large open spaces. Clans, led by the largest and oldest female, dominate the herds, while the males, in small, loose bachelor groups, roam along the edges of the herd, especially along the front edge. Since they are larger and stronger, they are better able to open up new areas. They are also more expendable. The loss of one male is the loss of an animal; the loss of a female, however, is the loss of all of her potential offspring.

Depending on the time of year, juveniles hang out within the protective confines of the clans. Here the young remain until their cranial decor and overall demeanor announce their sex. Then the young adult males leave or are driven from the clans by the adult females. This eliminates the possibility of inbreeding and allows them to interact with other males without the pressures or distractions associated with mating season. In this way, the subadult males have an opportunity to spar, test their strength, and ready themselves for the next rut.

In general, the horned dinosaurs move in relative safety within their herds. At times, however, the environment tests their stamina and endurance. Only the healthiest and strongest survive long enough to procreate. Once or twice a year, a severe storm hits the east coast of West America. Then, the normally slow-moving streams and small rivers meandering through broad, flat-bottomed valleys swell within hours into raging torrents that often overflow their banks and cause extensive sheet flooding. Still driven by the urge to move, the herds' attempts to cross these once placid waterways can end in disaster. Even if the lead animals are stopped by a river in flood, the pressure from those moving in behind can force them into the water, and, unless they are strong enough or large enough to reach the other side, they can drown. Sometimes, for a mile or so downstream, hundreds of carcasses line the banks of a river as its muddy waters slow and recede. Then the theropods arrive. Most of the successful packs of tyrannosaurs in Hell Creek have territories that border on one or more large streams. Sooner or later, while on patrol after one of these storms, a pack will discover the bloated bodies from one of these catastrophes. Even the close presence of smaller troodontids and dromaeosaurids is tolerated by the larger tyrannosaurs when the food is this abundant and widespread.

Usually, however, ceratopsid flesh is not at all easy to come by. The horns of *Torosaurus* and *Triceratops* can easily exceed five feet in length. Used mostly for sparring and wrestling with other males, the horns are still readily available to defend against a predator. Covered with dark, horny keratin, they taper gradually into narrow tips, concentrating all the energy of a charging six-ton ceratopsid onto a very small area with disastrous effect. Their first job, however, is to intimidate. They are displayed proudly at every opportunity. When facing an attacker, the eye horns can appear foreshortened and lose their intimidating effect. The larger neck frills of most centrosaurines—the ceratopsids with long eye horns—underscore the fact that the animal is facing full forward toward its opponent, and its horns, even if not readily discernible, are poised to wound or kill.

Size, attitude, weapons, and surprising agility might seem to make these herbivores invulnerable to predation. Only tyrannosaurs have the physique and technique needed to tackle ceratopsids with any regularity. Although tyrannosaurs can attack ceratopsids at any time, most attacks occur when the herds have stopped for the night. The animals are tired, and the clans tend to break up and spread out as their members seek one last mouthful of food or a place to lie down and rest, enjoy a dust bath, or wallow, depending on the circumstances. By attacking during these lapses in attention, tyrannosaurs can often provoke the momentary confusion that might provide the few, critical extra seconds on which they rely to increase the chance of a successful hunt.

As a tyrannosaur pack approaches the milling ceratopsids in the half light of dusk, the alert herbivores turn to face the predators. Young animals move away quickly and a few of the larger ones might even take a few steps forward, heads raised, eyes, ears, and noses directed toward the danger. The experienced adults appraise the situation and choose their best response—flee, move forward in a false charge to deter the attack, mount a real charge, or resume their early evening activities. Snorting, pawing the ground, and shaking their heads, they reach a consensus, and subordinate members of the herd take their cue from the dominant ones. This way, when and if the attack comes, it is not a surprise. Most of the herbivores usually respond in the same manner, avoiding most of the confusion and panic the tyrannosaurs try to engender. More often than not, the pack will move on without launching the attack for any number of reasons—the closest herbivores are too large, or apparently uninjured, or too densely clustered, or perhaps the terrain is wrong.

Scenes such as these play out every day throughout Hell Creek. The key is that everything is interconnected: No single force acts without influencing the others in subtle and not so subtle ways. Rivers run, plant life grows, landforms are worn down or thrust up, sea levels rise and fall, the wind blows, and the rain falls. Through it all move the animals, keeping to rhythms all their own. Hell Creek is no different from any other environment in either East or West America, or any other continent. Although the animals here are unique, their responses and reactions to the land and to each other are no different than those of any other wildlife populations of any other time. The plants and herbivores constantly experiment with ways of getting around each others' defensive and offensive adaptations, while the predators and herbivores continuously thrust at and parry each others' attempts to find and exploit any weakness. In these respects, this environment is a healthy, viable ecosystem populated by magnificent animals going about their mundane business and dealing with the daily rigors of survival among the pleasant climate, meadows of wildflowers, and overall idyllic feel of Hell Creek.

AFTERWORD

Prehistoric Life Today

Along the eastern coast of North America lie the remnants of an ancient mountain chain created when continents collided during the formation of the supercontinent Pangaea. The numerous gray-brown valleys and hollows that occupy the gently rolling flanks of these mountains are poised for the greening soon to come. Within these recesses, bare branches shed an early spring rain, waiting for their leaves to emerge. Below them, tightly coiled ferns tentatively poke through the ground cover, ready to quickly unfurl their intricate green fronds when conditions are right.

Gentle sounds fill the calm, damp air as tiny frogs peep away at each other, insects whir about, and newly arrived migratory birds set up their invisible, yet defined, territorial boundaries with endlessly repetitive calls. The only smells are of the rain, the wet earth, and last year's leaves slowly moldering into loam.

Opossums, shrews, and other small mammals are fully active now and move through the leaf litter in search of seeds, or insects, or whatever else suits their dietary fancies. Snakes slide along quietly, on the lookout for larvae, small lizards, salamanders, and small rodents. This is the quiet time preceding the flurry of life that typifies the summers in the region. Its pattern has been repeated here for the last sixty-four million years, and each time, the only creatures separating this scene from one of the Mesozoic Era are the pterosaurs and non-avian dinosaurs.

A pair of *Troodon* pause under the majestic sight of the Northern Lights. For the wildlife that spend their lives in the higher latitudes, such as smaller dinosaurs as these, the Aurora Borealis is a familiar sight.

It has been that long since the great extinction. Not as cataclysmic as the one that effectively silenced the Permian Period, and the Paleozoic as well, but one still severe enough to close not only the Cretaceous Period, but to start a new era, the Cenozoic. The extinction that ended the Cretaceous was a time in which almost three-quarters of all animals became extinct, including most of the dinosaurs. All that remains of these mighty beasts are a group of highly derived theropods, the birds, that can be found worldwide, sharing habitats with the more successful mammals.

A close look at these birds reveals traces of the extinct dinosaurs. Ostriches speeding along at twenty miles per hour recall visions of ornithomimids doing the same, and roadrunners pursuing, catching, and eating small prey bring to mind some of the tactics and maneuvers used by coelophysians. Although most of the dinosaurs are gone, their avian descendants have retained such features as air sacs in their bones and scales on their legs and feet. Others have re-evolved certain behaviors, such as the simple form of group hunting employed among hornbills, and the long north-south seasonal migrations developed and perfected by their forebearers.

Even mammals have emulated designs perfected by non-avian dinosaurs since their disappearance millions of years ago. If an elephant raises its trunk to an acacia tree in a motion reminiscent of a sauropod reaching for a conifer branch, it is no coincidence. A rhinoceros stamps its feet, shakes its head, and myopically charges an intruder just as an agitated stegosaur might have done. A deer runs, unerringly through woodlands it knows by heart, just like a hypsilophodontid.

If the scenes and descriptions of Late Cretaceous ecosystems like Hell Creek and the West American corridor seem vaguely familiar, it is because environments very much like these still exist. The major difference is that the lead players on these stages have been replaced; all of the minor roles, bit players, walk-ons, and extras remain basically the same.

The Niobrara Sea is long gone and has been replaced by a vast, fertile, featureless plain. North America now sits neatly between the equator and North Pole, having broken its ties with Asia and establishing a new one with South America. A visit to any modern, moderately well-watered valley, plain, or woodland of this continent reveals birds filling the air with their constant chatter, activity, and flash of color, while beneath crawl the reptiles and amphibians who seem to go out of their way to avoid notice as much as the birds seem to crave it. There are also small mammals living their lives as hastily as possible, in contrast to those like the tortoises who seem to have no place to go, and all the time in the world to get there. Bodies of water are alive with fish and frogs, and all throughout are the dragonflies and cockroaches, spiders and centipedes, and myriad other invertebrates still going about their daily routines as they have for millions of years, oblivious to the fact that tyrannosaurs, pteranodons, and all the non-avian dinosaurs no longer share their worlds. This is a testament to the adaptability and flexibility of these surviving animals, and the ecosystems that house them, but a bit disappointing for the world that the largest, most magnificent land animals the planet has, or will, ever see are gone for good.

Of all the species of animals on the planet today, there is only one that has even an inkling as to the majesty of the dinosaurs. We humans are the method planet Earth has chosen to remember them—not as dry, broken bones in a museum basement, or weathering tracks on a desolate hillside, but as the vibrant, fascinating groups of wildlife they once were.

APPENDIX ONE

CREATING THE ART

Science and History Rendered in Oil Paintings

What were dinosaurs really like? Since the early part of the 19th century, that simple question has generated as much curiosity as any mystery in science. Almost from the moment dinosaurs were discovered, the matter of what these incredible animals looked like and how they lived their lives has provided a source of endless speculation, not only for scientists but for the general public as well. Even today, with each new fossil discovery, as more is known about dinosaurs than ever before, the reality of what they really were remains an enigma.

It was with this combination of curiosity and frustration at the lack of hard facts that the artwork in this book was undertaken.

The evolution, as it were, of dinosaur illustration in many ways parallels the science of dinosaur paleontology. To begin with, for animals as old as they are, dinosaurs are a relatively new phenomenon. When the eminent British scientist Richard Owen coined the term *Dinosaur* in 1841, the only fossil remains known at the time were fragmentary and did not allow a complete picture of what the animals were really like. It must be remembered that we today are fortunate, in that we can go to a museum or open a book and see what dinosaurs are to believed to have looked like. Several hundred years ago, people noticed that the earth had stories to tell. For instance, Leonardo Da Vinci observed the fossils of seashells in rocks in Italy and had surmised that the mountains containing them had once been under water.

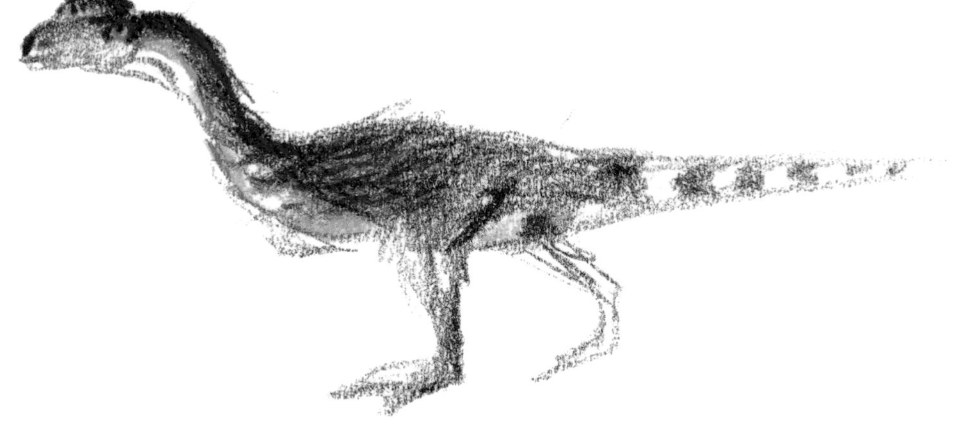

As with all the paintings in this book, *Dilophosaurus* "evolved" from a process of rough sketches. Once a design was chosen, rough color sketches were done; then, finally, the finished painting. The look of the animal is a simple countershaded pattern, combined with references from several species of hornbill for the head.

169

But in the early and mid-19th century, even the basic idea of what a dinosaur was, or how it looked, was only beginning to form in the minds of the people. There was no frame of reference to draw upon, and so the restorations that were done at the time reflected this. The only animals that influenced early attempts at restoring dinosaurs were the animals alive at the time, and so the first images of dinosaurs resembled huge frogs, huge kangaroos, huge lizards, and so forth. In retrospect, while these pictures had a charming naiveté, as it turned out, they were wildly off the mark. For instance, the first fossils of *Iguanodon* consisted of parts of the animal's jaw and teeth, which resembled the teeth of a living iguana, only much larger—hence the name given to the fossil, *Iguanodon*, or iguana tooth. The first attempts to illustrate *Iguanodon* looked like nothing more than a huge lizard. It wasn't until the latter part of the 1800s, when enough fairly complete fossil skeletons had been discovered, that a clear picture emerged of the kind of animal life that had once walked the earth. As a result, more accurate illustrations followed.

Then, a curious thing happened. Though for a while dinosaurs were thought of as active and dynamic creatures, by the time the 20th century had dawned, this view had begun to fall out of favor—interestingly enough, for no good reason. For a long time afterward, the prevailing scientific consensus was that dinosaurs were, at their best, little more than overgrown lizards. The disparaging term dinosaur, as in any person, place, or thing that has worn out its welcome, yet is too stupid to know that it already died out a long time ago, can trace its origins to this time. Dinosaurs were thought to be little more than evolutionary dead-ends, overgrown yet backward lizards that were more than deservedly succeeded by the smaller but smarter mammals. Much of the artwork of the time reflected this, portraying dinosaurs as mostly stuffed behemoths. Rare exceptions included the work of Charles Knight and Zdenek Burian.

It wasn't until the mid-1960s that a reevaluation began to take hold in dinosaur paleontology. Beginning with a second look at previous finds and leading to a whole new series of intriguing and provocative discoveries, a renaissance, as it has been called, emerged in the field. The result was an entirely new image of dinosaurs, even more complex than the original dynamic model. Dinosaurs are now seen as having been incredibly successful animals, active and alert wildlife with their own unique heightened metabolisms, and still living today in their last living line, birds. And all along the way, the illustrations that the fossils inspired have kept pace. It was within this context that the paintings for *In the Presence of Dinosaurs* were created.

More than anything, the goal for this book was to create a visual record of *live* animals—living wildlife in equally living ecosystems. It may belabor the obvious, but that simple reality is often lost sight of. Dinosaurs have grown to become such cultural icons, all the while breathing fire while they pilot ships through space, that it is easy to forget that once they were living animals and did all the things that living animals do today. The only slight drawback to illustrating these animals is that they are no longer alive. This is at once the most frustrating and at the same time the most fun aspect of bringing dinosaurs to life. The frustration lies in not having any living visual reference to draw upon. Birds remain an exception, but having descended from only one line of dinosaurs—small, carnivorous forms—it leaves every other group of dinosaurs having died out with no living descendants, and as such, no living models. So, in order to successfully bring dinosaurs to life, it requires the one part of dinosaur paleontology that is the most fun—imagination and speculation. This brings up a great dilemma in paleontology, and anyone who has chosen to be in the field has run up against it almost from the time they first started studying dinosaurs—where do you draw the line between science and speculation?

This stands as the great paradox of paleontology. In order to learn more about dinosaurs, you must do better science. But in its essence, science is a body of knowledge. And in order to increase your knowledge about something like dinosaurs, animals that are no longer living and are as such incapable of being observed, you must imagine and speculate. But once you have entered the realm of speculation, you have left the world of pure science. Where does one end and the other begin? Scientists have confronted this problem since dinosaurs were first discovered, and a rough consensus seems to have developed among them. There are some things that will never be known for sure, and many details concerning dinosaurs are at the top of that list. In a field given to constant change, as each new discovery transforms ideas, it remains the one single constant. The fun part about dinosaurs then is the speculation about how they looked and lived their lives. The fun that comes with speculating about dinosaurs often serves to compensate for the lack of knowledge about these animals, the reality about them that is the most frustrating. Dale Russell, of North Carolina State University, maintains: "You probably have ten wrong ideas for every one that's worth anything, but sharing this with other people is just great stuff. I so enjoy that. It's sort of like little boys hatching a plot together. If you can get something going, that's interesting and fun. I think you should enjoy science as much as you can. You can't enjoy science alone. You have to share it."

In this book, the key to successfully creating a visual record of dinosaurs as living animals was to keep the speculation believable. All speculation must be grounded within believable dimensions to successfully pull it off. The paintings for *In the Presence of Dinosaurs* are the result of a number of influences and source material, all of which are used by most dinosaur illustrators to various degrees.

First and foremost are the actual fossils themselves. Nothing takes the place of personal observation when it comes to trying to get a sense of what dinosaurs may have been like. Even when it is not feasible to study a fossil hands on, just going to a museum that has dinosaurs in it is enough to begin to get a sense of what the animals might have been like. For many artists and paleontologists, visiting the American Museum of Natural History as youngsters, for instance, and standing under the *Tyrannosaurus* was enough to hook them for life. Even as adults, the fossil conveys a sense of reality that still must be experienced. Since the mid-1990s, when the Dinosaur Hall's renovation led to a new and more dynamic pose to what had already been a most formidable animal, to stand and look at the mount is essential to even begin to understand what this and other dinosaurs may have been like. The sheer size of the animal, the elegance and power of its form, all speak of an animal that even today, sixty-five million years after its death, commands respect. To even begin to hope to convey a sense of the animal in illustrative or sculptural form requires that, at the outset, the fossils must be experienced firsthand. Even when a fossil can't be examined firsthand by touch, a good sense of the animal can be had just by observation. There isn't a dinosaur illustrator working today who does not have an extensive collection of photos from every museum they have ever been in, of every dinosaur they have ever seen, from every pose they were able to take. Even those times when a camera was not available, a sketchbook often did the trick and, many times, helped complement whatever photos were taken. Many of the paintings in this book had their inception as museum photos and sketches.

The wonderful proportions of *Sharovipteryx*, coupled with its webbing, provided an opportunity for a painting where the shape of the animal itself became the central design focus. The cardboard cutout was used as a tool for compositional purposes, but the basic design of this painting literally dictated itself. The positioning on the branch offered not only a visual balance to the animal, but a chance to introduce translucency as an additional theme.

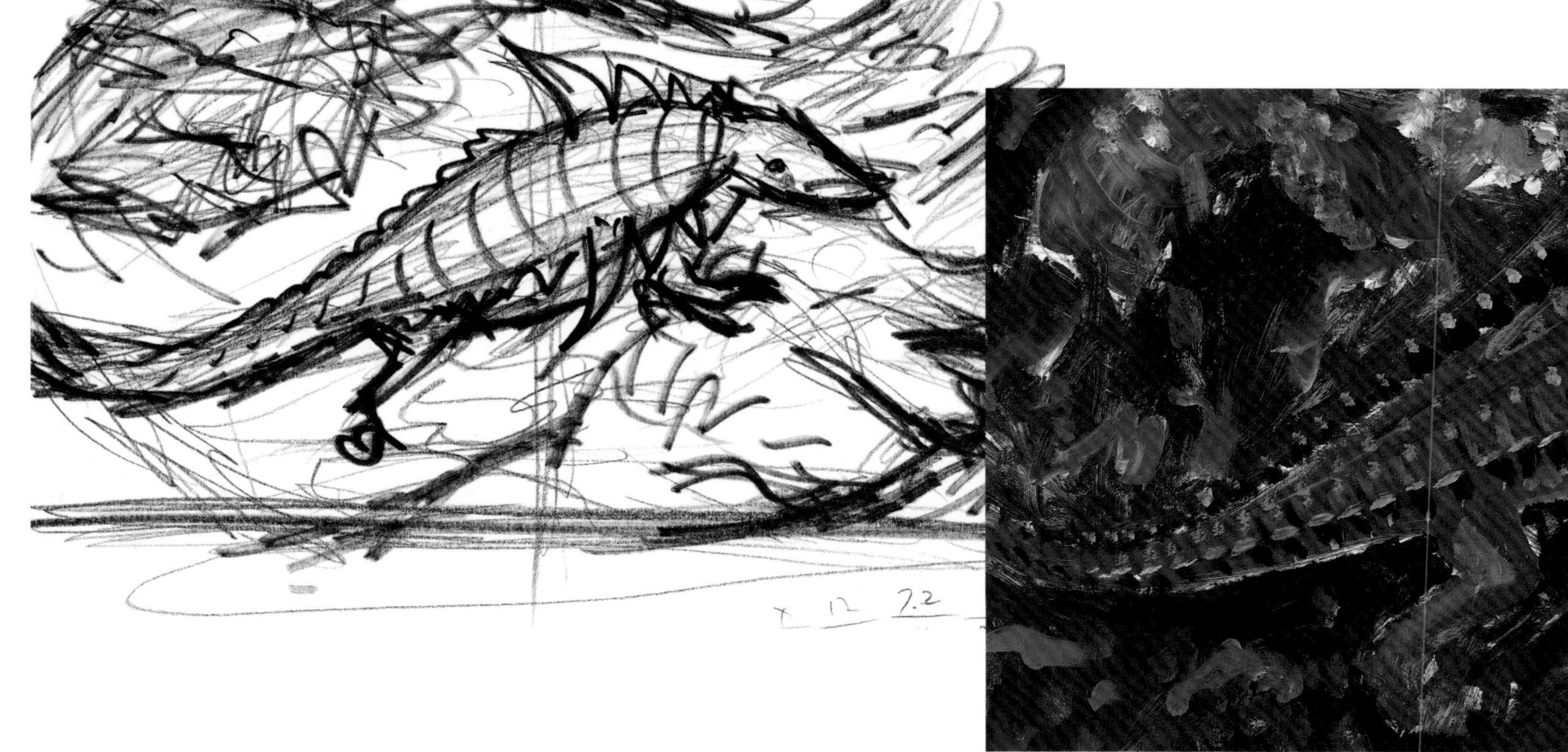

Often, as many as forty to fifty different reference sources provided the information that was used to create a single painting. For the final painting of *Desmatosuchus*, photo sources for foliage, plowed dirt, leaf litter, and the animal itself all came from different areas. The animal represents a combination of influences, ranging from several species of turtle, lizards, and crocodilians. Scale patterns, the texture of armor, and the subtleties present in keratin were all factors in the look of the animal.

An equally important source for information about dinosaur fossils are technical papers. When a new fossil is found, whether it is a new animal, or an important specimen of an already known species, the scientist heading the team in charge of its recovery publishes his or her findings in a paleontological journal, or an established science publication. Often, technical papers are the only accurate source materials for people in the field who could never have even observational access to the fossil, because of distance or the scarcity or paucity of the remains. For instance, Chris Bennett's extensive study of the large pterosaur *Pteranodon* is an invaluable resource for anyone seeking to illustrate this magnificent animal. One of his papers, in the December 1992 edition of the *Journal of Vertebrate Paleontology*, for instance, relays a detailed account of the animal's lifestyle, providing strong evidence for picturing this pterosaur as a species with wide variation between the sexes in size, the shape and size of its crest, numbers, and behavior. Any attempt to visualize and illustrate the lifestyle of this winged giant could not seriously succeed without a paper such as this.

That being said, reading a technical paper about a dinosaur fossil is to redefine the word tedious. Sitting down with one, a cup of coffee in one hand and a glossary of paleontological terminology in the other, brings new meaning to the experience of having one's eyes glaze over. No technical paper will ever break the *New York Times* Bestseller's List. But they are an essential tool in successfully rendering dinosaurs, and a little homework time spent reading a paper goes a long way in learning about these animals and especially about painting them.

The single most important quality to painting dinosaurs successfully, and the one common thread that runs through all of this, is observation. Nothing takes the place of a keen and intensely curious eye. The only difference throughout all of this is the source material the person uses. Many people have an image of artists and illustrators wildly thrashing at a canvas, all the while dripping paint on the floor. But the reality, at least for many artists and illustrators who work in a realistic style, is a lot more mundane. Most artists have an extensive library and filing system of source material, including books, magazine clippings, and photos. Much of the time that goes into completing a work consists of looking through this source material, laying it out in some sort of organized fashion to be able to be used without creating

too much of a cluttered workspace, and putting sticky notes on pages of books and magazines, all the while hoping there wasn't an important picture that you could be using that you have just forgotten about.

We are lucky enough today to be living in a world of color photography, where an intrepid group of wildlife, nature, and landscape photographers trek to all corners of the world to capture on film shots and scenes that most of us will never be able to experience in our lives. Bless them all, for they make the work of illustrating dinosaurs that much easier. Nothing takes the place of personal observation, whether the subject is wildlife or landscape, but the next best thing is to have a good photo of the thing that you can't experience yourself. Photo essay books, nature books, wildlife books, nature and natural history magazines—all make the rounds as sources of scenery and wild animal photos.

Among the photographers whose work inspired the work in this book are Art Wolfe, Thomas Mangelsen, David Muench, Marc Muench, Carr Clifton, Frans Lanting, Fred Hirschmann, and Pat O'Hara. They and many other talented photographers serve to create work that many illustrators can learn from, not to copy from but as an instructional tool. Studying the approach of a good photographer to his or her chosen subject can impart a wealth of information to any illustrator, even one whose subjects have been dead for one hundred million years.

Part of the goal of this book was to create an artistic rendering of dinosaurs that was the closest thing to a photographic record that had yet been done. Whether an animal or a tree is living today or died eighty million years ago, scales still photograph a certain way, hair still photographs a certain way, skin still photographs a certain way, and green leaves, blue skies and white clouds still photograph a certain way. When painting dinosaurs in a realistic style, once the correct anatomy is achieved, good photos of wildlife and landscapes provide an invaluable tool in getting information about how to best paint these other elements.

In addition to wildlife and landscape photos, videos with these are just as valuable. This is especially so in studying animal behavior and the interactions of animals in their environment. This is also one thing that studying dinosaur fossils cannot impart. A skeleton can give a wealth of information, but nothing beats watching living animals, in real life or on camera. For instance, the skull of an African lion and an Asian tiger are virtually identical. Even experts at times have trouble telling them apart, Yet, the lion and tiger are very different animals. They differ in appearance, habitat, and in their social habits. Anyone studying only the skeletons of these animals would probably miss all of this. This is also a big problem in studying dinosaurs —we missed observing them by sixty-five million years. But, some pretty good inferences can be made about dinosaurs by watching living animals. For instance, birds, the last dinosaurs, are invaluable as a reference for imagining the movements and behavior of theropods and small bipedal herbivorous dinosaurs.

Anyone who has ever watched an emu or a ground hornbill in a zoo will know what this is about. Each animal moves with its own particular grace and presence and with an instinctively keen sense of its own body. It is aware of its surroundings and of the animals it shares its environs with. This points up an important aspect of illustrating animals such as dinosaurs.

For a long time, bad art became the accepted standard by which most people got to know dinosaurs, so much so that it became easy to forget that these were once living animals. Though it is true that dinosaurs have been extinct for a long time, just because an animal has been dead for eighty million years, it doesn't mean that it has to be portrayed or painted without the same care and attention an animal living today would be rendered. This was an essential consideration in the creation of the paintings for this book. It is something that goes beyond just getting the correct color, outline, habitat, and activity that the animal exhibits. All wild animals have an unconscious sense of themselves that transcends the sum of their parts, their bones, muscles, etc. There is an added dimension there, the spark that comes with just being alive. And the only way to try and capture that something extra is to spend a lot of time observing living animals.

Every artist has a different approach to their craft, which is the product of their habits and the inherent realities of their subject matter. For instance, some artists find it necessary to produce intricate, highly detailed preliminary sketches in both black and white and color, before they attempt the final work. Others require no more than rough line drawings, and color studies, preferring to save the detail for the end.

Another area of reference material is the work of other illustrators. Dinosaur illustration is a very small field, with perhaps at most two hundred people worldwide who work at it for a living. In perhaps no other science does the art have as strong an influence on the subject at hand. This is true for the people outside the field, as art is the only way possible for people to connect with a sense of what the animals were like, other than museum mounts. But it is also true for the artists in the field. For many, it was the work of other artists who first got them into the field. And still, it is the work of now fellow artists that continues to attract notice. For many illustrators, there are still many things that can be learned (and avoided) by studying the approach that other illustrators have taken with their subjects.

The paintings in this book were all done with oil paint on gessoed Masonite. Masonite is a particularly good surface for highly detailed work. First of all, it is almost glass-smooth. This eliminates the painting surface as a possible visual distraction, as sometimes happens with canvas, for instance. Also, fine detail can at times get lost in the weave of the canvas. Both of these are no longer considerations when working on Masonite—the only visual element present is the image itself.

In addition, Masonite is a very forgiving and easy surface to paint on, especially with oil paint. It creates a firm resistance to a paint-loaded brush, and various techniques can be had just by the right touch. For instance, the *Tyrannosaurus* sniffing the carrion in Chapter 7 has between fifty thousand and fifty-five thousand scales that were painted on the animal. Each is outlined and has its own shadows and highlight. This would have been a lot more difficult to paint had not the surface of the Masonite created its own scale-like texture just by a quick touch of a wide brush that had a little paint on it. Instead of deliberately painting each scale, the brush created a hundred small scales at a time, which were just accented and fine-tuned. Finely detailed areas on the paintings were done with the help of a magnifying glass. The most common theme running through the paintings is the interplay between light and dark. Light, as an element of design, not only conveys information but mood, temperature, and a basic feel that lends an added dimension to the portrayal of any animal life, both in photography and painting.

A common question that is asked about the illustration of any animal life that is extinct is often "How do you know what color to make it?" The short answer is, you don't. But when the subject lends itself to being solved only by speculation, again, the speculation should be at least believable.

Because of the large amount of fossils that have come to light over the years, many dinosaurs can be restored with a considerable amount of confidence. For some, especially many of the duckbills, there are fossil bones, muscles, connective tissue, and skin. So, for many of these animals, a reasonable effort can be made to reconstruct them. But, the only element missing is color. There are some dinosaurs that sport patterns on their skin, of larger and smaller scales woven together, where color patterns can be inferred. But no one knows for sure.

Again, it's an area of dinosaur paleontology that enters the realm of speculation, and again, the goal for this book was to keep speculation as believable as possible. Animals living today throughout the world sport a riot of different colors and patterns to them. Often, certain groups of animals zero in on common themes. For example, many of the big cats are arrayed in various versions of spots or stripes. The gulls, on the other hand, have gravitated toward white, gray, and black, in various proportions.

But whatever color and pattern they happen to have, there is a consistency of believability to how an animal is adorned. Often, color patterns are countershaded, where a darker

color covers the top half of the animal, and a lighter color can be found on the bottom half. The point of this is to try and render the animal as inconspicuous as possible, as light will lighten the darker top, and shadows will darken the lighter bottom, making them, in effect, blend together. Often, natural selection will favor a camouflage pattern that blends in quite nicely to the surrounding landscape, as polar bears do in the far north. Regardless, though, for the most part, animals look like they *belong* where they live.

This same sense of believability should also apply when rendering animal life of the past. Dinosaurs do not all have to be one color. Even today, on the plains of Africa, large mammals, which are for the most part color blind, exhibit a wide variety of colors and patterns. Dinosaurs, which almost certainly had color vision, like their avian descendants, no doubt were arrayed in colors and patterns at the very least the equal of mammals today. But, these colors and patterns should at least have a sense of believability. True, who can really say, but if the goal is to try and convey the greatest sense of life to animals no longer living, these animals should be portrayed with colors and patterns that reflect their habitat, making them look like they at least fit into where they are being placed. For instance, the color pattern on the lam-

OPPOSITE

Landscapes are very important in this book. Not only do they provide a frame of reference for the animals that populated them, they convey a *feel* for the environments. Plants and animals can no more do without the proper ecosystem and landscape than a train can do without tracks. In fact, it is impossible to fully understand dinosaurs without the proper backdrop—the environment in which they were found.

beosaurine *Parasaurolophus* in Chapter 6 is the result of several lines of thought. *Parasaurolophus* was a thirty- to thirty-five-foot-long duckbill of the Late Cretaceous Period. Among the duckbills, there were two basic types of animals. One group, the hadrosaurines, had very wide muzzles and no crests. The other group, the lambeosaurines, had narrow muzzles and elaborate crests. *Parasaurolophus* was one of this latter group.

Among large herbivorous animals today, such as the antelope, there are differences among the animals of the woodlands and the open savannas. Animals that tend to more open areas travel in large herds, have little differences in appearance between the sexes, and have shorter horns and wider muzzles, like wildebeests. Animals of the woodlands, on the other hand, travel in smaller social units, where differences in the sexes are pronounced. They have narrower muzzles and longer horns in the males.

Parasaurolophus fits nicely into this latter description. The color pattern on the animal was based on several sources. First of all, the crest on the male was the largest to evolve on any dinosaur. The color of the crest was based on the cedar waxwing, a handsome crested bird of North America (and also a distant relative). The countershaded tan, white, and black of the animal's body was based on several antelope of wooded areas of Africa. But, because the animal is considerably larger than the antelope of today, a further element was added to help break up the animal's body outline—the narrow, white vertical lines along the animal's dorsal, or top, half.

As in many antelope of the woodlands, female lambeosaurines were different from the males. As a result, the color pattern given to them is different. It is more muted, with a much less ornate pattern on their considerably smaller crest. But one added feature is a pronounced eye ring, and also a white ring around the animal's bill. This was to serve as an imprinting device, to help newly hatched young imprint on the female. Many birds today sport such marks, and it is reasonable (and believable) to think that some animal life of the past had them as well. The bird analogy holds up well with respect to many dinosaurs. Until very recently, putting any feathers on small dinosaurs was frowned upon by many in the field as being too speculative and bordering on fantasy. But there were always very valid arguments that birds evolved from dinosaurs, and so, even as a matter of speculation, putting feathers on small dinosaurs was a reasonable choice. Dinosaur illustrator Gregory Paul used to make a strong case that, on an animal that does not have any fossilized skin remains, any covering that is put on the animal, be it skin, scales, or feathers, is speculation, so choosing to cover a small dinosaur with feathers was as valid a choice as covering it with scales.

Now, with the discovery of several fully feathered dinosaurs from China, the matter has been put to rest. As a matter of fact, at least a half-dozen small dinosaurs are now known to have been covered in feathers. Interestingly enough, several of these fossils show patterns on the feathers almost exactly like the patterns that can be found on many birds today. So, when contemporary models are sought as possible references for coloring dinosaurs, many animals living today are quite reasonable choices.

In the end, there will always be more questions about dinosaurs than answers, especially in trying to illustrate them. People will always believe and see what they want to believe and see, and not be confused or swayed by something as trivial as the facts. But, even in a field with as much subjectivity as dinosaurs, some decent guesses and inferences can still be made about how these incredible animals went about living their lives. Studying fossils, observing living animals, learning from the work of others, in science and art—all are important in bringing dinosaurs back to life. Oh, and one more thing—a good coffeepot.

APPENDIX TWO

ABOUT THE NARRATIVE

The text for *In the Presence of Dinosaurs* is constructed from evidence preserved in the fossil record. In addition to the bones we see reassembled in natural history museums, fossils also include footprints, foliage impressions, insects trapped in amber, and fallen trees that are now petrified logs. There are eggs in nests, internal organs, dung, all millions of years old. Under closer examination, the condition in which these fossils are found also tells a story, as when bones show evidence of combat injuries or disease, leaves of certain plants are found telling us about diet, and skeletons are found at one site suggesting that an animal traveled in herds.

Still, paleontologists and paleobotanists—and authors—are faced with the dilemma of where pure science stops and speculation starts. We are fortunate to be living in a "Golden Age" of paleontology, as the pace of discoveries continues to accelerate, and the variety and quality of the finds fill in substantial gaps of information, reducing the amount of speculation necessary. How those finds are analyzed has improved dramatically since the 19th century, when filling museums with immense skeletons was the focus, not gaining an understanding of the environment where the bones were unearthed, or carefully considering every fragment of information. Technology has changed, too, so scientists are now in a position to more precisely date and dissect fossils, without damaging them, which earlier scientists with their picks and brushes could not hope to do.

The narrative has been related in a positive tone, avoiding terms such as "probably" or "possibly" as they alter the sense of being immersed in the scene. Whenever possible the proper scientific terminology has been employed when referring to animals, because many have no modern counterparts or close, living relatives. With plants, however, wherever possible their common names, or names of closely related, more familiar, modern forms have been used. Each ecosystem is based on the fossils and other geological evidence collected from a particular area, and represents an accurate description, with certain embellishments added only to round out the scene or improve readability. Here are a few examples of how scenarios in our modern world have been woven into the text.

CHAPTER 2: VEILED WOODLANDS

This chapter is based on data from the Petrified Forest National Park and adjacent Painted Desert in north central Arizona, both of the Late Triassic Period. What existed there was very much like a modern rain forest habitat cut through by wide, sluggish rivers. Within this ecosystem dwelt a variety of wildlife including reptilian herbivores and predators. The dinosaurs, both literally and figuratively, played a very small part.

Phytosaur feeding and overall behavior are based on those of modern crocodilians. Other descriptions, such as metoposaur hunting and aetosaur feeding strategies were arrived at by determining which method would best be accomplished by each animal's particular adaptations and physical appearance. Rauisuchid behavior is based loosely on that of the large monitor lizards; that of *Icarasaurus*, on the gliding lizard *Draco*. Since there are plenty of small, nocturnal, insectivorous mammals around today, the speculation on the behavior of their Late Triassic relatives is straightforward.

CHAPTER 3: RIFT VALLEY

Evidence for the rifting that rent Pangaea occurs within the rocks of the Newark Series, which are exposed from Nova Scotia, down the east coast of North America, to North Carolina. Here are the tilted red sandstones, lava flows, numerous footprints, and less numerous bones that combined to provide the raw data for the ecosystem. The presence of the soda lakes are indicated by the mineralogy of the basaltic flows and inferred by their presence in the rift valleys of east Africa. The wet and dry cycles have been worked out by a close examination of the rocks, and brush fires were inferred as a natural consequence of prolonged periods of drought. These rocks sit right on the Triassic-Jurassic boundary and record the disappearance of many animals and the increased diversification of the dinosaurs in the wake of their extinction. The success of the dinosaurs is due, in part, to the void left by the extinctions which closed the Triassic, and in part to their bipedal habit, that aided in food gathering and manipulation, their metabolism, which allowed them to remain active, and their ability to survive extended dry seasons, excrete little water in their urine, and produce eggs with fatty yolks, two features lacking in many reptiles, but present in the theropods called birds. The lifestyles and coloration of the many species of *Semionotus* were modeled after the many species of cichlids, fish that are native to east Africa today.

The problems encountered when a carnivorous animal switches over to a diet of plants are many. Pandas have overcome many of them and served as a loose model for the feeding behaviors of prosauropods. Remains of these dinosaurs have been found in mass burials in Germany that indicate a probable herding behavior such as described here.

The prominent head crests of *Dilophosaurus* could only have been for display, and their delicate nature indicates that actual physical contact among the displaying animals had to be minimalized, lest the crests be damaged. Except for locally abundant fish remains, larger bony fossils are uncommon in the Newark Series. So, although actual skeletal material of dilophosaurs has not yet been unearthed, numerous three-toed footprints and trackways, of a size and shape comparable to ones they might have produced have been found, so their presence in this environment is not unlikely.

CHAPTER 4: PLAINS DOMINION

Although widespread throughout much of western America, the sediments of the Morrison Plain are not very thick. Still, it provides a glimpse of a vast, savanna-type environment, dotted with wooded and scrubby areas, especially near permanent water. That sauropod dinosaurs lived here is a fact. What they ate while here is a question that begs to be answered because the plant cover was sparse in many areas; locally dense only near permanent water. For this reason, they are depicted as seasonal visitors moving in response to the plants, which in turn are responding to the weather. The sensations of being near animals this size can only be extrapolated from those of being near any large animal such as an elephant. Their use and fastidious selection of gastroliths, the pebbles they would swallow to help them break down food, is well documented in the fossil record. Skeletal features determine the extent to which each kind could move its neck and rear up on its hind legs, and these led to the speculations concerning their feeding habits and styles. Ingesting clay, salts, and other minerals is common enough among other animals to be included as part of sauropod diet, as is the propensity for a nice relaxing mud bath. Ectoparasites, flaking skin, and overheating are, and undoubtedly were, problems for many large animals, so a behavior such as this is almost a given. Egg clutches have been discovered worldwide, and the arrangement of the eggs within them gives a fair indication of how they were laid.

Opinions as to the function and arrangement of stegosaur plates are as numerous and varied as the scientists who hold them. Display seems to be their primary function, both within their own species and with other species as well. The presence of the bony scutes evidently embedded in the skin of their necks could not, in any way, stop a predator's teeth, but required an explanation all the same. Cycad cones and seeds are not widely eaten today. These tiny bone plates seem to be just the trick needed for a stegosaur to get at them and avoid the serious consequences of a cycad's prickly leaftips. Their general territorial behavior and solitary lifestyle have been modeled after African rhinos.

Camptosaurs, dryosaurs, and othnielians have been cast as close approximations of the elands, kudus, and Thomson's gazelles that inhabit similar environments today. The association of *Dryosaurus* with sauropods is documented by the fossil record, but their exact relationship is speculation.

Ceratosaur fossils are not common and are found as isolated individuals, so a solitary lifestyle seems reasonable, just as the form and arrangement of their teeth and claws indicate the type of vicious attack described. Their feeding behavior is reminiscent of many modern carnivores. The tendency for allosaur remains to occur in clusters indicates a group behavior for these animals, more like that of ravens, who simply follow the lead of one animal in the group, usually the biggest and/or boldest rather than the much more complicated and intricate relationships and hunting techniques associated with animals such as wolves. The behavior of these animals and their prey during and just after an attack is one typical of the wildlife inhabiting the veld of east Africa today. Although conjectural, something like carcass etiquette is necessary for many different animals such as allosaurs, ornitholestians, and coelurans to all feed at the same carcass without someone getting seriously injured or killed. The behaviors and interrelationships described here are based on those of lions, hyenas, wild dogs, jackals, and vultures when they meet at a kill site.

The size and kinds of Jurassic mammals were determined by their fossils, their particular diets inferred from their teeth, and their nocturnal habits inferred from living a world dominated by large predators. The details of the first few minutes of the life of a baby pantothere are based on those of modern marsupials such as kangaroos, and their fecundity on those of opossums.

CHAPTER 5: WANDERING SHORES

The extensive Cretaceous chalk deposits that underlie so much of the central portions of North America provide both the geological and biological evidence for the existence of the vast Niobrara Sea and its amazing inhabitants. Elasmosaur diet is evident in the structure of their teeth and jaws, while their unique style of fishing is suggested by the form of their incredible necks. Nesting on land is inferred by their overall shape, size, and assumed strength of their paddles. Their behavior on land, and that of their hatchlings, is modeled after sea turtles.

Although no *Hesperornis* nests are known, they were birds and therefore laid eggs in some sort of nest. The exact shape, size, and composition of these nests, as stated here, are totally conjectural. Their general courtship and various nesting behaviors are an amalgam of those of various seabirds, and their fishing techniques, buoyancy, and ability to alter the shape of their eye lenses are based on surface diving seabirds such as cormorants. The description of their rookeries, and those of the pteranodons, are based on those of the albatross, pelicans, penguins and other large seagoing birds. Frigate birds regularly harass other seabirds into relinquishing their catches and provided a role for *Ichthyornis* as a result. Ever-present, scavenging gulls provided an additional pattern, not only for *Ichthyornis* but for *Nyctosaurus* as well.

The large head crests of pteranodons have been assigned as sexual display features. The fossil evidence indicates that there were two distinct crest sizes among the most common species of *Pteranodon*, which can be explained as sexual dimorphism and has been treated as such. Thermals are used by many types of modern birds when they soar, so were put to use here for the pteranodons. Contests among males for nesting sites, displaying and calling to establish and reinforce pair bonds, and preening are all common behaviors among birds of many kinds and have been liberally used here to give a picture of what it might have been like. The flying, fishing, nesting, and child-rearing aspects of pteranodon life were borrowed from those of pelicans and the albatross.

Using a "function follows form" guide, the swimming and feeding techniques for tylosaurs were deduced by combining a mixture of dolphin and shark behaviors. Their diet of coiled cephalopod and sea turtle is evident in the numerous cephalopod shells with neat rows of holes that correspond nicely with mosasaur tooth arrangement, and the occasional sea turtle skeleton complete, save for a missing paddle.

Although a contemporary image of seabirds is their establishing rookeries on rugged volcanic islands and cliff sites, neither are warranted here because there is no geological basis for them. The sediments are almost entirely of chalk. Barrier islands are, or at least until very recently were, used extensively by many kinds of wildlife for nesting because of the isolation and relative safety they afforded. Their tenuous and temporary nature, and subsequent vulnerability to powerful storms, is legendary and seemed a fitting end for them.

CHAPTER 6: CORRIDOR

Wildlife migrations seem such a fact of modern wildlife that its early beginnings are often taken for granted, or not considered at all. Up until the advent of dinosaurs with the metabolisms necessary for prolonged physical exertions, no other terrestrial animal had the stamina, let alone the ambition, to undertake such monumental journeys no matter what advantages these journeys had to offer. The paleogeography of the subcontinent of West America during the Late Cretaceous was ideally suited to migrations of the scope and magnitude described. The species of dinosaurs preserved in the rock sequences of what is known as the Judith River Wedge, which occurs throughout the western interior of the United States and extends some distance into southern Canada, provided a host of possible and probable migrants.

Starting with the sauropods in the Jurassic, dinosaur movements in response to seasonal changes culminated in the Late Cretaceous with the extended migrations of many of the hadrosaurines and the practically continuous migrations of many ceratopsids, who raised migration from a seasonal event to a lifestyle. The tension that builds among modern animals about to begin their migrations, such as their increased vocalizations that occur with migratory waterfowl before they begin their mass journey, and its apparent release once on the move, served as the model for the scenes and behaviors described here.

The accounts of ceratopsids and hadrosaurines congregating in vast herds have been deduced from the occurrence of layers of bones composed of a single species, and which cover many square miles. That the large herds indicated by these fossil deposits might stay in one place for any length of time is just not plausible. In addition, the occurrence of numerous nests close by each other, and piled on top of each other, layer upon layer, indicate that, at least for some of the hadrosaurines, communal nesting was employed, and that the animals were returning to these sites year after year. Migration seems to be the only explanation for these two facts.

Parasaurolophus behavior at a lek was modeled after that of prairie chickens, while their fixation on a boldly patterned signaling device while on the move is based on that of modern antelopes such as waterbucks. The interactions between female and young parasaurolophans such as imprinting are very similar to those of many kinds of birds, and the concept of feeding their young crop milk was borrowed from the behavior of pigeons, and used as an explanation for the extraordinary growth rates demonstrated by young hadrosaurines as documented in the fossil record.

The fossil record has preserved evidence of feathers in some types of theropod dinosaurs. Their existence in other types is a matter of conjecture, but smaller dinosaurs such as hysilophodontids and newly hatched hadrosaurids would stand to benefit greatly by their presence, so they have been included here. Fossil evidence also exists which indicates that some dinosaurs actually brooded their nests, so that behavior has been extended to some smaller, feathered dinosaurs such as hypsilophodontids.

Among modern antelopes, those which show little sexual dimorphism live and feed in more open environments, so this type of lifestyle was described for the hadrosaurids whose males and females also look alike. On the other hand, differences between the sexes are more noticeable among those antelopes that live and feed in more wooded areas, so this behavior seemed best suited to the lambeosaurines. The brighter colors and more striking appearance of lambeosaurines offered the advantage of being quickly noticeable to the opposite sex and resulted in a favorably adaptive trait because their narrow muzzles demanded more time devoted to feeding at the expense of other pursuits such as courtship.

Among modern hoofed mammals, like the wildebeest and zebra, horns and antlers are used for display, intimidation, defense, offense, and species identification. The presence of these same structures on ceratopsids is a strong indication of a similar function in them too. Ceratopsid skeletons with fractured forelimbs are known from the fossil record. The rearing up and dropping down of excited males during the rut is inferred from this fact.

During the migrations that occur in Africa each year, the animals invariably proceed in a definite order based on the feeding behavior and ability to tackle the food available to them. Leading are the zebras, followed by the wildebeests, and finally the gazelles. By the same token, and based on the physical attributes and inferred feeding habits of each type of migratory dinosaur, the sequence of ceratopsid, followed by hadrosaurine, and then lambeosaurine has been described, with the addition of requisite camp followers.

CHAPTER 7: GLENS OF HELL CREEK

Located in Montana and the Dakotas, the Hell Creek Formation is the uppermost layer of rock, and therefore the most recent, of the Cretaceous Period. The bones and other fossils preserved within its sandstones, siltstones, and mudstones literally represent the last chapter of the so-called "Age of the Dinosaurs." The plains represented by the rock layers of Hell Creek were repeatedly flooded by the Niobrara Sea as it valiantly, if unsuccessfully, tried to maintain its hold on central North America. And, for North America, this was the end of an era both biologically and geologically.

The discovery of skeletons of tyrannosaurs found together suggest a pack, or some sort of group behavior. Injuries inflicted on tyrannosaurs by tyrannosaurs provide evidence that indicates that serious altercations occurred, even if infrequently, giving rise to the pack hierarchy and behavior described. Modern predators such as lions and hyenas regularly hunt by moonlight, so it does not seem to be too much of a stretch to have tyrannosaurs do the same. The changes that occur in tyrannosaur skulls as they mature is well documented in the fossil record, and the differences in feeding styles are a logical extension of these changes.

Although no bone beds have been discovered for any chasmosaurines as yet, *Triceratops* are still described as living in family groups within herds, albeit the herds are of a much smaller size than those of centrosaurines. The structure and overall behavior of the family clans are patterned after those of elephants. The close association of these animals and their resident tick bird entourages were modeled after those of animals today such as the giraffe and rhinoceros. The horns of chasmosaurines, such as *Triceratops* and *Torosaurus* would only be effective against attack from a pack of tyrannosaurs if there were many individuals around. Because horns can appear foreshortened when their owner is facing directly at its opponent, the modern oryx has striking facial coloration that-sends the message that a head equipped with potentially dangerous weapons has been turned in your direction. The same function is assigned to the distinctively patterned head frills of the ceratopsids. The reactions of a group of ceratopsids confronted by a pack of tyrannosaurs is much the same as the way Cape buffalo and baboons would react to a similar threat.

SELECTED BIBLIOGRAPHY

Books and Articles

Andrews, H. N. *Studies in Paleontology.* New York: Wiley, 1961.

Ash, S. "Fossil Plants and the Triassic-Jurassic Boundary." In *The Beginning of the Age of Dinosaurs,* edited by K. Padian. New York: Cambridge, 1986.

Attenborough, D. *Life on Earth.* Boston: Little, Brown, 1979.

Bakker, R. T. "The Return of the Dancing Dinosaurs." In *Dinosaurs Past and Present,* edited by S. J. Czerkas and E. C. Olson. Vol. 1. Seattle: University of Washington Press, 1987.

Basinger, J. F. "Mesozoic Floras." In *Encyclopedia of Dinosaurs,* edited by P. J. Currie and K. Padian. New York: Academic Press, 1997.

Baur, E. A. *Yellowstone.* Stillwater, Minn.: Voyageur, 1993.

Behrensmeyer, A. K., L. D. Damuth, W. A. DiMichele, R. Potts, H. D. Sues, and S. L. Wing. *Terrestrial Ecosystems Through Time.* Chicago: University of Chicago Press, 1992.

Benton, M. J. "Dinosaur Summer." In *The Book of Life,* edited by S. J. Gould. New York: Norton, 1993.

——. *The Reign of the Reptiles.* New York: Crescent, 1990.

——. *Vertebrate Paleontology.* London: Chapman & Hall, 1997.

Benyus, J. M. *Beastly Behaviors.* New York: Addison Wesley, 1992.

Bigelow, P. "Cretaceous: 'Hell Creek Facies': Late Maastrichtian." 1998. At Web site http://www.dinosauria.com/jdp/misc/hellcreek.html.

Britt, B. B., and B. G. Naylor. "An Embryonic *Cammarasaurus* from the Upper Jurassic Morrison Formation." In *Dinosaur Eggs and Babies,* edited by K. Carpenter, K. F. Hirsch and J. R. Horner. New York: Cambridge, 1994.

Brower, K. *American Legacy: Our National Forests.* Washington, D.C.: National Geographic, 1997.

Carpenter, K., and J. McIntosh. "Upper Jurassic Sauropod Babies from the Morrison Formation." In *Dinosaur Eggs and Babies,* edited by K. Carpenter, K. F. Hirsch, and J. R. Horner. New York: Cambridge, 1994.

Carr, T. D. "Cranial Facial Ontogeny in Tyrannosauridae." *Journal of Vertebrate Paleontology,* 19: 3 (September 14, 1999).

Carrol, R. L. *Vertebrate Paleontology and Evolution.* New York: Freeman, 1988.

Chadwick, D. *The Kingdom: Wildlife in North America.* San Francisco: Sierra Club, 1990.

Cohen, S. A. *Bird Nests.* San Francisco: Collins, 1993.

Colbert, E. H. *The Triassic Dinosaur Coelophysis.* Bulletin Series 57. Flagstaff: Museum of Northern Arizona Press, 1989.

Cousin, R., G. Breton, R. Fournier, and J. P. Watte. "Dinosaur Egglaying and Nesting in France." In *Dinosaur Eggs and Babies,* edited by K. Carpenter, K. F. Hirsch, and J. R. Horner. New York: Cambridge, 1994.

Crompton, A. W., and J. Attridge. "Masticatory Apparatus of the Larger Herbivores During Late Triassic and Early Jurassic Time." In *The Beginning of the Age of Dinosaurs,* edited by K. Padian. New York: Cambridge, 1986.

Currie, P. J. *The Flying Dinosaurs.* Alberta, Canada: Red Deer College Press, 1991.

——. "Migrating Dinosaurs." In *The Ultimate Dinosaur,* edited by B. Preiss and R. Silverberg. New York: Bantam, 1992.

——. "New Approaches to Studying Dinosaurs in Dinosaur Provincial Park." In *Dinosaurs Past and Present,* edited by S. J. Czerkas and E. C. Olson. Vol. 2. Seattle: University of Washington Press, 1987.

——. "Theropoda." In *Encyclopedia of Dinosaurs,* edited by P. J. Currie and K. Padian. New York: Academic Press, 1997.

Czerkas, S. A., and S. J. Czerkas. *Dinosaurs: A Global View.* New York: Mallard Press, 1991.

Daws, G., and S. M. Gon. *Hawaii: The Island of Life.* Honolulu: Signature, 1988.

Diamond, J. "Eat Dirt." *Discover* (February 1998).

Dixon, D. *The Illustrated Dinosaur Encyclopedia.* New York: Gallery, 1988.

Dodson, P. *The Horned Dinosaurs.* Princeton, N.J.: Princeton University Press, 1996.

Dodson, P., ed. *Encyclopedia of Dinosaurs.* Lincolnwood, Ill.: Publications International, 1990.

Dott, R. H., and R. L. Batten. *Evolution of the Earth.* 4th ed. New York: McGraw-Hill.

Droscher, V. B. *The Friendly Beast.* New York: Dutton, 1971.

Eberth, D. A. "Judith River Wedge." In *Encyclopedia of Dinosaurs,* edited by P. J. Currie and K. Padian. New York: Academic Press, 1997.

Ehrlich, P. R., D. S. Dobkin, and D. Wheye. *The Birder's Handbook.* New York: Simon & Schuster, 1988.

Ethridge, F. G. "Paleoecology of the Morrison Formation." Personal Communication, 1988.

Fatovsky, D. E., and D. B. Weishampel. *The Evolution and Extinction of the Dinosaurs.* New York: Cambridge, 1996.

Fitzharris, T. *The Audubon Society Guide to Nature Photography.* Boston: Little, Brown, 1990.

——. *Wild Wings.* Minocqua, Wis.: NorthWord, 1992.

Forster, C. A. "Hadrosauridae." In *Encyclopedia of Dinosaurs*, edited by P. J. Currie and K. Padian. New York: Academic, 1997.

Forster, C. A., and P. C. Sereno. "Maginocephalians." In *The Complete Dinosaur,* edited by J. O. Farlow and M. K. Brett-Surman. Bloomington: Indiana University Press, 1997.

Gallagher, W. B. "Becoming a Modern World." In *The Ultimate Dinosaur,* edited by B. Preiss and R. Silverberg. New York: Bantam, 1992.

Galton, P. "Herbivorous Adaptations of Late Triassic and Early Jurassic Dinosaurs." In *The Beginning of the Age of Dinosaurs,* edited by K. Padian. New York: Cambridge, 1986.

Gardom, T., and A. Milner. *The Book of Dinosaurs: The Natural History Museum Guide.* Rocklin, Calif.: Prima Publishing, 1993.

Gillette, D. *Seismosaurus: The Earth Shaker.* New York: Columbia, 1994.

Haley, D., ed. "The Making of a Seabird." In *Seabirds of Eastern North Pacific and Arctic Waters.* Seattle: Pacific Search Press, 1984.

Hallett, M. "The Scientific Approach to the Art of Bringing Dinosaurs to Life." In *Dinosaurs Past and Present,* edited by S. J. Czerkas and E. C. Olson. Seattle: University of Washington Press, 1986.

Hare, T., ed. *Habitats.* New York: Macmillan, 1994.

Haubold, H. "Archosaur Footprints at the Terrestrial Triassic-Jurassic Transition." In *The Beginning of the Age of Dinosaurs,* edited by K. Padian. New York: Cambridge, 1986.

Herendeen, P. S., P. R. Crane, and S. Ash. "Vegetation of the Dinosaur World." In *Dino Fest,* edited by G. D. Rosenberg and D. L. Wolberg. Knoxville: University of Tennessee, 1994.

Horner, J. R. "Comparative Taxonomy of Some Dinosaur and Extant Bird Colonial Nesting Grounds." In *Dinosaur Eggs and Babies,* edited by K. Carpenter, K. F. Hirsch, and J. R. Horner. New York: Cambridge, 1994.

——. "Ecologic and Behavioral Implications Derived from a Dinosaur Nesting Site." In *Dinosaurs Past and Present,* edited by C. J. Czerkas and E. C. Olson. Vol. 2. Seattle: University of Washington Press, 1987.

Horner, J. R., and P. J. Currie. "Embryonic and Neonatal Morphology and Ontogeny of a New Species of *Hypacrosaurus* (Ornithischia, Lambeosauridae) from Montana and Alberta." In *Dinosaur Eggs and Babies,* edited by K. Carpenter, K. F. Hirsch, and J. R. Horner. New York: Cambridge, 1994.

——, and D. Lessem. *The Complete T. rex.* New York: Simon & Schuster, 1993.

Johnson, K. R., and R. K. Stucky. *Prehistoric Journey.* Boulder, Colo.: Roberts Rinehart, 1995.

Jones, D. L. *Cycads of the World: Ancient Plants in Today's Landscape.* Washington, D.C.: Smithsonian, 1993.

Kirkland, J. I. "Predation of Dinosaur Nests by Terrestrial Crocodilians." In *Dinosaur Eggs and Babies,* edited by K. Carpenter, K. F. Hirsch, and J. R. Horner. New York: Cambridge, 1994.

Knauth, P. *The North Woods,* The American Wilderness series. New York: Time-Life Books, 1972.

Lambert, D. *The Ultimate Dinosaur Book.* London: Dorling-Kindersley, 1993.

Lessem, D. *Dinosaur Worlds.* Honesdale, Pa.: Boyds Mills Press, 1996.

Lessem, D., and D. F. Glut. *Dinosaur Encyclopedia.* New York: Random House, 1993.

Levy, C. *Crocodiles and Alligators.* London: Quintet, 1991.

Lillegraven, J. A. "Reproduction in Mesozoic Mammals." In *Mesozoic Mammals: The First Two-Thirds of Mammalian History,* edited by J. A. Lillegraven, Z. Kielan-Jaworowska, and W. A. Clemens. Berkeley: University of California Press, 1979.

Lockley, M. G. "Dinosaur Ontogeny and Population Structure: Interpretations and Speculations Based on Fossil Footprints." In *Dinosaur Eggs and Babies,* edited by K. Carpenter, K. F. Hirsch, and J. R. Horner. New York: Cambridge, 1994.

Lofgren, L. *Ocean Birds.* New York: Knopf, 1984.

Long, R. A., and R. Houk. *Dawn of the Dinosaurs.* Petrified Forest National Park, Ariz.: Petrified Forest Museum Association, 1988.

Lucas, S. G. *Dinosaurs, The Textbook.* Boston: Wm. C. Brown, 1997.

McGowen, C. *Dinosaurs, Spitfires, & Sea Dragons.* Cambridge, Mass.: Harvard University Press, 1992.

McIntosh, J. S., M. K. Brett-Surman, and J. O. Farlow. "Sauropods." In *The Complete Dinosaur,* edited by J. O. Farlow and M. K. Brett-Surman. Bloomington: Indiana University Press, 1997.

McLoughlin, J. C. *Archosauria.* New York: Viking, 1979.

Miller, R. *Continents in Collision,* the Planet Earth series. Alexandria, Va.: Time-Life Books, 1983.

Milne, L., and M. Milne. *The Nature of Life.* New York: Crown, 1970.

Morris, D. *Animalwatching.* New York: Crown, 1990.

Morton, E. S., and J. Page. *Animal Talk.* New York: Random House, 1992.

Murry, P. A. "Vertebrate Paleontology of the Dockum Group, Western Texas and Eastern New Mexico." In *The Beginning of the Age of Dinosaurs,* edited by K. Padian. New York: Cambridge, 1986.

Norman, D. *Dinosaur.* New York: Prentice Hall, 1991.

———. *The Illustrated Encyclopedia of Dinosaurs.* New York: Crescent Books, 1985.

———. *Prehistoric Life.* New York: Macmillan, 1994.

Olsen, P. E. *Australian Birds of Prey.* Baltimore: Johns Hopkins University Press, 1995.

———. "Paleontology and Paleoenvironments of Early Jurassic Age Strata in the Walter Kidde Dinosaur Park (New Jersey)." In *The Geological Association of New Jersey, Contributions to the Paleontology of New Jersey,* edited by J. E. B. Baker. Vol. 12. Wayne, N.J.: William Paterson College, 1995.

Olsen, P. E., R. W. Schlische, and P. J. W. Gore, eds. *Tectonic, Depositional and Paleoecological History of Early Mesozoic Rift Basins of Eastern North America.* Washington, D.C.: American Geophysical Union, 1989.

Paul, G. S. "Dinosaur Reproduction in the Fast Lane: Implications for Size, Success, and Extinction." In *Dinosaur Eggs and Babies,* edited by K. Carpenter, K. F. Hirsch, and J. R. Horner. New York: Cambridge, 1994.

———. *Predatory Dinosaurs of the World.* New York: Simon & Schuster, 1988.

———. "The Science and Art of Restoring the Life Appearance of Dinosaurs and Their Relatives: A Rigorous How-to Guide." In *Dinosaurs Past and Present,* edited by S. J. Czerkas and E. C. Olson. Vol. 2. Seattle: University of Washington Press, 1987.

Psihoyos, L. *Hunting Dinosaurs.* New York: Random House, 1994.

Reader, J., and H. Croze. *Pyramids of Life.* New York: Lippincott.

Ricciuti, E. *The Natural History of North America.* New York: Gallery, 1990.

Rice, D. W. "Albatrosses." In *Seabirds of Eastern North Pacific and Arctic Waters,* edited by D. Haley. Seattle: Pacific Search Press, 1984.

Romer, A. S. *Vertebrate Paleontology.* Chicago: University of Chicago Press, 1966.

Ross, K. *Okavango: Jewel of the Kalahari.* New York: Macmillan, 1987.

Rue, L. L. *World of the White-tailed Deer.* New York: Lippincott, 1962.

Russell, D. A. *The Dinosaurs of North America.* Minocqua, Wis.: NorthWord, 1989.

Ryden, H. *God's Dog: A Celebration of the North American Coyote.* New York: Lyons & Burford, 1979.

Sattler, H. R. *Dinosaurs of North America.* New York: Lothrop, Lee & Shepard, 1981.

——. *The Illustrated Dinosaur Dictionary.* New York: Lothrop, Lee & Shepard, 1983.

Savage, R. J. G., and M. R. Long. *Mammalian Evolution: An Illustrated Guide.* New York: Facts On File, 1986.

Schaller, G. B. *The Serengeti Lion: A Study of Predator-Prey Relations.* Chicago: University of Chicago Press, 1972.

Scott, J. *The Great Migration.* Emmaus, Pa.: Rodale, 1988.

Shreeve, J. *Nature: The Other Earthlings.* New York: Macmillan, 1987.

Smith, A. *The Great Rift: Africa's Changing Valley.* New York: Sterling, 1988.

Smith, A. G., D. G. Smith, and B. M. Funnell. *Atlas of Mesozoic and Cenozoic Coastlines.* New York: Cambridge, 1994.

Spinar, Z. V., and P. J. Curie. *The Great Dinosaurs.* Stamford, Conn.: Longmeadow, 1994.

Steele, R., and A. Harvey, eds. *The Encyclopedia of Prehistoric Life.* New York: McGraw-Hill, 1979.

Stewart, D. "Fires of Life." *National Wildlife* (Aug.-Sept. 1994).

Stewart, W. N., and G. W. Rothwell. *Paleobotany and the Evolution of Plants.* New York: Cambridge, 1983.

Talbot, F. H., and R. E. Stevenson, eds. *The Encyclopedia of the Earth: Oceans and Islands.* New York: Smithmark, 1991.

Tidwell, W. D. *Common Fossil Plants of Western North America.* Provo, Utah: Brigham Young University Press, 1975.

Tiffney, B. H. "Land Plants as Food and Habitat in the Age of Dinosaurs." In *The Complete Dinosaur,* edited by J. O. Farlow and M. K. Brett-Surman. Bloomington: Indiana University Press, 1997.

——. "Plant Life in the Age of Dinosaurs." In *The Age of Dinosaurs, Short Courses in Paleontology.* No. 2. Edited by S. J. Culven. Knoxville, Tenn.: University of Tennessee.

Tilson, R. L. "Carcass Protocol." *Natural History* (March 1983).

Tufts, L. S. *Secrets in Yellowstone & Grand Teton National Parks.* North Palm Beach, Fla.: National Photographic Collections, 1990.

Varricchio, D. J., F. Jackson, J. J. Borkowski, and J. R. Horner. "Nest and Egg Clutches of the Dinosaur *Troodon formosus* and the Evolution of Avian Reproductive Traits." *Nature* 385 (Jan. 16, 1997).

Walther, F. R. *In the Country of Gazelles.* Bloomington: Indiana University Press, 1995.

Watson, L. *The Dreams of Dragons.* New York: Morrow, 1987.

Weishampel, D. B., and L. Young. *Dinosaurs of the East Coast.* Baltimore: Johns Hopkins University Press, 1996.

Wellnhofer, P. *The Illustrated Encyclopedia of Pterosaurs.* New York: Crescent, 1991.

White, M. E. *The Flowering of Gondwana.* Princeton, N.J.: Princeton University Press, 1990.

Zimmer, C. "Dinosaurs in Motion." *Discover* (November 1997).

Videocassettes

Forniz, C. *Horse Tigers.* Nature series. Bristol/WNET/Channel Thirteen: BBC, 1991.

Grossett, P., ed. *Super Predators.* Safari series. Produced by Sable Enterprises and Londolozi Productions, 1992.

Helton, D. *The Great Rift.* Nature series. Bristol/WNET/Channel Thirteen: BBC, 1988.

Joubert, D. *Zebra: Patterns in the Grass.* Washington, D.C.: National Geographic Society, 1991.

O'Dell, D. R. *Race for Life: Africa's Great Migration.* ABC World of Discovery series. ABC Kane Productions International, 1993.

Reader, J. *The Rains Came.* The Natural World series. Survival Anglia, 1992.

Reitherman, B. *Baja Lagoon.* Nature series. Produced by Educational Broadcasting System for Pandion Enterprises, 1986.

Root, A. *A Season in the Sun.* The Natural World series. Survival Anglia, 1982.

ACKNOWLEDGEMENTS

Life, as they say, is a learning experience, and if there's anything we've learned from writing this book, it's that it never could have been done without the help and support of some very special people.

The seeds of *In the Presence of Dinosaurs* were planted nine years ago, at monthly paleontological meetings and dinners. Bob and Jane Ramsdell, Grace and Dick Hancock, Wayne and Sue Callahan, Chris and Shar Kennett, and Fran and Charlie Rizzo grew so tired of us saying "We gotta do a book" that we thought we should spare them any further talk without action, and go ahead and finally write one. Their support and encouragement will always be appreciated.

Along the way, there were many individuals whose efforts and help, although downplayed by them, made things much easier for us. Rick Carmella, Dave Emma, Joe Esposito, Meg Feeley, Dave Felder, Howard Fenton, Pam Giordano, Melinda Hamilton, Erin Kelly, Paula Landau, Allan Lang, Dave Lawson, Dave Lott, Sheila and Marv Maltz, Lynne Mazza, Don Morgan, Theo Padavano, Jeff Picazio, Cyndy Rosen, Phyllis and Tedd Schwartz, Ian Schwartz, Neil Schwartz, Dave Slaman, Jane Smith, Mike Vecchiarelli, and Mike Yahr; all deserve our thanks. Thanks also to Tim Mulvey and Houston Art & Frame, upon whose gessoed Masonite the art in the book was painted.

A number of people are owed a lot of appreciation for their good wishes and moral support, which was of tremendous help, especially during our Dark Ages. Among them are Nicole Al-Aiday, Pam Barett, Elisa and Sam Bergman, Donna and Steve Burkat, Sue Champagne, Eilene and John Colagrande, Wendy and Sam Cooper, Marty and Marie Dowd, Marcy Dubinsky, Lisa Eisenberg, Ellen and Rob Essex, Marta Feinstein, Deb and Andy Felder, Linda Felder, Neal Fitzsimmons, Michele Franck, Sue Gebeloff, Bryna and Ben Gotlib, Joe Hughes, Gary Inzana, Deb Kammerman, Sandy and Morty Kammerman, Diane Kay, Jane and Jon Lakritz, Audrey Landis, Randy Lovrin, Pam Kaczowski, Meryl and Jeff Marias, Deb Meshulam, Lisa Meshulam, Tobia Meyers, Marie and Pat Martucci, Terry Millman, Marie and Larry Minion, Laura Mollé, Janice and Bernie Patlock, Lori Payne, Sue Polyn, Susan Rabinowitz, Audrey and Sid Rabinowitz, Lora Speiser, Caren Symchowicz, Christine Trcic, Janet Walton, Steve Weisberg, and Chrissy and Rich Zimmermann. Very special thanks to Ann Marie Fitzsimmons for her friendship, support, and much appreciated advise and comments on the illustrations.

Many critical areas of this book could not have been completed without the help and support of many of those in the paleo-art community. Dan LaRusso's friendship and guidance was always there at the right moments. Dave Peter's efforts and research aided tremendously, and Brian Franczak's support and advice will always be appreciated. Donna Braginetz and Mike Skrepnick were always generous with their support, and Mike Trcic's talents and frienship could always be counted upon. Jim Gurney, Dougal Dixon, Greg Wenzel, Bob Walters, Tess Kissinger, Bill

Stout—your help was much appreciated.

Several individuals in the scientific community were most generous with their help, and deserve our thanks. Jack Horner, who wrote the Foreword, deserves our most humble appreciation for his kind words and comments. Bill Gallagher, Dave Parris, Barbara Grandstaff, Roland Gangloff, Jim Kirkland, Jim Farlow, Paul Olsen, Lou Jacobs, Alex Kellner, Darren Tanke, and Larry Barnes were all generous and helpful, and have our thanks.

Attorneys Lloyd Jassin, Donald Myers, and Clara Harelik were of enormous assistance, and we thank them for their efforts on our behalf. Peter Jacobs, who photographed much of the artwork in the book, was always meticulous and accomodating, and deserves our thanks, as do Alan Goldstein, Brian Mohan, and the rest of the gang at Klein and Ulmes.

There are certain individuals whose generous support during the course of this project bear special recognition. Heidi Binz, Al Fraser, Sy Gelbard, Manny and Shari Haber, Dean Hannotte, Eddie Jastrzebski, John Lanzendorf, Annette and Greg Sarrazine, many thanks to you all. Many thanks also to Susan Rondeau, whose friendship and support will always be treasured.

Bob and Sue Gruning merit very special thanks for their friendship, support and faith, which will never be forgotten. Special thanks also go to Jesse Chan, Kimberly Gruning, Brian Gruning, Kevin Gruning, Kyle Fitzsimmons, Eva Marie Fitzsimmons, Katie Padavano, Eric Rondeau, Jeremy Felder, Casey Felder, Ryan Felder, and Zach Felder for their help and support. (Keep drawing, guys!) Thanks also goes to Harriet Felder, Joanne Bolick, Evan Bolick, Todd Bolick, Randi and Ed Garber, Robin George, Benjamin George, and Daniel George. And very special thanks and a belated apology go to Jeff Felder, who put up with all of those rocks in the basement for all of those years. And, to Bea and Art Felder, who would have been proud, and Vito and Evelyn Colagrande, who are.

This book is dedicated to Sandy Colagrande and Edwina Wong, whose support, enthusiasm, and love never wavered. Our eternal gratitude.

To our copyeditor, Lise Lingo, who was able to translate the meanderings of a couple of cases of arrested dinosaur development into a coherent narrative, many thanks. (How dja du dat?)

To our designer, Phillip Unetic, who created this elegant edition, allowing both the text and the art to shine, our sincere thanks.

And, finally. In the course of life, there are moments that occur which have been alternately described, depending on the source, as serendipity, karma, or just plain dumb luck. However we managed to meet up, to Anna Burgard, who shepherded this project along from inception to fruition, our most heartfelt thanks. To any aspiring writers and artists who think they have a good idea for a book, and who may be looking for advice, the best we could ever wish for you is that along the way, you, too, may come to have an Anna Burgard in your life.

J. C. *L. F.*

The illustrations were created
using Winsor & Newton and Grumbacher
oil paints on gessoed Masonite.

The text is set in Minion,
the captions in Franklin Gothic.
The display font is Trajan.

The book was printed on a 5-color Heidelberg press
on 80-pound Kinmari Matte paper.